Woolworth's

PALMOLIVE
SHAMPOO
3D EACH
6D EACH
OSLO
STABLOND
tonedints
drene
OUTDOOR GIRL
AMAMI
POND'S
2D

Woolworth's

100 Years on the High Street

Kathryn A Morrison

Historic England

Published by Historic England, The Engine House, Fire Fly Avenue, Swindon SN2 2EH
www.HistoricEngland.org.uk

Historic England is a Government service championing England's heritage and giving expert, constructive advice, and the English Heritage Trust is a charity caring for the National Heritage Collection of more than 400 historic properties and their collections.

First published 2015 by Historic England

ISBN 978-1-84802-246-1

British Library Cataloguing in Publication data
A CIP catalogue record for this book is available from the British Library.

For more information about images from the Archive, contact the Archives Services Team,
Historic England, The Engine House, Fire Fly Avenue, Swindon SN2 2EH; telephone (01793) 414600.

Brought to publication by Rachel Howard, Publishing, Historic England.

Typeset in Charter 9.5/11.75 and 9.5/12.75

Edited by Kathryn Glendenning
Indexed by Caroline Jones
Page layout by Tori Herries, Ledgard Jepson Ltd
Printed in the UK by Bell & Bain Ltd

Front Cover: Blackpool store at the junction of Adelaide Street and Promenade (see Fig 4.48). [FWW01/01/0066/022]

Frontis: Window display at Blackpool, 1938 (see Fig 4.89). [AL2203/014/01]

Back cover: Pic 'n' mix counters at Milton Keynes, 1988 (see Fig 9.9). [JLP01/10/33763]

CONTENTS

ACKNOWLEDGEMENTS

I am immensely grateful to Keith Austin, Jo Beach, Ian Leith and their colleagues for helping me to study the Woolworths Collection held in the Historic England Archive (formerly the National Monuments Record and latterly the English Heritage Archive) in Swindon. The task of trawling through thousands of architectural drawings and photographs would have been impossible without the careful sorting, cataloguing and archiving undertaken by Elaine Arthurs and David Birks in 2003, when the collection was first acquired.

Over the years I have received useful advice and information from the following people associated with Woolworth's: Tim Ayre (former Investment Director, Chartwell Land), Peter Dunn (formerly of the Construction/Architects' Department, Woolworth's), Paul Seaton (former IT Manager, Woolworth's), Nigel Stretch (former Estate Manager, Woolworth's), Pat Sullivan (former Project Manager, Woolworth's) and Ken Trimmer (former Architectural Manager, Woolworth's). I must single out Paul Seaton for special thanks: for being particularly generous with his information and for going beyond the call of duty to safeguard the company's history. In addition, the following friends and colleagues have kindly provided assistance, information or photographs, helping me to piece together and present the story of Woolworth's stores: Steven Baker, Ron Baxter, Jane Biro, Wayne Cocroft, Emily Cole, James O Davies, Emily Gee, Katherine Knights (née d'Este Hoare), Lindsay Lennie, John Minnis, Pat Payne, Tony Perry, Phil Sinton, Matthew Whitfield and Peter Williams. Jon Wilson, the Commercial Director of Shaws of Darwen, gave me generous access to his company's archives. Ron Baxter and Harriet Richardson read draft text, and I appreciate their observations and suggestions. In addition, I wish to acknowledge the assistance of archivists in various libraries, record offices and collections visited or consulted in the course of my research, including the British Library, Cambridge University Library, Cambridgeshire Record Office, Essex Record Office, Imperial War Museum, Lancashire Archives, Kingston upon Thames Museum and Heritage Service, London Metropolitan Archives, Marks & Spencer Company Archive, Museum of London, RIBA Library and SPAB.

I would like to thank John Hudson, Robin Taylor and Rachel Howard in the Publications Department at Historic England for commissioning this book and seeing the project through to fruition. I am grateful to Kathryn Glendenning for her astute and tactful copy-editing, to Caroline Jones for preparing the index and also to Tori Herries of Ledgard Jepson Ltd for designing this book.

INTRODUCTION

Woolworth's legacy

Woolworth's stores – with their bright red lettering, inexpensive toys and enticing sweet counters – were a joyous part of British and Irish childhood for a century. Or, to be pedantic, almost a century. For the last stores closed in January 2009, just six months short of the firm's centenary. Any celebrations that might have been planned were, quite understandably, aborted, as members of staff were laid off and receivers took possession of the company's assets.

The demise of Woolworth's was met initially with disbelief, followed by a welling of nostalgia and a sense of loss. Souvenir-hunters abounded, collecting everything from wire baskets to plastic bags, and poignant photographs of near-empty premises were posted on the internet. The extinction of no other high-street 'name' has inspired such an emotional reaction. The company's legacy, however, endures in British high streets and shopping centres. Many hundreds of purpose-built Woolworth's stores still stand, most of them now emblazoned with the liveries of new occupants. In addition, the abiding impact of Woolworth's cheap-and-cheerful approach to retailing is reflected in the myriad fixed-price 'pound' and '99p' variety chains that have colonised town centres in recent years, while 'pick 'n' mix' (or as it was later spelt, 'pic 'n' mix'), a Woolworth's invention, remains a favourite method of selling loose sweets. In many ways, the high streets of Britain and Ireland would be very different places today had Woolworth's never existed.

From metropolitan centres to Scottish islands, Woolworth's figured in everybody's life. It provided generations of young people, especially girls, with experience of the workplace. For consumers, it was the first port of call for a broad range of everyday items, from cosmetics and haberdashery to kitchenware and pop records. The variety and turnover of its affordable goods, many of them treats rather than necessities, injected colour and excitement into Saturday shopping trips. Woolworth's 'red fronts' seemed as ubiquitous, enduring and British as red telephone kiosks or red pillar boxes. Despite this, the company was not home grown. It was American in origin, with a head office in New York and subsidiary chains in countries around the world.

The formal name of the British and Irish chain, 'F W Woolworth & Co Ltd', was always abbreviated, by staff and customers alike, to 'Woolworth's' or, more affectionately, 'Woolies'. Variations on the name appeared on store fronts over the years, with 'F W Woolworth & Co Ltd' yielding to 'Woolworth' in the late 1960s, and this in turn being superseded by 'Woolworths' in the mid-1980s. To sidestep editorial confusion and maintain some consistency, the familiar colloquial form 'Woolworth's' is used here to refer to the British company throughout its history, while 'Woolworth' is reserved for the American parent. This is, of course, also the family name of the founder.

Numerous books, articles and websites have been devoted to Woolworth's over the years. The American biographer John K Winkler's book *Five and Ten: The Fabulous Life of F W Woolworth,* first published in America in 1940, is predictably hagiographic. Nevertheless, it is a fundamental and much-quoted source for the early years of the company. Information on the history of the British firm can be gleaned from annual reports, progress reports and staff magazines, as well as from contemporary press articles. A heroic contribution to the preservation of the Woolworth's story has been made by Paul Seaton. Formerly an IT manager with the company, Seaton set up and maintained the 'Virtual Museum' on Woolworth's own website between 2004 and 2009. This has been superseded by Seaton's more comprehensive website, www.woolworthsmuseum.co.uk, and his popular book *A Sixpenny Romance: Celebrating a Century of Value at Woolworths* (2009). A number of other websites offer insights into aspects of the chain, demonstrating its enduring fascination (*see* Bibliography).

Although this book is primarily about buildings, it does not set out to be a conventional architectural history. Essentially, it is the story of Woolworth's seen through the prism of its stores. Few of these buildings can be classed as great architecture. Most were designed by obscure company architects who received little critical acclaim, yet they allow one to track the development of mainstream commercial architecture over the course of a century. Additionally, they remain of huge cultural interest. They were the conduit by which American influences such as cheap westerns, soda fountains, cafeterias and lunch bars were introduced into many British and Irish towns. They sometimes shaped, and sometimes followed, fundamental changes – mostly American in origin – that took place in the nation's shopping habits. Through Woolworth's stores one can chart the move from personal counter service to self-service, from streets to precincts and shopping centres, and from town centres to the out-of-town retail parks and mega-malls where we carry out much of our shopping nowadays. Perhaps it is a fitting finale to this historical progression that 'Woolworths' exists today only as an internet shopping site: www.woolworths.co.uk.

This book is unlikely to be the final word on the subject. It enlarges upon a short overview of Woolworth's stores included in K Morrison, *English Shops and Shopping: An Architectural History,* published by Yale University Press in 2003. In that very year, a large collection of photographs, architectural drawings and ephemera was deposited by Woolworth's Architects' Department with the National Monuments Record (now the Historic England Archive), in Swindon. This rich mine of material was plundered for the present book, and is all the more valuable considering the destruction of much of the company's archive since 1982. It is worth noting that an incomplete set of board minute books is known to be held by Shop Direct, but was not available during the preparation of this book.[1] According to Paul Seaton, who read these minute books prior to 2009, they include 'details of all the leases and freeholds acquired, and every financial investment made in building, equipping and redeveloping the stores ... along with a commentary about the location'.[2] Obviously, the information in these minute books would add further depth and detail to the story of Woolworth's buildings, as would the relevant records that must be hidden away in local libraries, record offices and private collections throughout the country, many of them still uncatalogued and inaccessible. Above all, there is great untapped potential in the memories of those associated with Woolworth's, staff and customers alike.[3] This is a story which, with help from local historians, has potential to grow and grow.

Kathryn A Morrison

An American retail empire, 1879–1909

Frank Winfield Woolworth

The story of Frank Winfield Woolworth (1852–1919, Fig 1.1), a farmer's son, is one of the classic rags-to-riches tales of 19th-century America. Woolworth came from Rodman, Jefferson County, close to the Canadian border in northern New York State. Having completed his education he found farm labour distasteful and decided that he would prefer to work in a shop. Consequently, at the age of 21, Woolworth obtained a lowly position with Augsbury & Moore (later Moore & Smith), a dry-goods store – or, in British terms, a drapery – in nearby Watertown. Here he learnt the business of running a successful store from the ground up, and developed a particular talent for window dressing and display, though not for salesmanship. A move to a clerk's (sales assistant's) position with a rival firm, A Bushnell & Co, exposed Woolworth's weakness in this area and prompted a breakdown in his health. After convalescing he married a young Canadian woman, Jennie Creighton (1853–1924), and purchased a farm. But before long, in June 1877, the offer of a well-paid job with Moore & Smith enticed Woolworth back to the world of retailing and the farm was forgotten.

Around 1878 a former employee of Bushnell's visited Moore & Smith in Watertown and outlined to the proprietor, William H Moore (d 1916), the benefits of setting up a five-cent table.[1] This was a popular ploy in some American stores, but was as yet unheard of in Watertown. Since trade was slack, Moore decided to try out the idea. He bought a large quantity of five-cent goods in New York City and allowed Frank Woolworth to lay them out for sale. This was a great success. The experience enthused Woolworth, planting in his head the notion of not merely a five-cent table, but a five-cent store. With the support of his employer he sought premises of his own in a different town. He lacked capital, but Moore & Smith was in business as a wholesaler as well as a retailer and agreed to lend $300 on credit for stock.

Woolworth opened his first outlet on Bleeker Street in Utica, New York State, on 22 February 1879, with a large signboard proclaiming 'The Great 5¢ Store'. This enjoyed fleeting success. Custom tailed away after just a few months and so, before bankruptcy beckoned, Woolworth shut up shop, extended his credit with Moore & Smith, and in June 1879 tried again in a better location, on North Queen Street, Lancaster, Pennsylvania. Within a year this five-cent store had been reinvented as a five-and-ten (otherwise known as a nickel-and-dime or five-

Fig 1.1
Frank Winfield Woolworth (1852–1919) built up a phenomenally successful retail empire in America before exporting his nickel-and-dime-store format to the British Isles. This portrait was published as the frontispiece to the Fortieth Anniversary Souvenir, *produced just before his death in 1919. [Author's collection]*

and-dime), reputedly the first of its kind in America, meaning that it could trade in a much wider range of merchandise. This fine-tuning of the fixed-price approach was Woolworth's great breakthrough: he had invented – or, if not exactly invented, certainly honed to perfection – a new genre of retailing.

The risk taken by Woolworth and his backers paid off. The Lancaster venture proved so profitable that, within a few years, Woolworth was enjoying a prosperous lifestyle and opening stores in other towns. Family, friends and former colleagues were invited to share in his winning formula, either by entering into partnerships with Woolworth, creating a loose syndicate of 'friendly rivals', or by managing his stores. Two of his earliest partners were his younger brother Charles Sumner Woolworth and his cousin Seymour H Knox. By forging such partnerships, and sharing capital investment, Woolworth could build up a chain of stores without borrowing from banks. His partners managed their jointly owned stores and the entire group benefited from the discounts that could be obtained through central buying. By 1885 Woolworth was wealthy enough to rescue the ailing business of his former employer, William H Moore, by

transforming the old dry-goods store in Watertown into a five-and-ten (Fig 1.2). At this point, Woolworth controlled, or jointly controlled, seven stores, with an annual turnover of $100,000.[2] No longer involved in the day-to-day management of any individual outlet, he moved to New York City, establishing his family – Jennie and their three young daughters – in Brooklyn while he took charge of a central buying office in Manhattan.

Sourcing stock

The success of the Woolworth syndicate's five-and-ten policy relied on sourcing and purchasing the right stock for the right price, an operation that came firmly under Frank Woolworth's control. It was here that the true skill of the enterprise lay, not in the salesmanship of the stores' young and poorly paid clerks, nor in the eagle-eyed supervision of their managers. Initially, Woolworth had struggled to identify sufficiently varied and novel lines of merchandise within his prescribed price limits. He quickly realised, however, that great economies could be obtained by buying in bulk, for multiple stores rather than for a

Fig 1.2
Moore & Smith's five-and-ten store in Watertown, where F W Woolworth began his career, shown on a card posted in 1914. Following William H Moore's death in 1916, the store was rebuilt. It served as Woolworth's 'principal office' until 1971, when the company moved out. [Author's collection]

Arsenal Street from the Square, Watertown, N. Y.

single establishment, and by liaising directly with factories rather than placing orders with middlemen. Some of his first deals with manufacturers concerned sweets and Christmas decorations, lines that endured as Woolworth's staples to the bitter end. Another common source of cheap merchandise was bankrupt stock, but Woolworth instinctively steered clear of damaged goods, or 'seconds'.

In February 1890 Woolworth embarked upon the first of many transatlantic voyages, landing at Liverpool and spending three months touring Europe, mixing business with pleasure. This trip presented a dual opportunity, both to source stock and to investigate foreign stores. Thus Woolworth ordered large quantities of china from the potteries of Stoke-on-Trent, where he observed, 'The shops, we cannot call them stores, are very small and dark as a pocket.'[3] He ordered dolls, toys and Christmas baubles direct from their manufacturers in Germany and bought glass goods in Bohemia. In Vienna he declared, 'The store windows make the prettiest display of any city I was ever in,' while in Paris he devoted an afternoon to exploring the Bon Marché, perhaps, at that time, the most famous store in Europe.[4] Many businesses around the world adopted the name 'Bon Marché', despite having no connection with the Parisian original. Among them was a shop in Brixton, south London, which is often hailed as the first purpose-built English department store.

Expansion

Woolworth gradually imposed a consistent aesthetic on his stores. Initially, his pine signboards, or fascias, were hand-painted by local workmen and did not follow a rigid template. From the mid-1880s, however, most of them had shaped ends and displayed gilded lettering on a red background. This feature, which caused Woolworth stores to be dubbed 'red fronts', was standardised around 1900. By 1890 Woolworth had adopted the so-called 'diamond W' – a barbed crossed 'W' framed by a lozenge or diamond – as his emblem. Another characteristic of the stores was the provision of scales for customers to weigh themselves, a gimmick seen by Frank Woolworth in a rival store and taken up thereafter in his own outlets.

The expansion of the chain steadily accelerated, with 28 stores in 1895, 59 in 1900, 76 in

12250— Woolworth Building, Lancaster, Pa.

1903, 120 in 1904 and 189 in 1908.[5] Woolworth undertook his first ambitious construction project in 1899–1900, replacing the original store in Lancaster with new premises designed by the New York City architects Ditmar & Sheckels (Fig 1.3). The local supervising architect was C Emlen Urban.[6] This building resembled provincial European department stores of the previous decade. The sales area on the ground floor, befitting its senior status in the chain, was grander than usual. The show windows had mirrored glass and the structural columns were clad in imitation Siena marble. Behind counters of imitation mahogany, the walls were festooned with slogans, including the proud boast: 'This is the oldest established 5 and 10 cent store in the world.' Above the

Fig 1.3

The original Woolworth store on North Queen Street in Lancaster, Pennsylvania, was superseded by this new building in 1900. Initially, Woolworth shared the ground floor with 'The Bon Ton'. The neighbouring store glimpsed to the right was McCrory's, a rival chain of five-and-tens started up in 1882 in imitation of Woolworth. [Author's collection]

3

store were four floors of offices, rented out to various companies, and a rooftop garden with an open-air theatre. The tall façade was dominated by corner turrets with cupolas and flagpoles that gave it a festive air. This historic Woolworth store closed in April 1949, and was subsequently demolished.

Imprecisely dated photographs reveal the appearance of Woolworth stores in the early 20th century.[7] The windows were not yet uniform in design and were largely concealed by arrays of goods on the sidewalk. Inside, sales counters with panelled fronts ran along each side of the shop, beneath signs reading 'Any article on this counter 10¢' or 'Any article on this counter 5¢.' A row of free-standing (or 'island') display counters ran down the centre, their tops compartmentalised to keep goods as tidy as possible.

Frank Woolworth's personal wealth continued to grow and he moved his family to a mansion on Fifth Avenue in New York, a house from which his two eldest daughters were married. Until 1905 Woolworth owned outright the retail empire that bore his name. But with 120 stores to run, and suffering poor health, he became convinced of the wisdom of forming a corporation. Thus, on 16 February 1905, F W Woolworth & Co came into being under the laws of the state of New York, with a share capital of $10,000,000. A total of 50,000 shares of preferred and 50,000 of common stock were issued, each with a value of $100.[8] There was no public subscription. Unsurprisingly, Frank Woolworth was elected President, while his protégé Hubert Parsons became Secretary and Treasurer. The new company grouped its stores into regional divisions, each with its own superintendent and head office, creating an organisational hierarchy that would be emulated when a subsidiary was set up in Britain.

2

The pioneering years, 1909–1918

Launching the British operation

Frank Woolworth had contemplated opening stores in Britain for some time. He made a close study of London shops in the course of his first European trip in 1890 but was far from impressed. In one of the regular 'General Letters' he addressed to his employees, he wrote:

> They may have some fine stores here but we have not yet found them. Those we have seen are nothing but little shops and the way they trim their windows is new to me. They trim them close to the glass from top to bottom, and it is impossible to look into the store. The stores themselves are very small and are called 'shops' and not much like our fine stores. I think a good penny and six-pence store run by a live Yankee would create a sensation here, but perhaps not.[1]

Nineteen years later Woolworth decided to chance his hand, ignoring the misgivings of his senior executives. As a first step he issued a call for volunteers, seeking proven managers with an enterprising spirit who were willing to uproot their families and pursue a new life on the other side of the Atlantic. Carson Peck, Woolworth's general manager and right-hand man, warned employees against volunteering, claiming, 'It is a good deal like asking a boy to volunteer to go into a bear's den when he does not know whether he is to eat a nicely cooked luscious bear's steak or be eaten by a great, big black bear.'[2]

Regardless of Peck's concerns, Woolworth managed to recruit three able men, none of whom was familiar with Britain. Foremost among these pioneers was Frank's cousin, Fred Moore Woolworth (1871–1923), who had accumulated valuable experience working in diverse capacities for Woolworth in the States, latterly as manager of the Sixth Avenue store in New York. His new task was to set up and manage the British operation. With Fred Woolworth were Byron De Witt Miller

(1875–1960; superintendent of the Boston District) and Samuel Balfour (d 1911; manager of the Fourteenth Street store in New York). Fred Woolworth was to dedicate the remainder of his career to the British operation, but Balfour returned to the US in 1910 and Miller in 1921. On 29 May 1909, however, all three departed from Hoboken on the *Kaiserin Auguste Victoria* in the company of Frank Woolworth and their families.

Shortly after landing in Plymouth on 6 June 1909, Woolworth's party began to tour the country by train, searching (or 'scouting') for suitable sites for stores. In July the team was augmented by a new recruit, an Englishman, William Lawrence Stephenson (1880–1963, Fig 2.1), who may have been headhunted with a view to defusing anti-American prejudice, but also because of his established connections with British manufacturers. Known to

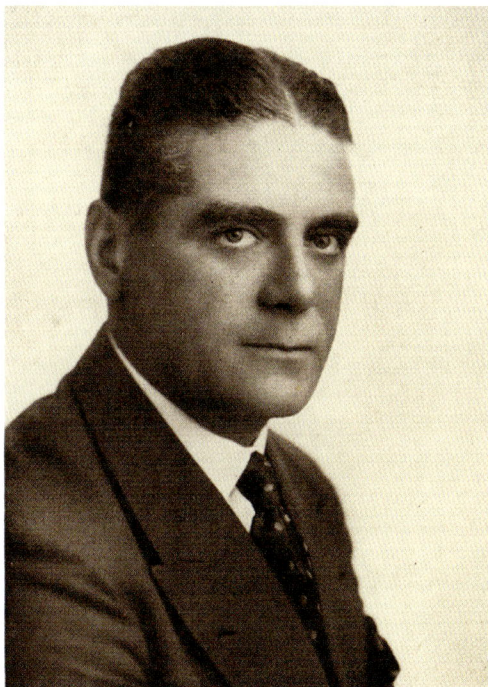

Fig 2.1
William Lawrence Stephenson, a wholesaler recruited by Woolworth in July 1909, led Woolworth's British operations from 1923 until 1948. He was 'an able, affable, and much-liked Englishman' and a most effective manager.[a] Thanks to his career with Woolworth's, he became one of the country's richest men. This portrait was published in Twenty Years of Progress in 1928.
[FWW01/05/01/04]

Figs 2.2 and 2.3
Henry Miles & Co, Nos
25–25a Church Street,
Liverpool, shown (on the left
of the street view) in a pre-
1909 postcard and in a
photograph of 2000. This
building accommodated the
very first Woolworth's store
in England, opening on 5
November 1909. Although
Woolworth's moved out
in 1923, the building still
stands, occupied by a
Clarks shoe shop.
[Author's collection;
AA011347]

appointed Managing Director, while Balfour became Company Secretary. Although Frank Woolworth had contemplated 'penny and sixpence' stores in 1890, the company now decided to open 3d and 6d stores. These prices were the closest equivalents in British currency to five and ten cents. Their modern value can be calculated in many different ways, but 6d in 1909 is (very approximately) equivalent to £2.50 in 2015.

Woolworth wished to forge a chain as swiftly as possible but choosing the right site for the very first 3d and 6d store was of paramount importance, to ensure that the business got off on the best possible foot. He reported in a letter that his team had visited Northampton, Southampton, Portsmouth, Croydon, Brighton, Reading, Hammersmith, Kensington, Birmingham, Wolverhampton, Coventry, Liverpool and Manchester, all of which were considered good locations for stores, though he complained that available shops were too shallow for the purpose. Manchester, with its vast working-class catchment area, and Northampton, with its central location, both received close scrutiny, but Woolworth's team thought Liverpool city centre looked more 'lively and up to date'.[5] When the pioneers signed the 21-year lease of their first shop, on Church Street in Liverpool, on Friday 13 August, Woolworth insisted, 'We are not superstitious.'[6]

Store 1: Nos 25–25a Church Street, Liverpool

The very first 3d and 6d store of F W Woolworth & Co Ltd opened its doors in the heart of Liverpool's thriving shopping district on Friday 5 November 1909. Tantalisingly, this was a preview day with nothing available for sale. This maintained an American tradition. Since the 1890s Frank Woolworth had opened his new stores for business on a Saturday, preceded by a reception on the Friday afternoon, with an orchestra or a band to draw and entertain the crowds. Liverpool followed this convention and also offered free teas. The Saturday takings amounted to the decent sum of £562 6s 11d.[7]

The store, at Nos 25–25a Church Street (Figs 2.2 and 2.3), stood opposite St Peter's Church, known as the Pro Cathedral. It occupied a four-storey commercial building with an Italianate façade, erected around 1858 for Elkington's, art

Woolworth since 1904, Stephenson had worked as a chief buyer for E Owen of Birmingham, a company that specialised in exporting goods to American stores, including John Wanamaker's great store in Philadelphia.[3] Stephenson undoubtedly had a more profound knowledge of the English retail landscape than any of his new American colleagues, something that would prove invaluable to the scouting process.

F W Woolworth & Co Ltd was registered as a private company on 23 July 1909. The American company took a 66 per cent stake in the business: the total capitalisation was £50,250, representing 5,000 seven per cent preference shares at £10 each and 5,000 ordinary shares of 1s each.[4] Fred Woolworth was metalworkers and electroplaters, to a design by Lewis Hornblower.[8] From 1889 this was occupied by the Glover, Milliner and Fancy Draper, Henry Miles & Co, and was known rather quaintly as 'The Sign of the Glove'. The shop was L-shaped, with a two-storey wing at No 8 Williamson Street.

As far as the outside of Miles's building was concerned, Woolworth's main alteration was the installation of a new shopfront (Fig 2.4), or rather two shopfronts, since the Williamson Street frontage would have been transformed in the same manner as the main entrance on Church Street. These were the first of hundreds of shopfronts that would be produced in a characteristic Woolworth's house style prior to the Second World War. The initial design is likely to have been created by the London-based shopfitter Frederick Sage & Co, a well-established firm which had recently fitted out the new Harrods store in Knightsbridge, London. Certainly, Sage was responsible for an almost identical shopfront designed for the Manchester branch of Woolworth's a few months later.[9] In its general lines, with tall display windows alternating with lobby entrances and topped by an eye-catching red and gold fascia, this design closely resembled American Woolworth shopfronts of the same period. No doubt Sage had been explicitly instructed to emulate these.

The Church Street frontage had two lobbies, replacing Miles's single entrance. These lobbies probably had mosaic floors displaying the 'diamond W', a feature of subsequent shopfronts, as well as panelled plaster ceilings, and single pairs of part-glazed double doors of natural wood with shiny brass push-plates and kick-plates. Double-action hinges allowed the doors to swing open for entrance or exit. The fanlights over the doors took the form of lunettes. Flanking the lobbies were bronze-framed plate-glass display windows with curved – or, more precisely, quadrant-shaped – corners that gently funnelled window-shoppers into the store. The large panes of glass were held in place by slender mullions in the form of barley-twist or cable-moulded colonnettes. These had an important secondary function, serving to distract the eye from the structural cast-iron columns that rose directly behind them to carry the superstructure of the façade. Along the tops of the windows ran a narrow ventilation strip which prevented condensation forming on the inside of the glass. The windows

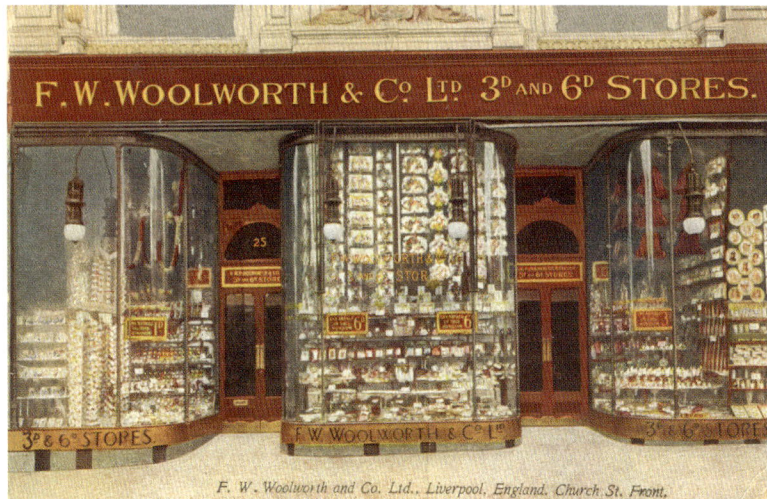

F. W. Woolworth and Co. Ltd., Liverpool, England. Church St. Front.

between the two entrance lobbies displayed 6d goods, while that on the far left showed 1d goods, and that on the right, 3d goods; this may have corresponded to the arrangement of merchandise on the counters of the salesroom inside the store. The backs of the shallow display areas were lined with mirror-glass and at night the shopfront was illuminated by arc lamps.

The name of the company, 'F. W. Woolworth & Co. Ltd.', was spelt out in gilded letters on the low emerald pearl granite stall-risers, as well as on the high red and gold fascia. It was, therefore, equally visible to those strolling along the pavement directly outside the store and those surveying the street from a distance. At the base of the fascia was a discrete housing for retractable canvas sun blinds, a ubiquitous feature of British shops in the Edwardian era. These blinds prevented goods from fading in bright light and also sheltered window-shoppers from sun and rain. Historic photographs of British high streets show that up to the mid-1930s the blinds of Woolworth's stores continued to be printed, in bold letters, with the full company name.

The interior of Miles's L-shaped shop had been lavish, with an elegant staircase, a gallery, a first-floor salon lit by a high clerestory, and bronze figurines which bore aloft electric lights.[10] It was depicted, shortly after its transformation by Woolworth's, in a series of tinted postcards. From these it is evident that while the company retained Miles's architectural features, it had no use for his shopfitting. The long, traditional counters lined by bentwood chairs, the impressive glass showcases and the overhead cash railway were

Fig 2.4
The new shopfront of Store 1 in Liverpool created a template for future Woolworth's stores in the British Isles. The company's contemporary American shopfronts were similar, but seldom included curved glass and usually had deep transom lights. [Courtesy of woolworths museum.co.uk, © 3D and 6D Pictures Ltd]

all replaced by Woolworth's own fittings, primarily mahogany-fronted island counters equipped with cash registers.

By the end of 1909 Charles Hubbard (1886–1945) had been recruited from America to manage the Church Street store and train up potential managers, known to the firm as 'learners'. He was responsible for introducing these men (for they were all men) to the arts of book-keeping, management, sales and display. Eventually, the learners would run stores of their own. One of them, John Cochrane, was recruited by Hubbard in February 1910 and remained in Liverpool until 1912. In 1959 his memory of the store remained clear: 'As one entered from Church Street, the lofty Sales Floor went through to Williamson Street, approached by steps – so the floor was on two levels, high at the front and low to the back.'[11] On the Williamson Street side, the staircase led to a very grand first-floor showroom (Fig 2.5) with special free-standing display units for china (Fig 2.6): these were evidently an American idea since similar tiered china

Fig 2.5
This first-floor plan of the Liverpool store dates from c 1909. It shows features such as the china counters (see Fig 2.6) and the tea room (see Fig 2.7). The faint red circles pinpoint the positions of five-light chandeliers.
[FWW01/02/0001/003]

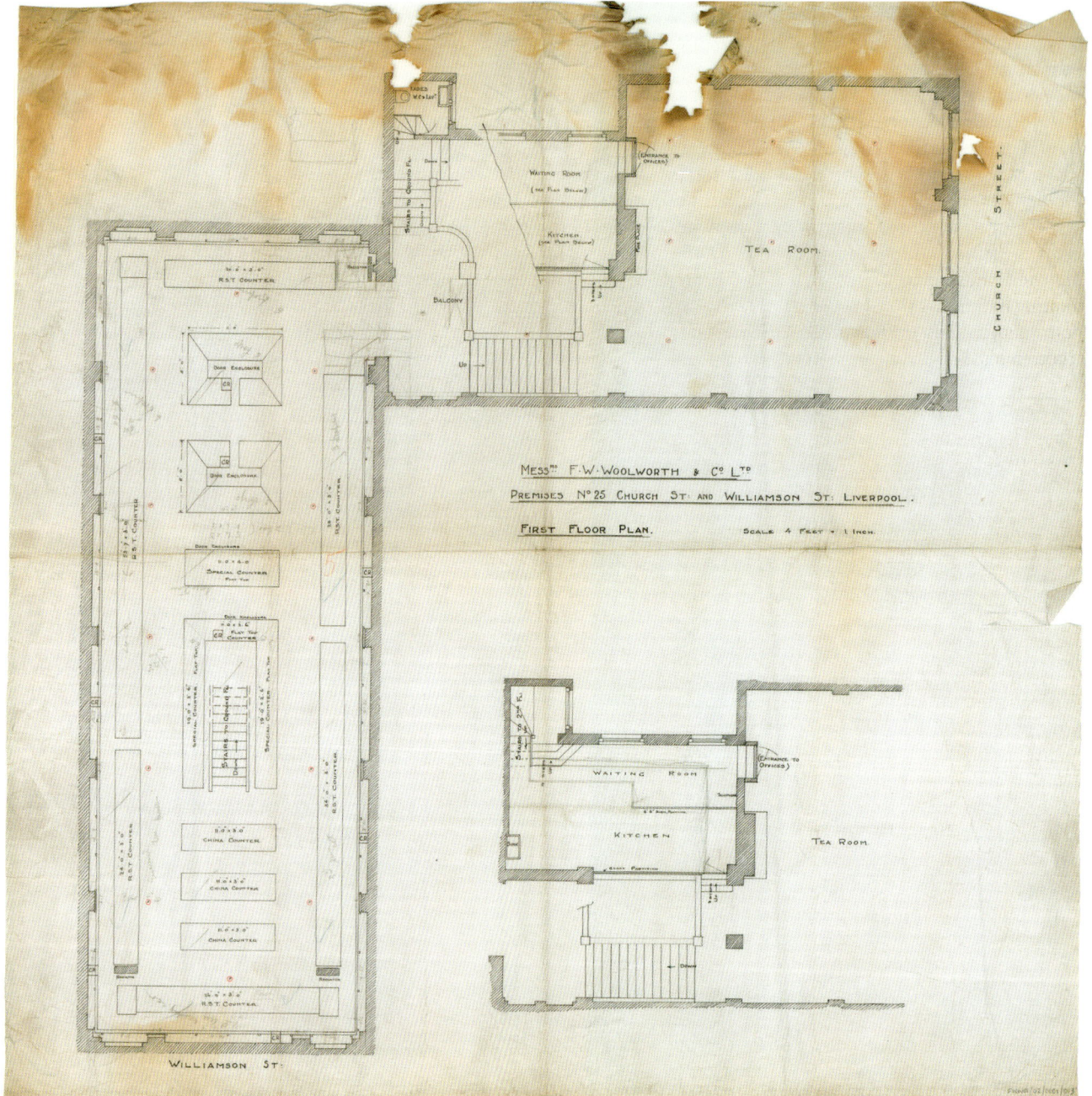

counters feature in a photograph of 1897, showing the first Woolworth store in New York.[12]

Over the Church Street salesroom was the tea room (Fig 2.7). This seems to have been an innovation for the company. The first Woolworth eatery in America was the 'Refreshment Room' that opened in the Fourteenth Street store in New York in August 1910; this was Balfour's old store, and so it is likely, in this rare instance, that the US chain was inspired by its British offspring rather than vice versa.[13] The offices and stockroom occupied the top floors, overlooking Church Street. In 1931 William L Stephenson reminisced: 'Over our one store was my office, a dingy little place where I used to buy goods. We did all the work ourselves, even to sweeping out the floors and hauling the cases about in the stock-room.'[14] Cochrane remembered 'the buying office of Mr W L Stephenson, and the office of the Construction Department, occupied by one elderly gentleman'.[15] This employee must have been instrumental in adapting and fitting out successive stores in the chain, and so it is unfortunate Cochrane had forgotten his name.

Figs 2.6 and Fig 2.7 Contemporary postcards show the interior of the Liverpool store. Miles's top-lit millinery show-room was stripped of its tall, glass showcases and furnished with freestanding china counters. On opening day, free teas were served in the tea room: note the doorway to Stephenson's second-floor Buying Office. [Courtesy of woolworths museum.co.uk, © 3D and 6D Pictures Ltd]

British antecedents and rivals

Naturally, great curiosity surrounded the opening of Woolworth's first store in Liverpool. Since the end of the Napoleonic Wars, British shopkeepers had tended to look for inspiration to Paris, with its elegant arcades and ornate *grands magasins,* but the sheer scale and bravado of American retailing was beginning to grab more attention.

Woolworth was not the first retailer to transfer an American commercial model to English soil, though he was probably the first chain store proprietor to do so. Indeed, in 1909 there was a suspicion that the Americans were plotting to invade the English retail scene, since, in March 1909, just as Woolworth was issuing his call for volunteers in New York, Gordon Selfridge had opened a mammoth new store at the west end of London's Oxford Street (Fig 2.8).[16] Perhaps these two events were connected: news of Selfridge's colossal enterprise may have spurred Frank Woolworth into action after years of cogitation.

Selfridge's background and experience were very different from Woolworth's. Back in Chicago, Selfridge had worked in the vast dry-goods store of Marshall Field, and he had briefly been proprietor of the Schlesinger & Mayer store. Selfridge was an adept retail showman, highly skilled in the arts of promotion, display and advertisement, and the opening of his Oxford Street store was oiled by a vast publicity machine. It was proclaimed as

'London's first great "Store" based on an American model'.[17] This statement, and its use of quotation marks, demands some explanation. British cities already had their fair share of large retail warehouses or emporiums: businesses like Whiteley's in Notting Hill or Bainbridge's in Newcastle. These are thought of, historically, as 'department stores', and it is certainly true that they were subdivided into shops or departments, selling different categories of merchandise, but in Edwardian Britain the word 'store' was applied principally to shops run by co-operative societies, or to local grocery shops. The term 'department store', though familiar to Americans like Woolworth, did not become common currency until after the First World War. Thus the deliberate adoption of the term 'store' by Selfridge, and by Woolworth in his turn, must have seemed curiously out of context, and distinctly, perhaps even exotically, American.

Other aspects of Selfridge's store would undoubtedly have been perceived as American. First of all, the sheer bulk of his brand new building must have impressed onlookers.[18] The London Building Acts prevented the structure soaring to the same heights as its skyscraping counterparts in Chicago, but the architecture drew on the latest technology and style. Its structural steel frame was designed by the Swedish engineer Sven Bylander and erected with unprecedented speed. The grandiose Beaux Arts façades were devised by the American architects Daniel Burnham and Frank Swales but executed under the auspices of the English architect Robert Frank Atkinson, who made a speciality of commercial buildings. The impact of these elevations, with their great bronze and glass panels and inherent verticality, cannot be underestimated. Their influence dominated British retail architecture into the 1930s.

Inside Selfridge's building, extensive open-plan floors permitted vast displays of goods and encouraged browsing, if not always handling. As yet, informal browsing was uncommon in high-class London emporiums, where goods were generally stowed behind counters and revealed to seated customers by obsequious sales staff. Selfridge's policy of allowing customers to study goods without interference was shared by Woolworth, who was highly critical of the intimidating courtesies of English shopping. However, in Woolworth's lowly five-and-ten stores, goods were piled on

Fig 2.8
The Chicago retailer Gordon Selfridge opened his impressive new store on Oxford Street, London, in March 1909, just three months before Woolworth arrived in England with his team of 'pioneers'. Selfridge's confidence may have strengthened Woolworth's resolve to open a chain in Britain. [BL20507]

Fig 2.9
In Britain, Woolworth's was regarded as a 'bazaar', a form of retailing rooted in the late Georgian period. As shown here – at the Pantheon (1834; Sydney Smirk), a former theatre on Oxford Street, London – bazaar goods were laid out on counter tops overseen by female sales assistants, encouraging browsing. This later became the site of a Marks & Spencer's store. [London Metropolitan Archives, City of London (Collage 26601)]

counter tops without the finesse of Selfridge's crafted displays. Furthermore, Woolworth's clientele was very different: few of his customers would have dared to cross Selfridge's threshold. If, at first, Selfridge and Woolworth were business rivals, it was simply as two wealthy Americans making dramatic entries onto the British retail stage, for they were not in direct competition for the same custom. The situation changed two years later, in 1911, when Selfridge opened the first bargain basement in the country, regarded as a 'store within a store'.[19] This may have anticipated the arrival, before too long, of a Woolworth's store on London's Oxford Street. It was 1924, however, before such a store eventually materialised (*see* Figs 3.14 and 3.15).

The Americans helped to popularise the browsing of open displays in British shops but they were not, as is so often asserted, responsible for its introduction. This was the peculiar contribution of British bazaars, which bore only the vaguest relationship to the exotic oriental bazaars whose name they appropriated.[20] To this day, the best-known type of bazaar is the charitable bazaar or sale-of-work: usually a one-off event held to support a deserving cause. In 1816, however, the opening of the Soho Bazaar, on Soho Square in London, heralded a particular genre of bazaar

retailing that remained highly fashionable among the middle and upper classes for about 50 years. Bazaar proprietors usually provided stalls in impressive buildings, such as the Pantheon on Oxford Street (Fig 2.9). These were rented to saleswomen, who displayed their goods openly on counter tops. Because the saleswomen were often 'distressed gentlewomen', rather than salaried shop girls, bazaars had a respectable and charitable appeal. At their height, long before the invention of the department store, they were places where the beau monde might promenade for pleasure, buy knick-knacks, take refreshments and enjoy entertainments such as dioramas and panoramas.

Victorian shoppers were constantly seeking novelty, just as consumers do today. Thus bazaars eventually lost their lustre and fell from fashion. As this happened, in the 1860s, bazaar retailing was given a spectacularly downmarket twist with the invention of the 'penny bazaar' (Fig 2.10), and variants such as the 'sixpenny bazaar'. These fixed-price 'bazaars' bore little resemblance to their polite predecessors of the same name. Often they were dark, pokey shops, or even market stalls, with open fronts and garish signboards. They shared one feature in common with the elegant bazaars of earlier decades: the practice

Fig 2.10
A typical open-fronted
British penny bazaar:
B A Gale's Premier Penny
Bazaar in Southampton.
As the card indicates,
Gale had a second
branch in Portsmouth.
This was posted in 1914.
[Author's collection]

Fig 2.10
A typical open-fronted
British penny bazaar:
B A Gale's Premier Penny
Bazaar in Southampton.
As the card indicates,
Gale had a second
branch in Portsmouth.
This was posted in 1914.
[Author's collection]

of displaying goods openly on counter tops, often in baskets, where they could be scrutinised and handled – and, it has to be said, pilfered – by customers. The adoption of the term 'bazaar' may have alluded to this method of salesmanship but, as with the widespread adoption of the name 'Bon Marché' (*see* p 3), it may also have been an attempt to acquire cachet through a spurious association with a more upmarket retail format. Either way, the rapid spread of the fixed-price bazaar hastened the decline of established bazaars by debasing the concept. In earlier bazaars the goods had often been handcrafted, prices had been moderate, saleswomen were genteel and customers well-to-do. In penny and sixpenny bazaars, cheap, mass-produced goods were displayed in the manner of market stalls and sold by poorly paid shop girls to working-class customers.

At almost exactly the same time that Frank W Woolworth was building up his chain of five-and-tens in America, entrepreneurs were beginning to set up chains of penny and sixpenny bazaars in Britain and Ireland. But this was a risky business and few enjoyed Woolworth's spectacular success. One of the most ambitious was a naturalised German, Erdmann Gottlieb Sellentin, who built up a large chain of sixpenny bazaars between 1883 and 1887, before going bankrupt.[21] He had established his central depot in Birmingham,

the centre of the fancy goods trade and an important source of merchandise for bazaar traders, and opened branches in cities such as York, Derby, Bradford, Coventry, Dublin and Edinburgh. Similarly, Edward Smith failed when he set up a chain of sixpenny bazaars in Scotland, including Perth, Kirkcaldy and Haddington, and north-east England.[22] In contrast, Marks & Spencer's penny bazaars went from strength to strength.

Just as Woolworth claimed to have invented the five-and-ten in America, so Marks & Spencer's claimed to have originated the concept of the penny bazaar in England, when Michael Marks opened a market stall in Leeds in 1884. By the late 1890s, Marks & Spencer's fascias were commonly inscribed either 'Original Penny Bazaar' or 'Originators of Penny Bazaars' (Fig 2.11).[23] This was largely puff. Penny bazaars are documented in the British Isles from around 1860, with sixpenny bazaars becoming popular rather later, in the 1880s. Marks & Spencer's, nevertheless, became the foremost penny bazaar company in the country, buying up several rival chains, such as the London Penny Bazaar Co. Buying up the opposition was a quick and easy way for a multiple retailer to expand. Although not a growth strategy adopted by British Woolworth's, much of Frank Woolworth's rapid expansion in America in the early 1900s had been achieved in just this manner.

With more than 50 shops and market stalls by 1909, Marks & Spencer's was undoubtedly one of Woolworth's principal competitors in the British Isles, especially in the south and south-east. In 1909 its shops had open fronts topped by bright red signboards, with prominent 'Admission Free' signs to encourage those unsure of the etiquette of entering a shop. Inside, goods were piled into baskets on horseshoe-shaped counters. Although the direction of travel is uncertain, this style of salesmanship indicates cross-influence between American and British fixed-price retail outlets. Furthermore, just as Woolworth stores had signs reading 'Any article on this counter 5¢', Marks & Spencer's displayed very similar signs reading 'Any article this section 1d', and so forth. Despite being named 'penny bazaar' and adopting a Britannia (reverse) one penny logo, Marks & Spencer's did not stick to goods with a value of 1d. Items could cost as much as 6d, and so there was a strong correspondence between its merchandise and that of Woolworth's. The arrival of Woolworth's prompted Marks & Spencer's to refurbish its shops, introducing glass-fronted shopfronts for the first time.[24]

In Britain, Woolworth's was regarded for many years as a 'domestic bazaar' (a type of bazaar specialising in household items). It was referred to as such, or as 'the American bazaar', by the public, in the press and even in post-office directories, though the word never appeared on the company's own signboards or in its literature. Frank Woolworth himself noted that he had a particular rival, whom he discussed in a letter of 1909: 'Our chief competitor, who has one hundred and thirty 6½d bazaars all over England, is rumoured ready to give up and not fight us. How can he when he confines himself to one price in his small stores and only carries china, glass and enamelware while we carry 1d, 3d, and 6d goods and our lines are unlimited?'[25] This description fits the Domestic Bazaar Co, which, despite Woolworth's braggadocio, traded until 1935.

Competitors were certainly alarmed by Woolworth's intention to establish a chain in Britain. Interrogated on this matter in an interview with *The Draper's Record* in August 1909, Frank Woolworth argued that his stores would prove a 'drawing force', stimulating trade for retailers coming within his orbit.[26] He continued: 'I am now running 230 stores in different parts of the States, and if I find there is

a market for my goods in this country I shall perhaps open as many in England; but at present we shall open a few, and continue as necessity occurs. But I do not want either drapers or any other tradesmen to regard this as an American invasion.'[27]

Links in the chain, 1909–1914

Barely pausing to relish the success of the Liverpool venture, the pioneers pressed ahead with establishing the chain, allocating sequential numbers to the stores as they opened, starting with '1' for Liverpool (*see* Table 1 and Appendix 2). At first they sought to lease and adapt prime sites in busy shopping centres, rather than buy freeholds and take direct charge of new building operations. This approach seems to have been preferred by the founder in the United States. It enabled the chain to grow speedily, involved less initial outlay and allowed the

Fig 2.11
Marks & Spencer's penny bazaar in Portsmouth was erected in 1910. At this time most of Marks & Spencer's bazaars were in market halls rather than purpose-built high-street buildings.
[The M&S Company Archive]

Table 1 Woolworth's Stores, 1909–1914

Store Number	Store Name/Address	Opening Date	Store Number	Store Name/Address	Opening Date
1	Liverpool 25 Church St	5 Nov 1909	23	Richmond 19, 20 and 21 The Quadrant	1913
2	Preston 9 Fishergate	5 Feb 1910	24	Southampton 100, 101 and 102 East St	1913
3	Liverpool 133–137 London Rd	Feb 1910	25	Cardiff 50–54 Queen St	Summer 1913
4	Manchester 10–12 Oldham St	1910	26	Wood Green 48 High Rd	1913
5	Leeds Exchange Buildings	1910	27	Newcastle-upon-Tyne 15–21 Northumberland St	6 Sept 1913
6	Hull 4–5 Whitefriargate	11 Nov 1910	28	Darlington 78–79 (later renumbered as 66–68) Northgate	27 Sept 1913
7	Brixton 415–417 Brixton Rd/ 2 Atlantic Rd	10 Dec 1910	29	Derby 29–30 Victoria St	7 Nov 1913
8	Middlesbrough 91–93 Linthorpe Rd	1911	30	Edgware Road 178–180 Edgware Rd	21 Mar 1914
9	Woolwich 26–28 Hare St	1911	31	Dublin 65–68 Grafton St	23 April 1914
10	Bristol 63 Castle St	1911	32	Dudley 38a Market Place	25 April 1914
11	Harlesden 37–39 High St	1912	33	Southend-on-Sea 29 High St	25 April 1914
12	Croydon 60 North End	4 May 1912	34	Clapham Junction 36–38 St John's Rd	1 Aug 1914
13	Wolverhampton 58–59 Victoria St	June 1912	35	Portsmouth (Landport) 164–166 Commercial Rd	22 Aug 1914
14	Swansea 243–244 High St	1912	36	Nottingham 22–26 Listergate	Aug 1914
15	Peckham 91–93 Rye Lane	13 July 1912	37	Bradford 12–14 Darley St	Aug 1914
16	Bolton 26–30 Deangate	9 Nov 1912	38	Swindon 92 Regent St	12 Sept 1914
17	Chatham 112 High St	16 Nov 1912	39	Glasgow 62–70 Union St	Oct 1914
18	Grimsby 58–59 Freeman St	1913	40	Colchester 48–50 High St	Sept 1914
19	Ilford 120–122 High Rd	1912	41	Hammersmith 90–92 King St	Oct 1914
20	Lewisham 142–144 High St	1913	42	Cricklewood 154–156 The Broadway	1914
21	Wimbledon 30 The Broadway	22 March 1913	43	Kingston upon Thames 6 Clarence St	14 Nov 1914
22	Warrington 19–21 Sankey St	26 April 1913	44	Norwich 21–25 Rampant Horse St	Nov 1914

company to relocate without too much difficulty if a site proved unprofitable or a better site became available. While Byron De Witt Miller and Fred Woolworth took responsibility for scouting in the south, Stephenson was assisted in the north of England by the American manager John Benjamin Snow (1883–1973), who joined the team in 1910.[28] Expert advice was received from E J Smith, Frank Woolworth's American location specialist, who travelled with his boss to England in the winter of 1909: they sailed home together on the *Mauretania* on 11 December, no doubt pleased with what they had seen in Liverpool.[29]

The geographical distribution pattern of the early stores reveals that Woolworth's scouts adopted several deliberate strategies. In the course of 1910–11, for example, Stephenson and Snow opened a string of stores across northern England, from west to east, following the line of the Lancashire and Yorkshire Railway. Reportedly Stephenson's brainwave, this allowed the railway to serve as a supply line, linking the European port of Hull with the transatlantic port of Liverpool, thereby connecting Woolworth's continental suppliers with the company's American warehouses via a chain of English stores.[30] The opening of these stores caused much excitement. Stores 2 and 3 opened within days of one another, in February 1910, on Fishergate in Preston and on London Road in Liverpool, respectively. The opening events were carefully planned by John B Snow, but a near-riot broke out at the opening of Store 3: 'The counters were mobbed by shawl-clad, bare-footed women in such number that the very sales counters were pushed about the floor; shop girls fainted; and the customers

helped themselves to the goods without the formality of paying for them.'[31] Barriers and ropes ensured less chaotic openings in Oldham Street, Manchester, and Exchange Buildings, Leeds, followed by Whitefriargate, Hull (Fig 2.12), and Linthorpe Road, Middlesbrough (Figs 2.13 and 2.14). Other northern stores followed, including Darlington (Fig 2.15).

Another deliberate tactic was to establish a presence in the major suburban centres ringing central London. The first of these stores opened on the corner of Atlantic Road in Brixton on 10 December 1910 (Fig 2.16). This may seem a surprising choice of location, but Brixton was one of the busiest shopping centres in south London, dominated by the Bon Marché emporium. Woolworth's store was sandwiched awkwardly between two railway lines, but since it lay opposite the Bon Marché, it was actually a prime retail position. Marks & Spencer's, with its focus on London, often had an established presence on the streets selected by Woolworth's scouts but, contrary to popular belief, Woolworth's did not open up directly opposite a Marks & Spencer's store in Brixton, quite the reverse: Marks & Spencer's relocated across the road from Woolworth's in 1931.[32] As yet Woolworth's had no presence in the West End, England's principal shopping district, though Frank Woolworth surely nurtured ambitions to open a large store near Selfridge's on Oxford Street.

In provincial cities, on the other hand, central sites were preferred from the outset and only much later did Woolworth's begin to target outlying shopping centres. Before long the company had a good spread of sites throughout

Fig 2.12
A display of lighting and Coleman's 'Vitacup' (tonic food) in the window of Store 6, No 5 Whitefriargate, Hull, in the mid-1920s. The shopfront was unchanged since 1910, when the store first opened. Features typical of Woolworth's earliest shopfronts included barley-twist colonnettes or 'sash bars' and large lunettes over doors. Store 6 closed on 7 April 1984. [FWW01/01/0006/001]

Figs 2.13 and 2.14 Contemporary drawings show the shopfront and the original first-floor counter layout of Store 8, at Nos 91–93 Linthorpe Road, Middlesbrough, which opened in 1911. This branch occupied a fashionable new building but its general arrangements emulated those of the first store in Liverpool (compare Fig 2.5). In 1926 Woolworth's moved to a larger site at Nos 51–67 Linthorpe Rd, but the building at Nos 91–93 still stands. [FWW01/02/0008/004; FWW01/02/0008/003]

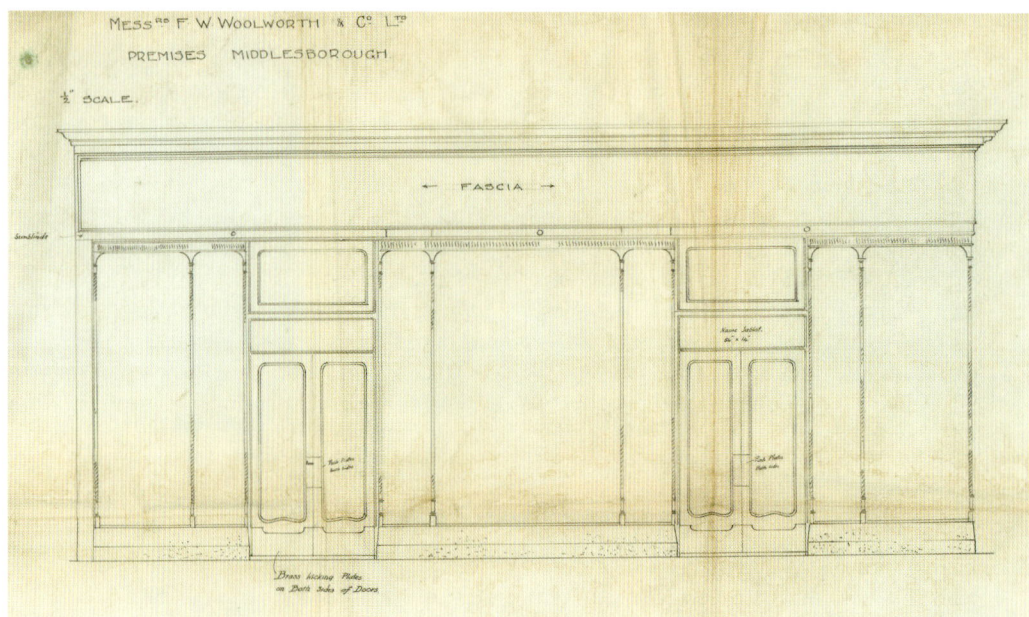

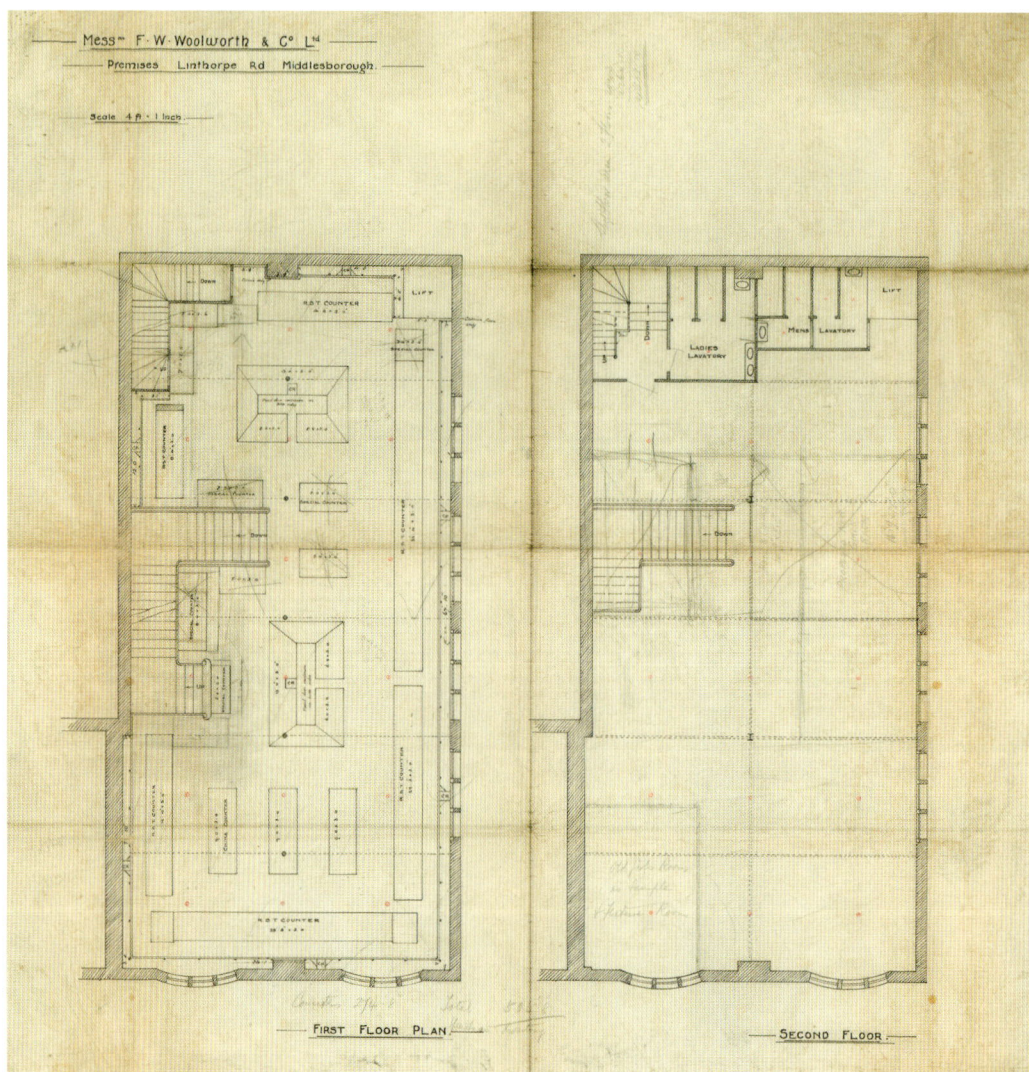

Fig 2.15
An undated photograph of Store 28 at Nos 78–79 (later renumbered as Nos 66–68) Northgate in Darlington, which opened on 27 September 1913. Although this shows the original building, the photograph may have marked the completion of alterations in 1927. Posters in the window announce a reduction in glassware prices, 'your requirements' for spring cleaning time, and an invitation to 'patronise our tea bar'. In 1940 Store 28 moved to the former King's Head Hotel at Nos 12–18 Northgate. [FWW01/01/0028/001]

Fig 2.16
This photograph of Woolworth's first London store, Store 7, which opened in Brixton in 1910, was taken around 1926 – the type of pedestrian crossing in the foreground was introduced in that year. The photograph marked the recent completion of a first-floor extension with Venetian-style glazing. Until this opened, the main sales areas had been restricted to the ground floor and basement, with stockrooms on the upper levels. The sign on the viaduct advertises Wallace Hughes, whose nearby drapery shop sold 'black wear' for mourning. Woolworth's relocated in the 1930s and Burton's built a new store on this site in the 1950s. [FWW01/01/0028/001]

England and began to cast its eyes on other parts of the British Isles. Between 1912 and 1914 stores opened in the most prestigious shopping districts of Swansea, Cardiff and Dublin. By the outbreak of war in August 1914 Woolworth's was operating 34 stores, and by the end of that year the number had risen to 44 (*see* Table 1).

In 1912 F W Woolworth & Co made a profit of £100,000 and its capital was increased through a further share issue to £100,000.[33] A year later the head office moved from Liverpool to London, to Central House on the newly created thoroughfare of Kingsway, which, with its metropolitan feel and spacious modern office blocks, was perhaps closer in ambience to the high-rise business districts of American cities than most other streets in central London. Moreover, Kingsway lay close to the Savoy Hotel on the Strand, which was favoured by Woolworth's executives. The former head office on Church Street, Liverpool, became the northern office, with oversight of Ireland, Wales and Scotland, as well as the north of England. Woolworth, Stephenson, Miller and Snow were all based at the new southern office. Snow now concentrated on his work as a buyer, while Miller, for the time being, scouted for store locations and supervised building works.

Building work, 1909–1914

In the early years, Woolworth's commissioned few new buildings, preferring to convert existing premises. Miller and his colleagues – including the unidentified 'elderly gentleman' in the Construction Department remembered by John Cochrane (*see* p 9) – generally liaised with reputable local architects, engaging those with proven experience of commercial building projects. Thomas Scamell & Son of Bristol designed Woolworth's new store on the site of the old Bristol Castle, on the corner of Castle Street and Queen Street. This was completed in 1911 (Fig 2.17).[34] Similarly in Nottingham, in 1914, Frederick Ball drew up plans for Woolworth's store on the site of the Caledonian Hotel, Listergate.[35] Right through to the 1960s, hotel sites were targeted by Woolworth's location scouts, probably because they occupied exceptionally deep, wide plots, offering more spacious sales floors than traditional shops and, often, rear access.

In Manchester, it is intriguing to find that Charles Heathcote was called upon in autumn 1913 to adapt the premises at Nos 6–8 Oldham Street as an extension to the original Woolworth's store of 1910 at Nos 10–12 Oldham Street.[36] As well as being one of Manchester's leading commercial architects, Heathcote could

Fig 2.17
Woolworth's Store 10, in Bristol – designed by Thomas Scamell and completed in 1911 – was one of the very first to be purpose-built for the company. It was bombed during the Second World War. This postcard dates from the 1920s.
[Author's collection]

count several American companies among his clientele, including Westinghouse, Henry Ford and now Woolworth's. Heathcote's extension of 1913 made Woolworth's Manchester store one of the largest in the chain. The sales area occupied the entire ground and first floors; the second floor was divided into a café to the front, and a stockroom to the rear, while the third floor was devoted entirely to stock. The main architectural feature was a central branching staircase under a glass roof. For a fixed-price bazaar, this was palatial, ranking alongside Woolworth's first store in Liverpool.

Increasingly, Woolworth's embarked upon the construction of new store buildings through intermediaries, notably Shop Properties Ltd. This was a subsidiary of Hillier & Parker, the commercial estate agents and property analysts founded by brothers-in-law William Augustus Hillier and Thomas Parker in 1896. Shop Properties was probably set up as Hillier & Parker's property-owning arm: the two companies shared an address, No 99 Regent Street, London, on the corner of Swallow Street (Fig 2.18), and had the same directors. Parker, in particular, is said to have acted as an adviser to Woolworth's, and to have acquired many of the firm's early sites around the country.[37] Woolworth's maintained its close working relationship with Hillier & Parker (from 1921, Hillier Parker May & Rowden) for decades.

One of Shop Properties' projects for Woolworth's was in Kingston upon Thames (Fig 2.19). In July 1913, having secured Woolworth's as a tenant, Shop Properties entered into an agreement with the owners of an irregularly shaped site running between Church Street and Clarence Street. This was a prime location in the heart of the town, directly opposite Bentall's store and next to a bank. Shop Properties assumed responsibility for replacing the existing buildings with new premises for Woolworth's at a cost of over £4,000.[38] Clearly, Woolworth's requirements were the defining factor in the design and layout of the building. Woolworth's was already trading from the new store by December 1914, when a 30-year lease was drawn up.[39] While Shop Properties held the site on a 99-year lease at £200 per annum, it received an annual rent from Woolworth's of £650, rising to £700 after the first seven years. Woolworth's 'repairing' lease was fairly restrictive. It stipulated that structural alterations could be made only with the agreement of Shop Properties (who, in turn,

had to seek permission from the freeholder), it forbade the sale of most fresh foodstuffs ('the trade of butcher, greengrocer or fishmonger') and specified maintenance, such as painting the exterior woodwork and metalwork every seven years. Woolworth's was, however, granted the freedom to change its shopfront without having to seek formal permission.

The architects of the new building were North & Robin.[40] This partnership had been formed in 1903 between Sidney Vincent North (1872–1951) and Charles Collas Robin (c 1876–1916), and one of their most significant buildings to date was the Heywood Library, Rochdale, of 1906, executed in a baroque style with strongly defined gables. Since North & Robin's office was at No 99 Regent Street (see Fig 2.18), alongside Hillier & Parker, it would appear they had developed a professional attachment to Shop Properties Ltd. They designed several buildings for Woolworth's between 1913 and 1919, no doubt with Shop Properties as the company's landlord in each case.

The Kingston upon Thames store opened on 14 November 1914, shortly after the outbreak of war. The style of the Clarence Street frontage, with its bold Classical flourishes, was much in

Fig 2.18
No 99 Regent Street: the offices of the commercial estate agent Hillier & Parker, with North & Robin's office above. While Hillier & Parker found and developed many sites for Woolworth's, North & Robin designed some of the company's first purpose-built stores. [London Metropolitan Archives, City of London (Collage 136603)]

Fig 2.19
Store 43 in Kingston upon
Thames was designed
by North & Robin and
erected in 1913–14.
This photograph of the
Clarence Street façade was
commissioned by a later
partner of North & Robin's,
Percy T Wilsdon, and was
taken on 2 November 1920.
A sign in the window reads
'Visit our Restaurant for
Luncheons and Teas' and
the menu includes plaice
and chips for 6d. By 1926
this restaurant had become
a sales area. Store 43
moved to a new site in
1930 (see Fig 3.40).
[BL25186]

vogue for commercial buildings. Above Woolworth's standard shopfront this façade was dominated by a strong centrepiece, with a tripartite window set beneath a cartouche within a deeply projecting open pediment. On the ground floor, the open-plan sales floor widened to the rear, corresponding to Church Street, where a secondary entrance had been created by 1916. It was encumbered with as few steel stanchions and columns as possible. The centre of the store, potentially a difficult area to light adequately, was served by windows overlooking a small light well. A narrow spur to

Wood Street contained the goods entrance: this was a partially covered yard with a goods lift as well as stairs to the first-floor stockroom. Staff lavatories opened off the stockroom, but there was no cloakroom or staffroom until 1916.[41] A straight public staircase to one side of the store led up to the first-floor café and a small kitchen. This arrangement recurred in other stores and probably represented Woolworth's preference.

Several other pre-1914 Woolworth's stores opened in new buildings which broadly resembled the Kingston upon Thames branch

Fig 2.20
Store 17 opened in
Chatham, Kent, in 1912.
Like many pioneering
Woolworth's branches, this
neo-baroque building was
replaced by a larger store
in the 1930s (see Fig 4.38).
[FWW01/01/0017/002]

and may also have been purpose-built for the company, including Chatham, Kent (Fig 2.20). Some might well have been designed by North & Robin. Few of the buildings occupied by Woolworth's at the outbreak of the First World War (*see* Table 1), however, fall into this category. As in Liverpool, Manchester and Hull, adapted premises were sometimes fitted with a new shopfront in Woolworth's house style, but this was not inevitable. Some inherited shopfronts conformed approximately to Woolworth's preferred style and appear to have been retained into the 1920s.[42]

Inside the pioneer stores

Visual evidence for the interiors of early Woolworth's stores is sparse, but architectural drawings reveal that they typically had matchboarded ceilings and walls, and bare wooden floors. They were brightly lit by electric lights with opaque glass shades suspended from the ceilings but, since electricity was still unreliable, supplementary gas lighting was always installed as an emergency backup, a safeguard that endured into the 1960s. The massive gas fittings appear to have been used at times as heaters, though stores were also equipped with radiators. The general layout derived from the American stores. Displays with sales points lined the side walls and, through the centre of each store, mahogany island counters were arranged to form oblong wells where sales assistants stood, waiting to serve shoppers. In addition, as in Liverpool, there were a number of free-standing 'special' display units.

Press reports of shoplifting cases clarify that just one girl was in charge of each counter and that goods were grouped by price as well as by category of merchandise. Arranging goods by price left no doubt in the customer's mind about the cost of individual items. These were mostly,

Fig 2.21
Identified by Woolworth's
historian Paul Seaton as
Store 12, which opened in
1912 at No 60 North End,
Croydon, this photograph
offers a rare glimpse inside
an ordinary, and rather
chaotic, early Woolworth's
store. This was one of the
few pioneering sites to
be retained – though
hugely extended – into
the 21st century.
[Courtesy of woolworths
museum.co.uk, © 3D
and 6D Pictures Ltd]

at this date, unpackaged and unbranded. Adjustable glass dividers were used to separate batches of items on counter tops, and large square notices in metal frames clearly identified the prices as 1d, 3d or 6d. A rare undated photograph of a counter has been identified as the Croydon branch, which opened on 4 May 1912 (Fig 2.21).[43] Sales were cash only, no credit, and the counters were equipped with cash registers. In America, Woolworth had abandoned centralised cash systems – the cash railways and pneumatic tubes so common at this time – for cash registers in 1900.[44] As yet, these did not add up automatically, but Woolworth's fixed-price approach meant that sales staff seldom had to deal with complicated arithmetic. Just in case, they often kept a jotter and pencil tied around their waist.

Woolworth's attempted to stock British-made goods, to pacify critics and appeal to customers' innate patriotism. In 1909 Frank Woolworth, writing from England, observed: 'Most goods here are better made and cheaper than in America ... Five cent goods can be bought for two or three cents. This means that when we open in England we shall sell very few American goods.'[45] Nevertheless, some merchandise was certainly imported from

America. Liverpool was a major port on the transatlantic route, and quite a number of American 'gadgets', even tomahawks, found their way onto the counters of the Church Street store.[46] Other items, such as dolls and Christmas baubles, came from continental Europe. In 1931 Stephenson admitted: 'In our first store we sold a variety of goods like we are selling today; but there was one great difference. At that time 85 per cent of our goods were foreign novelties brought over from Japan, Germany and other countries, whereas today only 15 per cent of the articles we sell come in from abroad.'[47] It was no doubt difficult to persuade British manufacturers to deal with the company directly, rather than, in the time-honoured manner, through wholesalers.

Some indication of the range of goods typically sold in Woolworth's British stores prior to the First World War was provided by a reporter for the *Derby Daily Telegraph*, who was given a preview of his local store prior to its opening on 7 November 1913:

The firm are making special features of toys, sweets, toilet goods, haberdashery, stationery, ironmongery, as well as mantles, burners, and globes and all articles in connection with incandescent gas lighting. Other special lines are ewers, basins, large jardinières, umbrellas, ladies' velvet slippers, vases, a choice assortment of pictures and electro-plated goods; jewellery, celluloid goods, and all kinds of fancy and useful articles too numerous to classify.[48]

Further insights into the merchandise carried by the early stores are offered by reports of shoplifting. Such cases abounded since many people, often with hitherto spotless reputations, had never encountered 'open access' shopping before and were sorely tempted. Stolen items included soap, mirrors, combs, scissors, packets of jelly, rubber balls, paintbrushes and even a live tortoise, taken from the Hull store by a 14-year-old errand boy. A report in the *Hull Daily Mail* revealed: 'The manager, after giving evidence, said that they got the tortoises in lots of a hundred and fed them on lettuce. They got the tortoises in the morning and sold them in the evening. They were good for killing beetles and insects.'[49]

Noting the sheer volume of shoplifting cases relating to Woolworth's, the Hull magistrate advised the company to cover its counters with sheets of glass. The manager retorted that this would not be possible because 'the people really enjoy handling the goods', and besides, it would cost £500 to £1,000 to implement.[50] The magistrate then suggested that a piece of wood a few inches high be fitted to the front of the counters, to make it more difficult to reach the goods. The manager promised to put this suggestion to his employers, surely knowing they would be unreceptive. Open access was crucial to the appeal of Woolworth's.

Shoplifting reports suggest that Woolworth's staff were trained to be store detectives as much as sales assistants. Invariably, young women were recruited in this role: advertisements for staff in Hull strictly specified 'young ladies ... age 17–19'.[51] As well as being cheap to employ, young women had sharp eyes and quick reflexes. Some required special skills: an advertisement for a young lady pianist in Liverpool in March 1914 reflected the fact that sheet music was a popular line, and an assistant was required to play tunes requested by customers.[52] Woolworth's 'girls', as they were invariably known, were expected to work long hours. In Derby this triggered a strike that was resolved only when the manager, acknowledging that the girls habitually worked overtime, reinstated two assistants whom he had dismissed.[53] Labour relations remained

Fig 2.22
Before the 1920s most Woolworth's stores had a café or a simple tea bar. Here we see Woolworth's rudimentary refreshment counter at Nos 164–166 Commercial Road, Portsmouth, with a display of mineral waters and custards. This was Store 35: the first to open after the outbreak of war in August 1914. The undated postcard appears to date from the earliest years of the store's existence. [Author's collection]

Fig 2.23
At Store 60 in Cheltenham –
which opened in the former
Public Office on the High
Street in December 1915 –
Woolworth's was charged
with maintaining the
enormous Town Clock,
a local landmark installed
on the façade in 1828.
It was modernised during
Woolworth's extension
works of 1933–4, which
were opened by the Mayor.[b]
The clock was removed in
1959, when Woolworth's
moved to a new store on
the site of the Royal Hotel at
Nos 123–125 High Street.
The building shown here
was destroyed by fire a
round 1969.
[FWW01/01/0060/001]

strained, and the same branch got into trouble for failing to give staff the correct local half-day holiday in accordance with the Shops Act of 1911.[54]

From the start, most Woolworth's stores offered refreshments: not always in a tea room with seating and tables like that in Liverpool (see Fig 2.7); sometimes from a simple counter or tea bar, placed to one side of the sales floor (Fig 2.22).

The First World War

It is often assumed that normal commercial life stands still in time of war, but the conflict of 1914–18 did not check Woolworth's expansion. On the contrary, by the time the Armistice was signed on 11 November 1918, the chain had grown from 34 to 77 stores. Admittedly, most of the wartime stores opened in 1914–16, with just a handful following in 1917–18, and expansion remained sluggish through 1919. By this time, however, Woolworth's was represented in many significant shopping centres throughout England, including Norwich, Leicester, Cheltenham (Fig 2.23) and Blackpool, with several stores further afield, for example in Glasgow, Belfast and Dublin.

For the four years of war, trading conditions were fraught. Several managers were upbraided, or even fined, for leaving lights showing on their premises, but illuminating the stores on dark winter evenings was the least of their worries. No fewer than 52 of Woolworth's managers joined the forces and there was a general shortage of male staff. As a result, women began to work in stockrooms, and some were promoted to managerial roles (see Fig 4.4). Frank Woolworth had appointed a handful of female managers to American stores in the past, but these tended to be favoured friends or family, such as his sister-in-law, Mary Ann Creighton. Now, due to the pressures of war, ordinary talented female employees had a chance to prove their worth. Few, however, secured further promotion after their male colleagues resumed their former jobs in 1919, and none, in this generation, ever achieved a post in the company higher than that of store manager.

War also brought severe disruption to Woolworth's supply chain. It became increasingly difficult, nigh impossible, to take deliveries from Europe and America, and so the company turned, as never before, to native producers. The same phenomenon occurred in America, where the brand name 'Woolco' came into use for haberdashery lines.[55] This reliance on home manufacture endured long after hostilities ceased, heightening the distinctiveness of the two companies, on either side of the Atlantic, at least in terms of their merchandising. British Woolworth's continued, perhaps wisely, to resist own-branding, except for a handful of items such as greetings cards and packets of seeds. It also managed to hold its 3d and 6d fixed-price policy throughout the war. Marks & Spencer's, in contrast, was compelled to abandon its penny limit, together with the strapline of 'penny bazaar'. In fact, the war seems to have wiped out the phenomenon of the penny bazaar.

During the war, Central House on Kingsway was requisitioned by the government, being used by the Air Ministry and by the Secret Intelligence Service, among others, and so Woolworth's Executive Office had to move into

temporary premises in Midland Bank Chambers at Nos 196–198 Oxford Street. Responsibility for identifying locations for stores now resided with Louis Denempont (c 1889–1944), a protégée of E J Smith, Woolworth's chief American scout.[56] The business of fitting out new stores became increasingly difficult as the premises of shopfitters were taken over for war work: Sage's Peterborough factory, for example, began to produce seaplanes rather than shopfronts and showcases.[57] This might explain why some wartime stores, such as Stockport, made do with existing or temporary shopfronts for several years.[58]

Despite the inevitable disruption suffered by building trades, several new-build stores were completed in the first two years of the war. Plans for the Putney store, by the local architect J P Matthews, are dated 13 October 1914, just two months after the declaration of war.[59] Although built for E J Jones, the store was obviously designed for Woolworth's tenancy.

In addition, North & Robin continued to work for Woolworth's, probably through Shop Properties Ltd. In November 1915, however, Robin joined the 28th Battalion London Regiment (Artists' Rifles), leaving North to continue on his own. Robin's name lived on in that of the practice after his death in 1916. The frontages of several wartime Woolworth's stores, including Hanley (Fig 2.24), Watford (Fig 2.25) and Ealing (Fig 2.26), were broadly similar to Kingston upon Thames. Each combined an open pediment with a Venetian window. This characteristic feature of North & Robin's work appeared in their designs for

Fig 2.24
Store 55, Hanley. This store opened at Nos 9–7 Upper Market Square on 25 March 1915. It spread into the building to the left at a later date and was rebuilt in the 1930s. [FWW01/01/0055/001]

Fig 2.25
Store 68, in Watford, was designed by North & Robin to replace a fish and poultry shop at No 124 High Street and opened in May 1916. It was photographed on 12 October 1920, possibly in relation to a new shopfront. Shortly afterwards, the central entrance was doubled in size. The sign above the door states that perambulators are not admitted at certain times. It is easy to imagine how these might have caused congestion in such a small store. Store 68, however, soon grew. As adjacent properties were acquired it was progressively rebuilt on a larger scale, first of all c 1936 (see Fig 4.41), then again c 1972. Having become one of the largest stores in Woolworth's portfolio, it was disposed of in 1983 and the site was redeveloped.
[BL25185]

Fig 2.26
Store 74 in Ealing, west London, was probably built specifically for Woolworth's in 1916, the date displayed in the pediment, and the architects may well have been North & Robin. The photograph was taken on 28 November 1930.
[FWW01/01/0074/001]

other clients, for example the Lucania Temperance Billiard Hall at No 242 Pentonville Road, London, of 1923.[60]

A less conspicuous architectural element shared by Hanley and Watford was a parapet in the form of a Classical balustrade. This also featured at the pedimented Bromley branch, which opened shortly after the war, probably in 1919 (Figs 2.27 and 2.28). In the meantime, similar Classical balustrades had crowned two other stores designed by North & Robin, which both opened for trading on 5 August 1916. That on Western Road in Brighton was designed in January 1915 and took a year and a half to build: a measure of the state of the building trade at the time, and also an indication of Woolworth's determination to forge ahead regardless (Fig 2.29).[61] The very similar store in Ramsgate was erected on the site of the Bull &

Fig 2.27
Store 80, Nos 33–34
(later renumbered as
Nos 140–142) High Street,
Bromley, Kent, after
doubling in size in 1926.
Drawings reveal that in
1926 Woolworth's architect
contemplated removing the
original pediment of 1919
and installing a straight
balustrade, but the idea
was discounted. Clearly,
the left-hand side of the old
discoloured balustrade was
dismantled and re-erected to
the left side of the extension.
Arc lights were left in place
in front of the original
façade, but not added to
the extension. Notices
on the doors forbade
perambulators 'in this store
after 2.30pm today'; it was
probably a Saturday. A new
faience front was designed
for this store in autumn
1939, but never built.
[FWW01/01/0080/001]

Fig 2.28
The Bromley store with
a new shopfront in
1969. The lettering was
ridiculously out of scale
with the building.
[FWW01/01/0080/002]

George Hotel, which had been badly damaged during a zeppelin raid in May 1915 (Fig 2.30). The grid-like, or trabeated, façades of these stores lacked the pediments and Classical flourishes typical of North & Robin's other Woolworth's stores and were more expressive of modern steel-frame construction. In each case, above the standard shopfront, red-brick pilasters with plain white plinths and caps flanked large first-floor windows; this was topped by a broad cement-rendered band. The store that opened at The Square, Bournemouth, in 1915 may also have been the work of North & Robin: its square quoins, tripartite upper-floor window and fielded pilasters were typical of their work (Fig 2.31). Woolworth's seems to have made a strategic decision to move into English seaside towns like Bournemouth, realising that its 3d and 6d fixed-price offer made its stores a magnet for British holidaymakers: one of the first was Southend-on-Sea, Essex, in 1914.

Stateside developments

While Fred M Woolworth and his team were busily setting up the British operation, things did not stand still for the American parent company, which continued, for the time being, to dwarf its offspring.

In January 1912, Frank W Woolworth effected the merger of several chains of five-and-ten stores owned by friends and family (the 'friendly rivals'), together covering much of North America. These included S H Knox & Co (112 stores), F M Kirby & Co (96 stores), E P Charlton & Co (53 stores) and C S Woolworth (15 stores), together with two stores owned by William H Moore; Woolworth himself had 318 stores, including the British outlets.[62] All of these stores thenceforth traded under the Woolworth banner. Their former owners, known collectively as 'the founders', became millionaires. They assumed important positions on the board of the new company, while F W

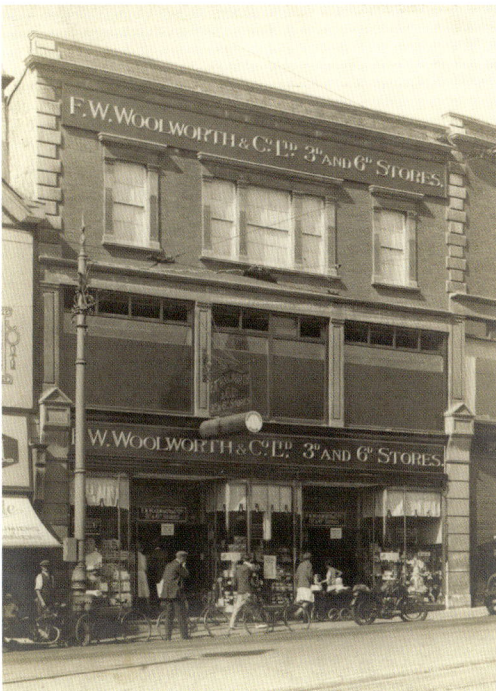

Fig 2.31 (left)
Store 54 opened in Bournemouth in 1915: it was photographed in the 1920s, before being rebuilt in the 1930s (see Fig 4.40). Note the unusual hanging sign incorporating a stick of Bournemouth rock. The windows display piles of buckets and spades, and are plastered with advertisements offering photographic films, developing and printing. Cameras were coming within the budget of ordinary working-class families in the 1920s. In the mid-to-late 1930s, one of Woolworth's most popular items was the sixpenny VP Twin Pocket Camera, manufactured from Bakelite.
[FWW01/01/0054/001]

Fig 2.32
The Woolworth Building
(often referred to as the
'Cathedral of Commerce')
on Broadway, New York,
was designed by Cass Gilbert
and caused a sensation
when it opened in 1913.
It was the tallest building
in the world, a record it
retained for many years.
The site had been acquired
in 1909 and this photograph
shows the structure nearing
completion in 1911. Despite
having the classic tapering
profile of an American
skyscraper, it was dressed
in an ornate French
Gothic style.
[Prints and Photographs
Division, Library of
Congress, LC-USZ62-100109]

Woolworth, inevitably, became the President. The share capital of the new corporation was $65,000,000.

Internationally, the company attracted a vast amount of publicity when Cass Gilbert's Woolworth Building (Fig 2.32) opened on Broadway in New York in 1913. Standing 792ft high (913ft if the basement was included), this aspired to be the highest habitable building in the world at a time when the Eiffel Tower (1,050ft) held the record as the tallest structure. It retained this status until 1930. In fact, only two of its 55 floors (the 23rd and 24th floors, the latter housing the executive offices and Frank Woolworth's private Empire Room, Fig 2.33) were occupied by Woolworth: the remainder was rented out. Businesses flocked to occupy the office suites, and their prestigious address served, indirectly, to advertise the Woolworth name far and wide. The fireproof structure had a steel frame, with internal walls of hollow tiles, and external walls clad in granite and glazed terracotta, highlighted with touches of colour and gilding. This famous Gothic skyscraper symbolised the dominance of the Woolworth Corporation,

especially since F W Woolworth boasted that he had not borrowed a cent to finance its $13.5 million (£3 million) construction cost. Sold to the Woolco Realty Co by the family for $11 million (£2.2 million) in 1924,[63] the building remained the company headquarters until 1998, when it was sold for $137.5 million (£84 million).

American Woolworth, like its British off-shoot, continued to grow during the First World War, and Store 1000 opened in New York in 1918. But Frank Woolworth's personal life was overshadowed by misfortune. His new weekend home, 'Winfield Hall' at Glen Cove on Long Island, burnt down in 1916. More seriously, Woolworth had suffered from ill health for many years, and now his wife, Jennie, lost her short-term memory. Jennie's mental problems may have been exacerbated by the alleged suicide of their middle daughter, Edna Hutton, in 1918. Her body was discovered in her bedroom by her young daughter, Barbara (*see* pp 67–8).

On 8 April 1919, just months after the First World War ended, Frank Winfield Woolworth died rather unexpectedly, at the age of 66, at

Glen Cove, which had been rebuilt following the fire to a design by Cass Gilbert. He was interred in the Egyptian-style family mausoleum at Woodlawn Cemetery.[64] Woolworth had contracted septic poisoning from an untreated tooth infection. At the time, the company had just issued a souvenir booklet to celebrate its 40th anniversary, listing its 1,038 stores in the US and Canada. Woolworth's personal estate amounted to $30 million (£8 million). *The Times* declared, 'Even in the United States, that land of vast fortunes and multi-millionaires, few commercial careers can have been more remarkable than that of Mr Woolworth.'[65] Settling Woolworth's estate was problematic: the only legal will, drafted after an illness in 1889, bequeathed everything to Jennie, who

had been declared legally incompetent in 1918. Although Woolworth had started to compose a new will, it had not been signed. His principal heirs, who inherited following Jennie's death in 1924, were his two surviving daughters and his granddaughter, Barbara Hutton. Frank's brother, Charles Sumner Woolworth, rose through the ranks of the Woolworth Corporation to become Chairman, while the former company Treasurer, Hubert Parsons, became the new President. Byron De Witt Miller was recalled to the US from England to become Finance Director and Senior Vice President, with Snow becoming chief buyer for the British operation in his stead. In 1932, on Parsons' retirement, Miller was appointed President of the company.

3

A roaring trade, 1918–1930

Expansion

British Woolworth's entered a period of frantic expansion after the First World War (*see* Table 2 and Fig 3.1). Local authorities are said to have approached the company in droves, requesting a 'red front' on their own high streets. This was largely because Woolworth's created much-needed jobs at a time of unprecedented unemployment. In 1924, upon the opening of a Woolworth's store in an old terraced building at No 310 Hessle Road, Hull, the local paper praised 'this progressive firm' for creating employment for 60 Hull girls. With the exception of the manager, the entire male staff was 'drawn from the ranks of Hull unemployed'.[1] In addition, Woolworth's was regarded as a magnet that drew other businesses: an irresistible prospect for any ambitious town council. As a result, few planning obstacles were placed in Woolworth's path when it wished to redevelop sites and the company was able to grow rapidly, opening its 100th branch in Mansfield in July 1921, and its 400th in Southport in July 1930.

In 1923 Fred Woolworth died from the effects of a stroke at the age of 52, at the Ritz Hotel, London.[2] Subsequently, this dynamic phase in Woolworth's growth was overseen by his successor, William L Stephenson. Woolworth's Executive Office remained on Oxford Street, London, until around 1921, when the company returned to Kingsway, to a new building called Victory House (1919–20; Trehearne & Norman). This stood just down the street from the former head office, Central House. Yet another move took place in 1929, to New Bond Street House (1929; E A Stone; Fig 3.2) at Nos 1–5 New Bond Street. This large block of shops and offices, distinguished by unusual Byzantine-style domes, stood at the southern end of the street, close to Piccadilly and St James's Street – not the natural habitat

for a variety store like Woolworth's, but the perfect stamping ground for its increasingly wealthy executives and buyers.

For a short time after the war Woolworth's continued to work with the architects North & Robin who, in March 1919, were engaged on alterations to the store at Nos 50–52 St Nicholas Street, Aberdeen, including a new

Fig 3.1
An illustration showing Woolworth's growth, from Twenty Years of Progress, 1928. The two buildings pictured are the original Store 1 in Liverpool and its successor of 1923.
[FWW01/05/01/03]

Fig 3.2
New Bond Street House was home to Woolworth's Executive Office from 1929 until 1959. The sample display room was on the first floor, accounting and imports on the second, buyers on the third (in individual offices), while the boardroom, the Construction Department and architect's office were on the fourth. This view was published in The New Bond, **2**, *12, December 1937, 425.* [FWW01/04/02/425]

Table 2 Number of Woolworth's stores in operation, 1918–1939 (Figures compiled from Woolworth's annual and five-yearly reports)

1918	78	1929	375
1919	81	1930	428
1920	92	1931	458
1921	108	1932	486
1922	126	1933	529
1923	155	1934	598
1924	177	1935	638
1925	207	1936	678
1926	242	1937	711
1927	299	1938	737
1928	343	1939	759

Fig 3.3
William Priddle (1885–1932), photographed in 1928, was Woolworth's Chief Architect from 1919 – if not earlier – until his death. [FWW01/05/01/09]

shopfront by Curtis of Leeds.[3] By this time, however, Woolworth's had appointed its own architect, based at the Executive Office. The first holder of this post was William Priddle (1885–1932, Fig 3.3).

Regrettably, nothing has come to light regarding Priddle's architectural training, although at the time of the 1911 census he was described as an 'architectural assistant' living with his parents and siblings in West Hampstead, London.[4] A year later he married a grocer's daughter, Gwendoline Thompson, who lived at No 15 Broadway, Cricklewood. This is where Priddle practised as an architect and surveyor until 1916, when he enlisted to serve as a draughtsman with the Royal Engineers in France. Very shortly after being demobilised on 22 February 1919, Priddle, at the age of 34, set to work as Woolworth's architect: by 26 March he was signing papers relating to a café extension at Southend-on-Sea.[5] The speed of Priddle's transition from military life to his role with Woolworth's seems remarkable, suggesting that his appointment pre-dated his service in France. Plans for a store in a terrace in Stoke Newington, north London, had been signed by Priddle in December 1915; earlier still, he may have had a hand in the store that opened on Broadway, Cricklewood, in 1914.[6]

Priddle's arrival did not mark an obvious watershed in the architectural treatment of Woolworth's buildings, which maintained continuity with North & Robin's designs to a remarkable degree. As for North & Robin, the firm continued to thrive in the commercial sector. By 1920 North had taken Percy T Wilsdon into partnership: significantly, Percy's brother, Herbert H Wilsdon, had been a director of Hillier & Parker since 1917. Thenceforth practising as North, Robin & Wilsdon, they went on to design a chain of high street stores for the Dutch clothing retailer C&A (Modes) Ltd, as well as taking on numerous other projects, mostly shops, pubs and restaurants, all over the country, through the middle decades of the 20th century. No doubt this continued to be abetted by their close connection with Hillier, Parker, May & Rowden, and from time to time their path crossed with that of Priddle and his team.

Priddle worked closely with William Stephenson, travelling with him to New York in January 1924, probably to look at American stores.[7] Many of Woolworth's architectural drawings from the 1920s and 1930s were marked 'for WLS', or otherwise endorsed by 'WLS', showing that Stephenson kept a close eye on the design of the stores.

Beneath Priddle in the Woolworth's hierarchy were two construction supervisors: A Barton in the southern office in London, where he was succeeded in 1929 by his colleague William Arthur Sherrington (1902–72), and Bruce Campbell Donaldson (1896–1977, *see* Fig 4.10) in the northern office in Liverpool. Little is known of the professional training of these men. Although they regularly signed off plans as 'architect', they evidently deferred to Priddle and may have lacked formal training. Rather more is known about Donaldson than Barton. Although of Scottish extraction, Donaldson was born in Ireland, where his father was manager of the Waterford Gasworks. He moved to London as a schoolboy, with his widowed mother and siblings, and served with the Northumberland Fusiliers in the rank of 2nd Lieutenant during the First World War.

The construction supervisors managed all building projects. On site, their foremen coordinated the work of different contractors, including specialist suppliers and local building firms.[8] Some companies were engaged on a regular basis: steelwork, for example, was usually provided by the constructional engineers Banister, Walton & Co Ltd, a firm founded in 1919 and based at Trafford Park, Manchester. Glazed terracotta or faience, used for several significant façades, was supplied by Shaws Glazed Brick Co Ltd of Darwen in Lancashire. Woolworth's Construction Department also developed longstanding arrangements with particular shopfitters. Projects in the north were generally assigned to John Curtis & Sons of Leeds, while A E Lindsey & Son of Edmonton, north London, undertook work in the south. Woolworth's early association with Sage seems to have been discontinued.

Occasionally, Woolworth's collaborated with outside architects. The store in Tottenham Court Road (Fig 3.4), London, for example, was designed for Woolworth's in May 1924 by Peter Dollar (1847–1943)[9] – an architect credited with introducing sloping floors in early cinema buildings. The store that opened next to The Savoy Hotel on the Strand in 1925 was part of a mixed commercial development (later known as Norman House) for Strand & Savoy Properties Ltd, designed by Trehearne & Norman, who customised the main shop unit for Woolworth's and the offices above for Shell-Mex.[10] Trehearne & Norman had recently designed Woolworth's Executive Office, Victory House, and were themselves based on Kingsway, so this was a close relationship.

Woolworth's property portfolio was still largely leasehold in the 1920s, but included some freeholds. Branches ranged from tiny single-storey shops to premises on the scale of small department stores. Some stores occupied old buildings that were far from ideal from an operational viewpoint, while others were purpose-built and precisely suited to Woolworth's requirements. Whether a store was located in the metropolis, a provincial city, small town or suburb, its scale was determined by the size of the community it aspired to serve, taking into account additional custom that might be drawn in from the rural or suburban hinterland, or from tourists and other visitors. Old photographs often show a pedestrian crossing or a bus stop right outside Woolworth's front door, and if these did not already exist they were readily introduced by eager local authorities. Similarly, many stores were situated close to railway stations: the Edinburgh branch, for example, lay directly across the road from the Waverley Station steps, ready to receive an influx of visitors to the city. The stores came to be graded by size, the largest being referred to as 'superstores'.

As business burgeoned, established stores strained at the seams. Some – including Liverpool (Store 1), Preston (Store 2),

Fig 3.4
Store 175, Nos 20–21 Tottenham Court Road, London, was designed for Woolworth's by the architect Peter Dollar but built under the auspices of Woolworth's Construction Department. This photograph dates from the mid-1960s. In the 1970s the building, with its neighbours, was replaced by a large office and retail development designed by Sidney Kaye for EMI. [FWW01/01/0175/002]

Fig 3.5 (below left)
Store 120 at Bridgend in
north Wales, photographed
around 1930. The frontage
was emblazoned with signs
advertising H Woodward's
paper showrooms. As shown
here, Woolworth's window
dressers often used rows
of baubles as pelmets to
enhance festive displays at
Christmas time. Poundland
opened in this building in
June 2009.
[FWW01/01/0120/001]

Fig 3.6 (below right)
Store 97 opened at Nos
38–39 O'Connell Street,
Limerick, Ireland, on 7 May
1921. This had previously
been the Limerick
Furnishing Warehouse. The
store was rebuilt in 1963.
[FWW01/01/0097/001]

Manchester (Store 4) and Leeds (Store 5) – relocated to larger sites. Another common strategy was to acquire and demolish the premises next door, then rebuild them in a style that matched the existing Woolworth's store, as at Bromley (see Fig 2.27). This resulted in a neat, uniform façade, and eliminated awkward discrepancies in floor levels. Sometimes the original Woolworth's store and the newly acquired neighbour were rebuilt together, usually in carefully planned phases that enabled the company to continue trading while work was underway. In this period of rapid expansion, some of Woolworth's buildings had very fleeting existences on high streets before being displaced by bigger and better stores, as the opportunity arose. The metamorphosis of some branches through successive stages of acquisition and rebuilding illustrates the ephemeral nature, not just of Woolworth's, but of retail architecture in general. Marks & Spencer's expanded in a very similar way, and was equally concerned to maintain architectural homogeneity across its principal street frontages.

Many Woolworth's stores were restricted to the ground floors of old buildings, beneath showrooms, offices, flats or billiard halls (Figs 3.5–3.8). If a location was deemed suitable from a commercial standpoint, Woolworth's scouts were unconcerned about the age or style of the building, and by 1930 the company's property portfolio included an assortment of Georgian terraced houses, commercial Victorian buildings and Edwardian villas. But above all, as noted in Chapter 2 (see p 18), Woolworth's scouts favoured hotel sites. Many old established hostelries succumbed to redevelopment at Woolworth's hands: the Spread Eagle in Lincoln, the Albion in Manchester, the Crown in Edinburgh, the Roebuck in Oxford (Figs 3.9 and 3.10) and the King's Head in Chelmsford, to mention just a few.

Fig 3.7
Store 75, No 5 Commercial Street, Aberdare, shared the premises of the Lucania (Temperance) Billiard Hall. The name was taken from the Cunard liner, Lucania, which was broken up in Swansea in 1909 and its fittings bought to furnish a chain of billiard halls. There were Lucania billiard halls above Woolworth's stores in Cardiff (Store 25) and Great Yarmouth (Store 134), while Bedminster (Store 195) cohabited with a YMCA billiard hall. Initial architectural plans for the Liverpool and London superstores, dated 1922–24, show that each was to include a billiard hall. The company, however, changed its mind and these never materialised. [FWW01/01/0075/001]

The design of Woolworth's standard shopfront did not change substantially in the 1920s, but was subjected to fine-tuning. Since 1914, for example at Putney, small pediments had been positioned over entrance doors, rising into rectangular fanlights. The barley-twist colonnettes were superseded by simpler mullions of square section, but articulated in the same manner as before, with miniature capitals and bases. Maroon-coloured notices were displayed in windows declaring 'Nothing in these stores over 6d' (popularly translated as 'nix over six'). The arc lamps that had illuminated shopfronts after dark were gradually replaced by internal lighting, positioned directly above the window display. As a direct result of this, from around 1922 fringed pelmet cloths were hung from rods in the upper part of display windows to conceal the light fittings and suppress glare (Fig 3.11). These cloths always had the same floral pattern. They were used into the 1940s, but at Christmas time were often replaced by rows of hanging baubles or supplemented by a tier of garlands or festive scenes – apparently stuck on the inside of the glass. A more variable element of shopfronts was the design of the moulded consoles (called 'trusses' by Woolworth's)

Fig 3.8
Store 40 in Colchester, Essex, photographed around 1930 when the upper floor was occupied by Burton's billiard hall. The entire building was taken over and extended by Woolworth's in 1934. At that time the billiard room was reglazed and brought into use as a stockroom. Unlike Montague Burton ('the tailor of taste'), Woolworth's never made a deliberate policy of opening billiard halls in conjunction with its shops. In Burton's case, this was a philanthropic endeavour to keep young men out of public houses – but with a clever commercial twist since the very same youths were, often as not, potential customers. [FWW01/01/0040/001]

that book-ended the fascias. Meanwhile, the 'diamond W' was increasingly evident. As well as ornamenting lobby floors, it began to appear in a simplified form on fascias, for example in Bangor, Wales (Fig 3.12).

*Figs 3.9 and 3.10
The Roebuck Hotel, an
18th-century building at
Nos 8–10 Cornmarket
Street, Oxford – shown in
Fig 3.9 in a photograph of
1907 – was acquired by
Woolworth's in the early
1920s. Commencing in
January 1925, under
Priddle's direction, the
interior was gutted and
the façade remodelled.[a]
Although this was deplored
by some, Woolworth's
architectural approach here
was relatively conservative,
befitting the location in
the heart of a hallowed
university city.[b] By autumn
1925, the building had
reopened with an H Samuel
jewellery shop as well as
Woolworth's Store 189
(Fig 3.10). Note the Easter
advertisements and displays:
from its earliest years,
seasonality was central
to Woolworth's
merchandising policy.
[CC51/00692;
FWW01/01/0189/002]*

Fig 3.11
This design of pelmet cloth hung in the majority of Woolworth's windows between c 1922 and c 1945. The photograph here, taken c 1932, shows Store 463, Nos 150–154 Oxford Street, Woolworth's second store on the street located close to Tottenham Court Road tube station. The freehold site of the old Princess Theatre had been bought in 1931 by Second Covent Garden Properties Ltd, and was cleared for new premises shared by Waring & Gillow and Woolworth's, designed by Elcock & Sutcliffe.
[FWW01/01/0463/007]

Fig 3.12
Store 105, No 234 High Street, Bangor, north Wales. This view of the shopfront, taken shortly before the store opened for inspection on Friday, 11 November 1921, shows typical displays of handkerchiefs and tin goods. The 'diamond W' was now commonly displayed on fascias, often breaking up a blank area or adorning a splayed corner, as here. This site was abandoned by Woolworth's after new premises were erected at Nos 277–279 High Street in the 1930s.
[FWW01/01/0105/001]

As in America, a penny-in-the-slot weighing machine was positioned just inside the main entrance, and moved into one of the lobbies outside opening hours. Photographs show several different makes and models. The most common were supplied by the Peerless Weighing Machine Co Ltd of Detroit and incorporated a height measure. The customer stood on a platform and watched the dial until the hand stopped, before dropping a penny in the slot to receive a ticket printed with his or her weight. In the days before bathroom scales became commonplace, these machines were money-spinners.

Superstores

Woolworth's architects, like those of other large-scale multiple retailers, contributed to the transformation of commercial high-street architecture after the First World War, with the introduction of new technologies, materials and styles. The robust and effusive baroque style of the Edwardian era was displaced by a more austere neo-Classicism. Shopping streets gained new buildings with fashionably restrained façades of Portland stone (often reconstituted as 'Empire Stone'), stucco (or cement render) or glazed terracotta tiles (usually called faience). Popular ornamental motifs included swags, garlands and Roman fasces (bundles of rods): these were not novel in themselves, but they were now executed sparingly, in low relief, quite unlike the sturdier forms favoured before 1914. The widespread use of steel framing liberated the frontages of buildings, in part, from their traditional weight-bearing purpose and, as if to demonstrate this, windows were commonly set within large metal infill panels that spanned two or more floor levels of a structure. This approach had been innovative when it was adopted by Selfridge's architects in 1909 (see Fig 2.8); now it entered the architectural mainstream.

In the context of prevailing architectural fashion, the façades of the most advanced Woolworth's superstores of the early 1920s represent extravagant hybrids of Edwardian and 1920s approaches. William Priddle's designs for prominent sites in Liverpool (1922–3) and London (1924–5) exhibited more panache than many other commercial buildings of the same period, although these must have been particularly challenging projects for a relatively inexperienced architect.

In Liverpool, Woolworth's had outgrown Henry Miles's old glove shop and acquired a 999-year lease on a site across the street, at Nos 22–36 Church Street. This had been occupied by St Peter's church until 1919, when it was cleared to make way for new developments. In fact, Harrods had considered building its first provincial store here, but backed out, allowing Woolworth's to step in.[11] The superstore (Fig 3.13), which opened for business on Saturday 4 August 1923, formed the principal component of a large commercial block.[12] While the central unit was occupied by Woolworth's, the slightly lower side ranges, completed in 1924, housed Burton's and C&A, neither of whom was in direct competition with Woolworth's since they specialised in clothing. Notably, C&A's shop was designed by North, Robin & Wilsdon.

The centre of Woolworth's five-storey Portland stone elevation contained a huge recessed panel, three storeys high and three bays wide, fitted with metal-framed windows within a framework of bronze panels. This extraordinary 'complete metal front' was executed by Crittall, an Essex-based firm rapidly becoming famous for its metal windows. In later years the eminent Liverpool architect C H Reilly described it as a 'howler', complaining that the central feature was 'big enough to drive the *Queen Mary* through'.[13] To modern eyes, however, this exaggerated panel is one of the most appealing aspects of the building. Such designs anticipated the curtain walling that appeared from the late 1930s and characterised much commercial architecture of the 1950s and early 1960s.

Priddle's biggest project after the completion of Liverpool was No 311 Oxford Street (Figs 3.14 and 3.15), the firm's first incursion into the West End of London and its first direct challenge to Selfridge's bargain basement. The store was positioned on the south side of the street – the less desirable aspect – opposite John Lewis's and some distance to the east of Selfridge's. Designed in 1923, this building had been completed by 1925, when upper-floor office suites were advertised for rent. Some of the offices were used by Woolworth's itself: the construction supervisor A Barton had a

Fig 3.13
The new Store 1 on Church Street in Liverpool was built in 1922–3 to a design by William Priddle, while B C Donaldson oversaw the construction. This was by far the largest Woolworth's store to date. In remembrance of its predecessor on the site – St Peter's Church – the crossed keys of St Peter were flanked by Roman fasces at the apex of the façade. The building was remodelled in 1967–70, but sold by Woolworth Holdings in 1983. Although the store was gutted for conversion as part of the Liverpool One Shopping Centre around 2009–10, this confident façade can be regarded as one of the most impressive remnants of Woolworth's to survive anywhere in the British Isles.
[FWW01/01/0001/001]

room on the fourth floor, next to a drawing office for his staff, before moving to New Bond Street around 1930. The building closely resembled the new Liverpool store, but the central feature of the façade was subdivided, probably in response to criticism from the architect Stanley Gordon Jeeves (1888–1964), who seems to have intervened on behalf of the freeholder.[14]

Many of the architectural motifs deployed on the Liverpool and London superstores recurred on the frontages of smaller Woolworth's stores in the mid-1920s. Among these was a lion's head motif (Fig 3.16), which seems to have featured for the first time at Liverpool. It may have been inspired by the British Empire Exhibition held at Wembley in 1924, which also took a lion's head as its symbol. Subsequently, lion imagery often featured on commercial buildings, suggesting a commitment to home trade. This would not have been lost on Woolworth's executives, who were very concerned with such matters at

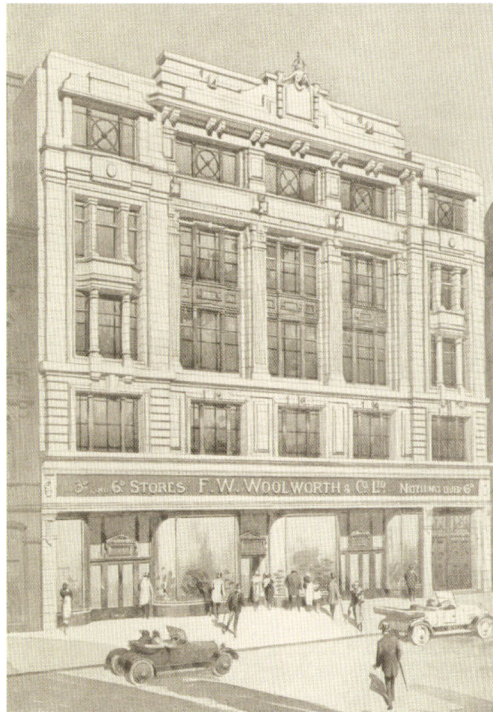

Figs 3.14 and 3.15
Store 161, No 311 Oxford Street, London, shown (above) in a photograph of c 1960 and (left) in an illustration published in The Builder *(7 March 1924, 378). The faience façade was manufactured by Shaws of Darwen and the steelwork was by Banister, Walton & Co, companies which worked regularly for Woolworth's. Repeatedly remodelled and extended over the years, this was one of three large London stores that were sold to fund the purchase of B&Q in 1980. Since then it has been occupied, in turn, by Tesco and Uniqlo.*
[FWW01/01/0161/001; Reproduced by kind permission of the Syndics of Cambridge University Library]

41

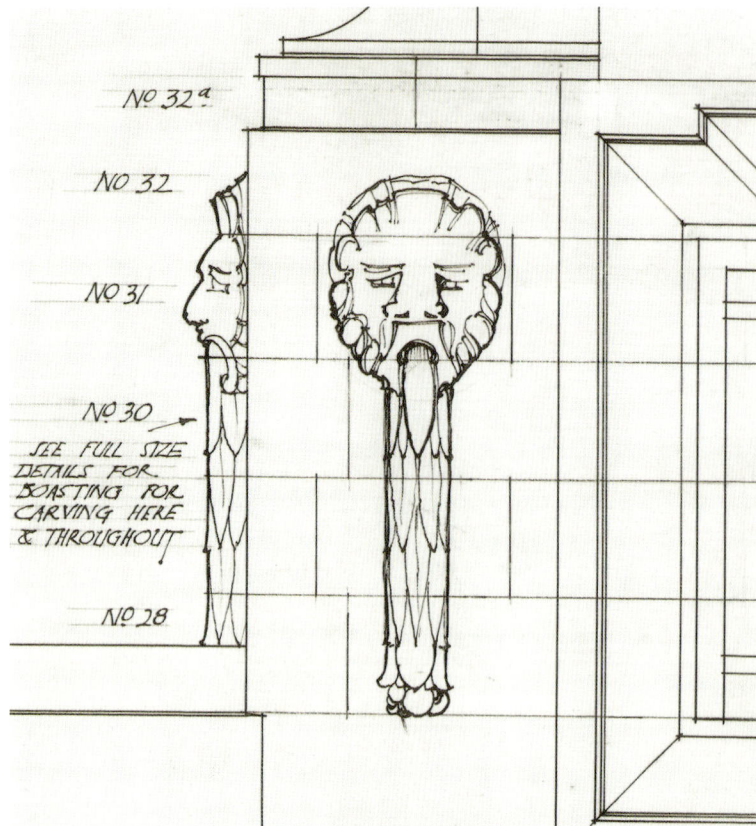

Fig 3.16
From 1923 until the mid-
1930s a lion's head motif
commonly adorned
Woolworth's store fronts.
Here we see (clockwise from
top left): a) detail of
an elevation drawing for
Store 1, Liverpool, 1923;
b) console, Store 207, Bath,
1928–9; c) keystone over
oval window, Store 184,
Bedford, 1934; d) capital,
Store 46, Walsall, c 1930–5.
The lion's head emphasised
Woolworth's efforts to
stock goods of British
manufacture in the
aftermath of the First
World War.
[a) FWW01/02/0001/001;
b) DP163714; c and d) Ron
Baxter]

this date. On Woolworth's façades, the lion's head assumed various guises, but it was most commonly depicted on consoles with a shield suspended from its mouth by a rope. This shield contained the letter 'W' and was surrounded by husks. The lion's head also appeared on capitals, keystones, gables and parapets. For a number of years, it ranked as a second logo for Woolworth's, alongside the established 'diamond W'.

For some reason, probably expense, Woolworth's did not adapt the grandiose style of the two principal superstores for other branches. Liverpool and London remained in a league of their own. The stores on Argyle Street, Glasgow (1922, Fig 3.17), and High Street, Oldham (1925, Fig 3.18), were oddities, with larger windows than other Woolworth's stores. Spelt out in large raised letters on these façades was 'Woolworth's Stores' (in Glasgow) and 'Woolworths' Stores' (in Oldham), the apostrophe being inconsistently applied in these early days. Other superstores adhered more closely to mainstream architectural fashion by assuming a chaste neo-Classical style with small metal infill panels and restrained

Figs 3.17 and 3.18
Lettering forming an integral part of the façades of Store 118, Argyle Street, Glasgow (Fig 3.17, above), and Store 181, High Street, Oldham (Fig 3.18, left), of 1922 and 1925 respectively. Both stores had unfeasibly large windows for Woolworth's, and those at Oldham were partly blocked-up in later years. Neither building survives.
[FWW01/01/0118/001; FWW01/01/0181/001]

Figs 3.19 and 3.20
Store 103 stood on Spiceal
Street, opposite St Martin's
church in Birmingham's
main market place, the
Bull Ring. Built c 1921–3
to a design by William
Priddle and faced in Shaws
'Marmola' faience, this was
one of the company's largest
stores. The exact date of the
daytime photograph (Fig
3.19) is not known, but it
was evidently taken around
Easter, in the mid-1920s. In
the early 1930s the building
was extended to the left in
a matching style, with a
rather magnificent arched
centrepiece (compare Fig
3.21 and, indeed, Fig 1.3)
and dazzling night-time
illuminations, shown here
(Fig 3.20) in an undated
interwar photograph taken
at Christmas. The area was
redeveloped in the early
1960s as the Bull Ring
Shopping Centre (see Figs
7.9 and 7.10).
[FWW01/01/0103/001;
FWW01/01/0103/002]

ornamentation, the favourite decorative motifs of Priddle's team being paterae, rusticated pilasters and garlands. Stores of this type were built in Birmingham (*c* 1921–3, Figs 3.19 and 3.20), Coventry (1922, Fig 3.21), Kensington (1924, Fig 3.22), Accrington (1925), Huddersfield (1927), Leeds (1928, Fig 3.23) and Plymouth (1930). These resembled contemporary Marks & Spencer's superstores.

The large stores designed in the mid-1920s for Edinburgh (Fig 3.24), Bath (Fig 3.25) and Manchester (Figs 3.26 and 3.27) presented a more conservative image of the company. Their traditional façades were classically conceived, with natural stone facings and attic storeys. This approach no doubt helped Woolworth's to secure planning permission without prolonged debate.

In Manchester, Woolworth's purchased two large sites in close succession. First of all,

in November 1925, the company acquired the L-shaped Victorian Exchange Arcade, connecting St Mary's Gate with Deansgate. The arcade shopkeepers were evicted and the interior was remodelled to accommodate a large new store. Then, in February 1926, the company bought up the old Albion Hotel, which stood close to Store 4, on the corner of Oldham

Street and Piccadilly. Here Woolworth's decided to erect a new three-storey building, to replace the existing store, but the Manchester Improvements Committee insisted on a height of five storeys, to preserve the balance of the square (see Figs 3.26 and 3.27).[15] The third and fourth floors were conceived as offices, but were soon incorporated into the store.

The flagship store for Scotland was built at Nos 10–14 Princes Street in Edinburgh (1925–6, see Fig 3.24). This substantial sandstone building had an octagonal corner turret and a giant elevation. All the windows had cross-banded margin lights, but only those on the top floor incorporated a central arched section with an opening fanlight. The same trick was used for the new stores in Manchester (1926–9, see Figs 3.26 and 3.27) and Leeds (1928, see Fig 3.23),[16] both designed by Donaldson under Priddle's supervision, and even featured in the relatively small-scale Brixton extension of 1925 (see Fig 2.16). A simplified version of Edinburgh's giant elevation was adopted elsewhere, for example Norwich (1928–9, Fig 3.28), Doncaster (1929–30, Fig 3.29) and the Renfrew Street façade of the branch on Sauchiehall Street in Glasgow, rebuilt after a fire (1929). Yet another example was prepared for a new location in Brixton in 1929, but by the time work started there in the mid-1930s, the elevation had been completely recast in an art deco style.[17]

Fig 3.21
Store 123 opened on Smithford Street, Coventry, on 25 November 1922 and was enlarged in 1931 and 1938. In February 1939 incendiary devices – toy balloons filled with powdered nitric acid and concealed in envelopes – were left on the counters, triggering a minor incident but causing little damage. The Irish Republican Army (IRA) was probably responsible. The following year, on 14 November 1940, the building was destroyed, together with much of the centre of Coventry, by German bombs. [FWW01/01/0123/001]

Fig 3.22
Store 162 opened at Nos 201–207 Kensington High Street in August 1924. This building housed a new district office from 1954. In November 1963, the store relocated to Nos 54–60 Kensington High Street, premises formerly occupied by Barker's and converted by R Seifert & Partners, working in close collaboration with Woolworth's. This closed in 1985. The building of 1924 is now shared by Robert Dyas and other retailers. [FWW01/01/0162/001]

Fig 3.23
Store 5 in Leeds relocated from its original premises to a new building on the site of the Albion Hotel on Briggate, opening on 1 December 1928. Designed by B C Donaldson, it had two sales floors, a second-floor café and third-floor stockroom. In December 1938 Woolworth's bought the adjacent Victory Hotel for an extension that would reach back to Central Road.[c] Although the hotel was demolished in 1939, work ground to a halt at the outbreak of war, leaving gaping holes on both Briggate and Central Road until construction could resume in the mid-1950s (see Fig 6.40). [FWW01/01/0005/001]

Fig 3.24
Store 213 stood at the east end of Princes Street, Edinburgh's famous shopping street. Opening in March 1926, this may have been the first of several Woolworth's elevations to combine a giant order of Roman Doric pilasters with arched upper-floor glazing units. Occupying the site of the Crown Hotel, it vied for importance – if not custom – with many older, established department stores such as nearby Jenner's. This store closed in 1984 and was completely gutted in 2012, prior to conversion to a hotel and shops. It was the first (and only) purpose-built Woolworth's store in Scotland to be listed, at Grade C. [FWW01/01/0213/001]

Fig 3.25
William Priddle's new store in Bath, Store 207, was built on the corner of Stall Street and Abbeygate Street in 1925. The Architect & Building News admired its ashlar elevations – a rare experience for Woolworth's.[d] But the journal pronounced that the building had 'one conspicuous defect': the way the glazed shopfront continued across the canted corner bay. Though this was deemed 'inexcusable', the faux pas was one of Woolworth's favoured devices. Bath, like Edinburgh, no doubt received special architectural treatment by Woolworth's, as a city of the highest historical pedigree. The building still stands, though Woolworth's moved out in 1963. [FWW01/01/0207/001]

Fig 3.26
Store 4, Oldham Street, Manchester. Woolworth's built a large new store on the site of the Albion Hotel in 1926–9. While this was in the process of being erected, in April 1927 a quarter of the old store was badly damaged by fire: remarkably, 600 to 700 people were evacuated in three minutes.[e] The new store – shown here in a postcard dated 1928 – suffered an appalling fire 52 years later in 1979 (see Fig 8.9). Store 4 finally closed on 28 June 1986. [Author's collection]

Fig 3.27
The Piccadilly elevation
of the Manchester store,
endorsed by 'WLS' on 22
December 1926. Note the
characteristic arched
glazing units on the upper
floor. This was a signature
feature of many large
Woolworth's stores of the
mid-to-late 1920s.
[FWW01/02/0004/002]

Fig 3.28
Store 44, Norwich. Around
1928–9, Woolworth's
relocated across the road
from its original premises to
a new building at Nos 21–25
Rampant Horse Street,
seen here in a photograph
dated 28 September
1940. Displays include
'splinterproof net' and the
windows of Richard Shops
next door are taped in case
of bombing. Woolworth's
building was, in fact,
bombed in 1942, and so
Store 556 at No 5 Magdalen
Street had to serve the city
for the next decade. Store 44
was eventually rebuilt in
1950–3 (see Fig 6.15a).
The department store next
door, Bunting's, became
a branch of Marks &
Spencer's, and this absorbed
Woolworth's store following
its closure in the 1980s.
[FWW01/01/0044/001]

Fig 3.29
This shows Store 193 at Nos 11–12 Baxtergate, Doncaster, following the completion of extension work undertaken in 1929–30. Free teas – with bread and butter, a roll or a pastry – were served in the self-service first-floor cafeteria from 10am on inspection day, Friday 4 April 1930. Following a fire, this was superseded by a new building in the art deco style in 1938. Store 193 relocated to the Arndale Centre in Doncaster in 1974, but the building of 1938 still stands. [FWW01/01/0193/001]

Standard stores

New-build Woolworth's stores of the 1920s rarely assumed the scale of the superstores discussed above. Typically, they stood no more than two storeys high and five bays wide, inviting an architectural treatment that was very different from the city-centre stores.

Woolworth's did not apply a rigorously uniform house style to the façades of these standard-size stores until around 1928. Nevertheless, their elevations exhibited variations on a relatively tight theme. The majority were designed with two formative constraints: the buildings they fronted were two storeys high, reflecting the preferred

Fig 3.30
Store 174 at Nos 48–60
Murraygate, Dundee,
opened in November 1924.
The broad, flat frame with a
shallow pedimental parapet
to the central three bays
was a typical Woolworth's
motif throughout the mid-
1920s, and the circular
(superimposed 'O' and 'X')
glazing units were borrowed
directly from the attic
storeys of the Liverpool
and London superstores.
Though initial plans to face
this building in cream-
coloured terracotta were
abandoned, it was succeeded
in the late 1930s by a three-
storey building with a
faience front. This closed
in March 1984, and is now
a Tesco Metro.
[FWW01/01/0174/001]

arrangement of a ground-floor salesroom and upper-floor stockroom, and they had flat asphalt roofs. Setting aside the inevitable presence of the standard shopfront with its red and gold fascia, this was sufficient to impose an architectural kinship – a Woolworth's 'look' – that spanned the store portfolio. Repetition of the lion's head symbol (Fig 3.30) enhanced this. Occasionally some other form of architectural branding was tried out: a 'W' flanked by small lozenges over the central window at York (1924), for example, or a 'diamond W' in the parapet at London Road, Brighton (1927).

Working within this format, Woolworth's architects introduced countless variations through their choice of cladding materials, style and ornamentation. Further minor variations at a technical level, such as the choice of English bond rather than Flemish bond brickwork, were perhaps imparted by local building contractors. While most store fronts were primarily of red brick, materials such as stone, faience or cement render were also used. Classical touches such as rusticated quoining and moulded architraves were sometimes added, and the effect veered between neo-Classical and neo-Georgian, but could equally be astylar. The symmetrical rhythm of the first-floor windows varied, its original balance often being destroyed in later years by extensions, and the glazing units were not standardised. Both sashes and casements were used, but in each case cross-banded margin lights were widely favoured, probably for their decorative and fashionable appearance. Upper-floor windows (or at least the lower panes) were usually fitted with 'cathedral' or rough plate glass. Their 'hammered' surface meant that untidy boxes and shelves in the stockrooms could not be seen clearly from the street, where they might detract from the neat outward appearance of a store. This became a Woolworth's signature, as did pyramids of goods in stockroom windows – not readily visible, but adding a decorative

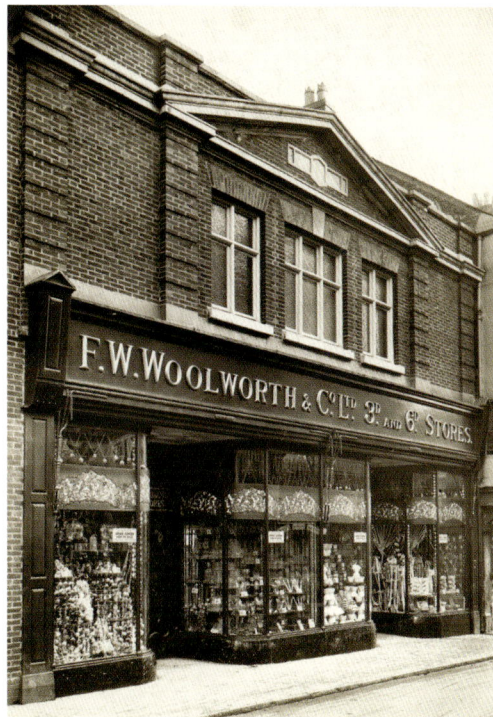

Figs 3.31 and 3.32
Store 214 in High Wycombe
(Fig 3.31, far left) was built
in 1926 and Store 250 in
Abergavenny (Fig 3.32, left)
in 1927. They were not
identical but obviously
shared several architectural
ideas. The banner motif
in the pediment at
Abergavenny was popular
with Woolworth's architects
through the 1920s. At Store
234 on Church Street,
Croydon, of c 1926, a lion's
head was added to the
centre of the banner.
[FWW01/01/0214/001;
FWW01/01/0250/001]

touch (*see* Fig 3.18) – something that can also be seen in early images of the American stores. Lastly, a shaped parapet or pediment concealed the flat roof, and sometimes added artificial height to the building.

Some designs were recycled with minor variations at two, three or even four sites. Thus, to pick random examples, the branches at Weymouth, St Helen's and Sheffield, all of 1923, had a family resemblance, as did Hereford and Sheerness in 1925, High Wycombe and Abergavenny (Figs 3.31 and 3.32) in 1926–7 and Poplar (*see* Fig 5.13) and Falmouth in 1928. The most likely explanation for the occurrence of groups of related store fronts is that particular projects happened to be on the architects' drawing board around the same time. Ideas were probably repeated more for economy and speed than with the aim of establishing a house style.

Around 1928 a particular design was embraced as Woolworth's standard style. This can be regarded as a miniaturised version of the large neo-Georgian fronts that were introduced at Doncaster and elsewhere in the same period (*see* Fig 3.29). It enjoyed great longevity, being rolled out to hundreds of Woolworth's stores throughout the country over the next 12 years. Admittedly, slight variations were introduced to adapt the design to the idiosyncrasies of individual

locations, but uniformity was maintained to an unprecedented degree. Although alternative designs continued to be produced, the dominance of this standard front was striking, and it must have become nationally recognisable very quickly. Woolworth's clearly found that it conveyed the character of its typical high street stores especially effectively. Moreover, since it incorporated prefabricated elements, it entailed an element of mass production and would have been erected easily and quickly by local building contractors.

The new standard front was most commonly applied to stores that were two storeys high and five bays wide. The material of choice was red brick with pale grey concrete or reconstituted stone dressings. The windows were fitted with fixed metal glazing, with margin lights and the usual rough plate glass. The three central bays broke forward very slightly and the central trio of windows was framed by pilasters with moulded caps. These supported a cornice with paired modillions that carried a shallow, stepped and/or pedimented parapet. Initially, the precast consoles at the ends of the fascia had a standard moulding profile; the upper half of the pilasters were also of concrete, while the lower half was clad in thin pearl granite slabs. One of the first stores of this type to open, in early summer 1928, was Bow, in east London (Fig 3.33). It was quickly

Fig 3.33
Store 314, Bow. This east
London branch was one
of the very first to adopt
Woolworth's new standard
front.[8] As proclaimed by
the notices plastered to
the windows, it opened for
inspection on Friday 4 May
1928 at 2.30pm. According
to another notice, over
88 per cent of the goods
on sale were 'British Made'.
Patriotic statements of this
nature were common at
a time of economic gloom,
in the late 1920s and
early 1930s.
[FWW01/01/0314/001]

Fig 3.34
Store 344, Bognor Regis.
In February 1929, while
the King was convalescing
in Bognor, the Queen and
Princess Mary made a much
publicised 20-minute visit
to Woolworth's store at
No 20 London Road, which
had opened on the 2nd
of the same month. They
examined 'pearl' necklaces
with 'gold' clasps, and made
several sixpenny purchases,
including bottles of smelling
salts and six novels by Edgar
Wallace. This photograph
was taken two years later,
in 1931. In subsequent
years, Woolworth's spread
into No 18 London Road.
The premises were rebuilt
in 1961–2, but suffered
damage when an IRA
bicycle bomb exploded
across the street in 1994.
[FWW01/01/0344/001]

Fig 3.35
Store 356, Letchworth.
This branch, on Leys Avenue
in the centre of the world's
first garden city, had one of
Woolworth's new standard
fronts. The store opened in
1929, but the precise date
of this interwar photograph
is not known. At a later date
Woolworth's spread into the
shop on the left, shown as a
tailor's, and the end pilaster
was reset. A poster in the
window advertises
'Horticultural Supplies', one
of Woolworth's most reliable
specialities. The branch
closed on 28 June 1986.
[FWW01/01/0356/001]

Fig 3.36
Despite serving the
county town of Suffolk,
Store 148, on Carr Street,
Ipswich, opened in an
unprepossessing single-
storey building on
3 November 1923.
The only architectural
embellishment was a
parapet. In a sequence
typical of Woolworth's
growth, this was replaced
by a two-storey store with
a faience frontage in 1939,
and then by a three-storey
superstore – the largest
branch in the county –
between 1963 and 1968.
[FWW01/01/0148/003]

followed by many others, including Islington (1929), Bognor Regis (1929, Fig 3.34) and Letchworth (1929, Fig 3.35).

The flexibility of the standard front was soon demonstrated. It could be contracted or stretched to suit branches ranging in width from three bays (for example in Wellingborough) to seven bays (such as Harrow). Single-storey stores, however, continued to open with frontages that comprised little more than a shopfront, usually – but not invariably – topped by a parapet or a blind gable, this being the sole architectural intervention required from Priddle and his colleagues (Fig 3.36). Inside, these stores often made up for their lack of height and breadth by extending far beyond the street line, their interiors lit by roof lanterns.

Some stores were far from typical, perhaps reflecting concerns for the integrity of the built environment that are not always preserved in accessible historical records. The Cambridge store of 1925 resembled nearby Sidney Sussex College (Fig 3.37).[18] It featured a gable, a first-floor oriel, leaded casements, a tiled roof and an armorial cartouche incorporating a bend taken from the arms of the founder of Sidney Sussex College, Frances Radcliffe, Countess of Sussex. This architectural approach was probably imposed on both Woolworth's and its next-door neighbour, Sainsbury's. Also illustrating Woolworth's willingness to embrace traditional architectural styles in the 1920s and 1930s is a small clutch of stores which, most unexpectedly, were given half-timbered gabled façades topped by pitched roofs. Other national multiples which made use of this neo-Tudor style in the 1920s included the bookseller and stationer W H Smith's and the hatter Dunn's.

How timber-framing came to appeal to Woolworth's is unknown, but Priddle – or one of his managers – may have been inspired by Liberty's newly completed department store on

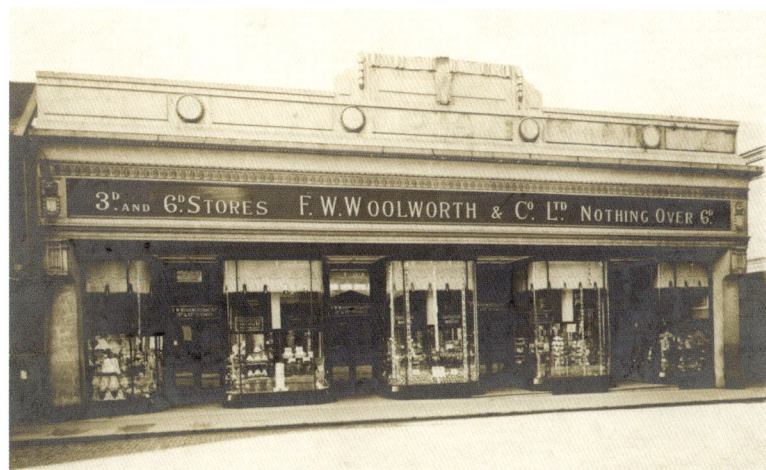

Fig 3.37
Store 194 at Nos 14–15 Sidney Street, Cambridge, echoed the architectural style of nearby Sidney Sussex College, founded in 1596. Built in 1925 (as was its neighbour, J Sainsbury's, seen beyond Woolworth's), it was extended in 1929 (as shown here) and in 1959. A planning condition in 1959 stipulated accommodation for 140 cycles. The roof of the structure was bogus, the front slope screening Woolworth's usual asphalt flat.
[FWW01/01/0194/001]

Great Marlborough Street in London (1924; E T and E S Hall), which represented a novel approach to commercial buildings. Nikolaus Pevsner disapproved of Liberty's, and his comments of 1957 seem even more applicable to Woolworth's efforts in the same genre: 'Technically there is nothing wrong – but functionally and intellectually everything … and the goings-on of a store behind such a façade are wrongest of all.'[19] One or two of Woolworth's stores, such as those in Chester (1924, *see* Fig 7.24) and Newcastle-under-Lyme (1928), occupied genuine timber-framed buildings, but others simply had mock-timber façades. In Wigan, the company acquired the Royal Hotel in 1924 and rebuilt the

Standishgate elevation, together with the splayed corner to Station Road, in a half-timbered style, including curved bracing and gables with decorative bargeboards (Figs 3.38 and 3.39).[20] Somewhat later, a half-timbered building with oriel windows and eyebrow dormers was built on the Market Place in Kingston upon Thames (Fig 3.40), and the Spread Eagle Hotel in Lincoln, which became a Woolworth's store in 1923, was refaced with a mock-timber front. Smaller timber-framed fronts were erected in Canterbury and Northwich. It seems that the taste for old England reflected in these façades never extended to Woolworth's internal fixtures and fittings.

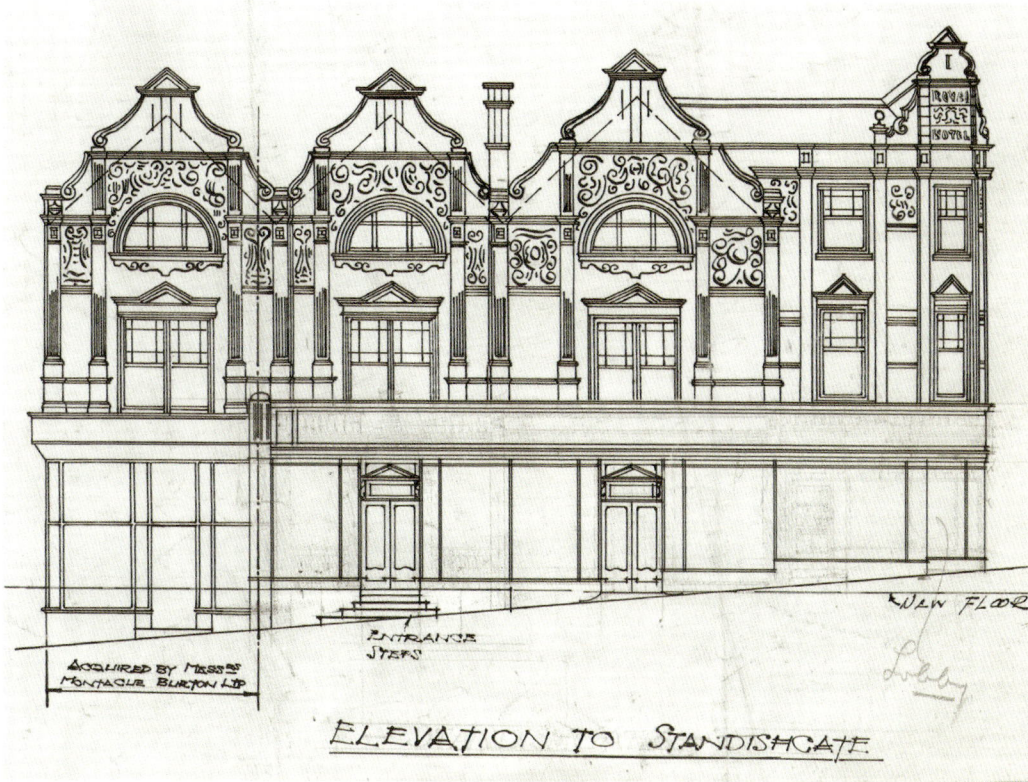

ELEVATION TO STANDISHGATE

Figs 3.38 and 3.39
The elevation of the Royal
Hotel site on Standishgate,
Wigan, before (Fig 3.38,
left) and after (Fig 3.39,
below) Woolworth's
rebuilding programme. In
1924 Woolworth's Store 187
occupied a shop on the
ground-floor of the hotel
(although not identified by
name on the drawing, the
shopfront is unmistakable);
by 1925 the company had
acquired the site and rebuilt
the store with half-timbered
frontages. The site to the
left was redeveloped by
Burton's shortly afterwards.
The Grand Arcade now
abuts what was once
the right-hand side
of Woolworth's store.
[FWW01/02/0187/001;
FWW01/01/0187/001]

Fig 3.40
Store 43 in Kingston upon
Thames (see Fig 2.19)
relocated to the site of the
Sun Hotel in the Market
Place in 1930. The new
building had a mock-timber
front, but was refaced
in a neo-Georgian style
in the 1960s.
[FWW01/01/0043/002]

Fig 3.41
The interior of Store 95,
St Helier, Jersey, decorated
with lanterns at Christmas
1921. Sales girls – wearing
their own clothes rather
than uniform – pose
with Father Christmas.
This small store seems
to have been quite unlike
mainland Woolworth's
stores of the same date.
[Société Jersiaise
Photographic Archive,
Jersey]

Inside Woolworth's

Woolworth's interiors usually comprised a ground-floor sales area (Fig 3.41), a first-floor stockroom and staff rooms. Only the largest stores, in city centres and seaside resorts, now had a large public café, and some earlier cafés and tea bars were removed to increase sales space. By 1920 the 'American habit' of drinking ice-cream sodas was becoming popular in Britain, and so Woolworth's established soda fountains in eight stores.[21] Plans show that an ice-cream counter (or 'Frigidaire' cabinet) was often positioned to the left of the main entrance. If there was no café kitchen, a separate small kitchen or scullery was provided to prepare food for staff who, by the end of the decade, were allocated a separate lunch room and a cloakroom with lockers, even in small branches.

Flat roofs were used for tea and cigarette breaks and as a popular spot for staff photographs (Fig 3.42). Staff rooms were usually reached via an enclosed staircase or a lift, located to the rear of the store, close to the delivery entrance. Not all sites permitted rear or side deliveries, and some façades had to include a 'goods entrance': merchandise was transported to stores by suppliers' vans, or railway goods lorries, and it was not desirable for these to clutter up store frontages. On occasion, stockrooms had to be located in a basement, or even in a sub-basement, as was the case on the Strand in London. Stockrooms always had separate secure enclosures – either rooms or cupboards – for sweets, biscuits and jewellery (Fig 3.43). These items were locked away to prevent 'shrinkage': losses through breakage or pilfering. The unheated spaces behind the scenes must have been bitterly cold when annual stocktaking

Fig 3.42
A staff group, with the
manager in the centre,
poses on the flat roof
of Store 86, Stratford,
London, in the 1920s.
[Courtesy of Jane Biro]

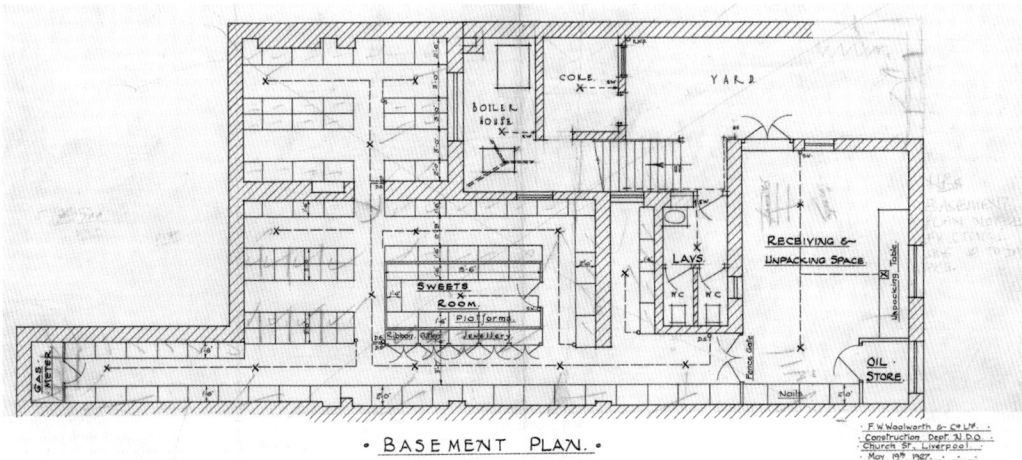

• BASEMENT PLAN. •

Fig 3.43
A plan of the yard and
stockroom in Store 90,
Kingstown (later renamed
Dun Laoghaire), Dublin,
in 1927, showing the
secure room for sweets
and cupboards for ribbons
and jewellery.
[FWW01/02/0090/001]

was undertaken immediately after Christmas, with all hands on deck.

The sales floors of Woolworth's, in the mid-1920s, looked very like those of Marks & Spencer's. Goods were displayed on the sloping tops of long mahogany island counters, with wells in the centres for the assistants and the bulky cash registers (Fig 3.44). Part of the weekly routine for Woolworth's girls was to clear and clean their counters on Mondays. The special free-standing display units of the pre-1914 period vanished. Floors were constructed of herringbone strutting laid with deal boards. Over the heads of Woolworth's customers, the ceilings were divided into compartments by the hefty downstand beams of the steel-frame structure and, from the mid-1920s, were usually covered in ornamental pressed-steel panels which imitated Lincrusta.

Steel or 'tin' ceilings (Figs 3.45 and 3.46) were an American idea. In the early 20th century they featured in shops and stores throughout the US. In Britain they were more of a rarity, although they had been used at the new Savoy Hotel in 1904. The principal manufacturer was the Steleonite Metal Stamping Co Ltd, known from 1928 as Steel Ceilings Ltd, which had a factory at Old Ford in east London.[22] Woolworth's, which favoured the 'Plastele' pattern of Steleonite tiles, was one of the firm's principal customers; other chains, such as Marks & Spencer's and J Lyons, also made use of its 'tin' ceilings. When Woolworth's added steel tiles to old plaster ceilings, they referred to this as 'Steleoniting', a term no doubt invented by the construction team.

Steleonite ceilings survived in several Woolworth's stores until 2009, often concealed above later suspended ceilings, and one or two are still on view, for example at Ely in Cambridgeshire. In contrast, no original internal wall finishes from the interwar period are known to have survived, though some may be hidden. Walls were painted pale primrose matt with white mouldings, and were enriched by pressed-steel friezes, with panels containing a red 'diamond W' under gold swags, topped by a fleur-de-lys. These steel decorations superseded an earlier version of the same design, introduced at Liverpool in 1923 and manufactured from wood. They remained prominent features inside stores, large or small, throughout the interwar period.

Fig 3.44
This photograph was taken at Store 273, Salisbury, just after Woolworth's had converted 'Salisbury House' at Nos 55–59 Silver Street, around 1927. It provides a rare uncluttered view of a newly fitted interior, before the counters were loaded with merchandise. Typically, this store had both electric and (emergency) gas lighting, pine floors and 'tin' ('Steleonite') ceilings and walls (note the pressed steel 'diamond W' swags on the far wall). In March 1957 this branch moved into a new building nearby, at Nos 22–30 High Street. Both buildings survive. [FWW01/01/0273/002]

Figs 3.45 and 3.46
'Steleonite' ceilings in Store 548 in Saffron Walden (right) and Store 524 in Ludlow (far right), both photographed in 2000. Steel tiles supposedly had fire resisting properties, as well as being cheap, decorative and low maintenance. [AA008686; AA009246]

Trials and tribulations

Although the 1920s was a decade of unchecked growth, Woolworth's encountered obstacles on the road to success, particularly in Ireland, where the Irish Republican Army (IRA) had been formed in 1919 to bring about independence. A period of violence and political tension culminated in the partition of Ireland and the creation, in 1922, of the Irish Free State. After this, Woolworth's set up a separate Irish subsidiary in the Free State, F W Woolworth & Co (Ireland) Ltd, which existed until 1931.

Seemingly oblivious to the raging civil war, Woolworth's pursued its expansion in Ireland. The opening in 1918 of a second Dublin branch, on Henry Street (Fig 3.47), was followed in 1920 by stores in Cork (Fig 3.48), Londonderry and Kingstown (Dun Laoghaire), Dublin (see Fig 3.43), followed in 1921 by Portadown, then Limerick (see Fig 3.6) and North Street, Belfast. By this time, protectionism and anti-British sentiment were combining to arouse strong antipathy against any retailer selling non-Irish, and in particular British-made, goods. Protestors caused disruption at several Woolworth's stores. Most notably, Sinn Fein boycotting campaigns spurred activists to plaster the windows of the Dublin stores with bills reading: 'Warning. This shop is selling boycotted goods.'[23] Although such prejudice waned in later years, for political expediency Woolworth's became increasingly reliant on Irish suppliers to fill its counters in the Irish Free State.

Fire precautions, by modern standards, were generally lax in the 1920s. Conflagrations erupted in many retail premises, including Woolworth's stores. In March 1921, for example, a serious fire broke out in the central well of the store on Union Street and Mitchell Street in Glasgow, affecting not just Woolworth's but also several neighbouring businesses.[24] A fire at North End, Croydon, in early December 1927, destroyed the Christmas stock.[25] And early one morning in 1928, the café on the upper floor of the Belfast store caught fire.[26] This spread to other premises, including Burton's; Woolworth's store was gutted and its stock destroyed. In all of these cases, trading continued in temporary accommodation until buildings could be repaired or rebuilt (Fig 3.49). Such experiences may have encouraged the firm's preference for steel-lined ceilings and walls (see pp 57–8), but expensive sprinkler systems appear to have been installed only occasionally, at the insistence of the most safety-conscious planning authorities, notably those complying with the London Building Acts.[27]

Despite the impromptu strike in Derby in 1913 (see p 23), it was unusual for Woolworth's staff to rebel openly against the terms and conditions of their employment. This was, perhaps, surprising, since an unfortunate tendency to view sales staff as dispensable had been inherited from the American parent company, reflecting the personal attitude of Frank W Woolworth himself. Woolworth's resisted the unionisation of staff throughout the 1920s, and generally ignored grievances, which usually related to salaries. Disputes did escalate from time to time. One in Cork (see Fig 3.48) in January 1922 led to the suspension of trading from that store for 18 months: when its doors reopened, no union members were

Fig 3.47
Store 76, Henry Street, Dublin. This building was erected in 1916–17 – note the date in the gable – after its predecessor on the site had been destroyed in the Easter Rising of April 1916. The store opened in 1918 and was larger than the first Dublin branch on Grafton Street.
[FWW01/01/0076/001]

employed.[28] Disputes seldom became violent, but in June 1922, during a strike at the original Dublin branch, on Grafton Street, a group of armed men entered the store and smashed it up, destroying the mirror glass and plate glass windows, apparently because the manager had ignored pickets. In May 1924, the same unlucky store was subjected to a dramatic armed robbery, during which the manager (not the same man) was held at gunpoint.[29]

Those with most to grumble about were the sales girls, whose paltry wages occasionally made the news. When Gladys Edwards stole 1s 6½d from the branch in Hare Street, Woolwich, where she worked as a 'half-timer', the magistrate was persuaded to be lenient on account of her low wage.[30] Store managers were better paid, but led disrupted lives, since they could be relocated from one branch to another at short notice, as they climbed the rungs of the company ladder. Each trainee or 'learner' spent a few years on the shop floor, graduated to become an 'advanced trainee', then a 'ready man', ready for promotion to an assistant manager position. A new manager was first allocated a small branch, then moved to a larger store. If he did well, he might become an area superintendent, a peripatetic role which involved reporting to either a district office or the Executive Office in London. Eventually a particularly successful man might obtain a settled office position, perhaps as a buyer, or manager of a superstore. As in the American parent company, promotions were always made from within the company itself, but it took a long time to complete the journey from the shop floor to the boardroom.

Buyers were not always scrupulous in sourcing and labelling Woolworth's stock and frequently landed the company in trouble. In 1921, for example, the Dover Police Court heard a case in which Woolworth's was accused of selling 'a certain article of food, strawberry cordial, which was not of the nature, substance and quality demanded, being a flavoured solution of phosphoric acid'. [31] Since the bottle had been carelessly mislaid, the case was dismissed. In 1928 the

Fig 3.48 (opposite) Store 83, Cork. This branch opened at Nos 39–41 Patrick Street on 6 February 1920. Trading here was suspended for 18 months in 1922–3 due to a labour dispute. [FWW01/01/0083/001]

Fig 3.49 Store 59 in Belfast opened in 1915. It suffered a serious fire in 1928 – a brave police inspector entered the burning building to rescue the money in the safe – and was subsequently rebuilt together with Burton's store next door on a much grander scale (see Fig 4.20).[h] This image illustrates how stores continued to trade, even at the height of rebuilding works. The steelwork is in the process of erection by Banister, Walton & Co, Woolworth's usual contractors. [FWW01/01/0059/001]

Oxford store was held to account for selling cheap knives with celluloid handles and blades made from 'a kind of zinc' as 'Best English Cutlery, Sheffield', implying that they were of the finest steel.[32] Also in 1928, a magistrate ordered the destruction of 'obscene postcards' sold at the Taunton branch.[33] In Ireland, the managers of stores in Waterford, Cork and Sligo had to defend prosecutions for selling banned – that is obscene or pornographic – books.[34] On Ireland's list of banned books was *The Girl from Woolworth's* by Karen Brown, the story of an American working girl with 'pep', which was based on a talkie made by Warner Brothers in 1929.

Woolworth's stores, with their invitingly open countertops, continued to be plagued by shoplifting, which was often reported in local newspapers. Shoplifters included men and women, of all ages and backgrounds, and on occasion involved the company's own staff. As in the case of Gladys Edwards, mentioned above, magistrates often blamed Woolworth's itself: either for putting temptation in people's way, or for paying insufficient wages to its girls. Following the suicide of a young man who had been accused of shoplifting from the Exeter store, despite maintaining his intention to pay, the magistrate strongly criticised the company for failing to apply greater discretion in such cases.[35]

But despite these unfortunate episodes, Woolworth's continued to go from strength to strength.

'The long long chain', 1930–1939

Flotation

The Wall Street Crash of 1929 dealt a blow to Woolworth's American investors, as the company's share price plummeted. To restore their shrunken fortunes, its managers decided to transform their British subsidiary from a private limited company into a public company. According to the prospectus issued on 11 June 1931, the capital share value was £8,750,000; net assets were valued at £10,027,132 and annual profits stood at £3,281,489. Woolworth's shares were being offered to the public for the first time in the midst of an economic slump, yet the issue was highly successful.[1] Remarkably, Woolworth's had not been adversely affected by recent trade conditions. Free from loans, the business was still expanding on the back of profits, which continued to grow from year to year. In fact, British Woolworth's now yielded larger profits than American Woolworth. As observed by Frank Woolworth's biographer, John K Winkler: 'Lush British Woolworth, in many respects, became the tail that wags the dog.'[2]

Flotation reduced the American holding of ordinary shares to 52.7 per cent, but reaped a profit of $9,977,452. As well as restoring the wealth of Woolworth's executives, it solved another problem. Apparently it had been illegal for the British company to buy freeholds (classed as 'overseas property holdings') under the laws of the state of New York.[3] From 1931, with revised Articles of Association, the British company operated under British law and could acquire property without having to obtain permission from New York District Court. Subsequently, more capital than ever before was set aside for the purchase of freeholds. The store at No 32 High Street, Weston-super-Mare, for example, had been leased at £700 per annum, but the freehold was bought in 1932 for £26,000.[4] By 1938, the freehold stores were valued at £6,305,565 and the leasehold stores at £3,218,532.[5] As well as running a spectacularly successful retail enterprise, Woolworth's had amassed a hugely valuable property portfolio.

While British Woolworth's was riding the crest of a wave, the experience of other Woolworth subsidiaries was less buoyant. Eight Cuban stores, established between 1924 and 1929, were badly hit by the Depression, as were the 144 Canadian stores.[6] Meanwhile, the German chain faced unique problems. The first 25 and 50 pfennig store of the Woolworth Company GmbH had opened in Bremen on 30 July 1927. In Britain, *The Observer* reported this development, noting: 'The sixpenny bazaar is unknown in Germany in quite this form; the ninety-five pfennig or eleven penny departments of the big stores are the nearest approach to it.'[7] The chain had grown to 82 stores by 1933, making it one of the largest multiples in Germany, when expansion was halted by Hitler's regime. Stores suffered physical attacks: in August 1932 tear-gas bombs were thrown into the premises in Krefeld;[8] in March 1933 a branch at Gotha was 'wrecked', while a store in Essen was picketed with placards reading 'Germans buy only in German shops.'[9] Restrictions imposed on foreign firms meant that the Woolworth Company was unable, for many years, to send profits out of Germany.

Competition

To retain its position as the unrivalled jewel in the international Woolworth crown, British Woolworth's had to bat away intense competition from other, newer, variety chains. Addressing shareholders in January 1938, William L Stephenson remarked: 'It would be futile for anyone, particularly myself, to say that we are not conscious of new competition.

Imitation is the sincerest form of flattery.'[10] Several fixed-price variety chains now adopted a wide price range of 3d to 2s 11d or 3d to 5s and, consequently, could offer a greater range of goods than Woolworth's. American Woolworth had raised its upper price limit from 10¢ to 15¢ in 1929, then to 20¢ in 1932, before dropping it altogether in November 1935. Despite pressure from its rivals and from its American bosses, the British company doggedly retained its 3d and 6d prices until 1940. This posed a challenge, and Woolworth's had to adopt crafty ruses to keep some lines going. Ingeniously, and notoriously, socks were priced and sold singly, and saucepans were offered separately from their lids (see Fig 4.5). Some items, such as gramophone records, had to be abandoned altogether.

Among Woolworth's foremost rivals in the 1930s was British Home Stores (BHS), founded in Brixton in 1928 and developed into a chain of 3d to 5s stores. By 1932, when the

business went public, it comprised 15 outlets.[11] Another new chain of 3d to 5s stores was Green Shops, which was founded in 1936.[12] It merged with BHS in 1943. Woolworth's kept a photograph on file, dated 15 July 1937, of Green's branch in Hounslow: unarguably, it resembled a standard new-build Woolworth's store. Another newcomer was Littlewood's. This company, founded by Littlewood's Pools, had started selling through mail order catalogues in 1932 before opening its first 3d to 2s 11d variety store in Blackpool in 1937. By 1939 it had 24 outlets. The general lines of Littlewood's stores were clearly inspired by Woolworth's, and at the seaside town of Morecambe the lobby floors even displayed a red letter 'L' in a lozenge, aping the famous 'diamond W' (Fig 4.1). Meanwhile, Woolworth's foremost competitor from years gone by, Marks & Spencer's, sold 'nothing over 5/-'. Marks & Spencer's had pursued a business model akin to Woolworth's well into the 1920s (Fig 4.2). It had dropped the British tag of 'bazaar' in favour of the more American 'stores', and started erecting shopfronts like Woolworth's, with quadrant-shaped corners and pelmets. Things began to change in the mid-1920s: not only did the upper price limit rise, but Marks & Spencer's red and gold livery was dropped in favour of a green and gold scheme, to avoid confusion with Woolworth's. The two chains nevertheless remained neighbours and, to a degree, look-alike rivals, with Marks & Spencer's opening café bars similar to Woolworth's in 1935.

When Stephenson mentioned Woolworth's imitators in January 1938 he was most probably referring to Metropolitan 3d and 6d Stores Ltd, which was operating firmly within the same price brackets. This company had been formed in 1937 to take over the business of Metropolitan Chain Stores. Shortly afterwards, in March 1938, Metropolitan Chain Stores went bankrupt. The takeover of the previous year had been fraudulent, leading to a high-profile trial and the liquidation of Metropolitan 3d and 6d Stores.[13] Woolworth's seized the opportunity to acquire at least one of its would-be rival's premises, in Watford (Fig 4.3). A more blatant, and ultimately more long-lived, imitation of Woolworth's was F A Wellworth & Co. The first Wellworth's store was opened in 1936 by the brothers Frederick and Charles Moore in East Bridge Street in Enniskillen, Northern Ireland. Based

on Woolworth's retail methods, and even sporting red and gold fascias, Wellworth's evolved into a successful supermarket chain in Northern Ireland.

Woolworth's people

Woolworth's British executives relished life at the top. In 1933 the Chairman and Managing Director, William L Stephenson, acquired a racing yacht which he named *Velsheda* after his three daughters, Velma, Sheila and Daphne. John B Snow, the head buyer until his retirement in 1936, was a bachelor with a taste for the high life, including horse racing, fox hunting and polo.[14] To unwind, he would ride around his estate, Highfield Farm near Hoddesdon in Hertfordshire, dressed as a cowboy, smoking a large cigar. At Highfield he established a stud and a polo field. He built a Spanish-style bungalow for himself, with a separate house for his guests, and inscribed over the fireplace in his lounge was the motto 'keep on soaring'. Charles McCarthy, an Irishman who joined the company in Liverpool in 1910 and became the buyer of china and glass, owned several private aircraft. By the late 1930s, Woolworth's flamboyant first-generation executives were approaching retirement. Stephenson began to plan his departure by appointing Charles Hubbard and Louis Denempont joint managing directors. After the outbreak of war, however, his retirement was deferred: he retained the role of Chairman until 1948, after the deaths of both would-be successors, Hubbard in 1945 and Denempont in 1944.

Woolworth's employed around 25,000 people in the mid-1930s. Excluding the co-operative societies, this was many more than any other multiple retailer, including Boots (with 18,500), Home & Colonial (15,000) or Marks & Spencer's (11,555).[15] In 1934 and 1938, following earlier exercises in 1924 and 1928, the company published progress reports illustrated with photographic portraits

Fig 4.3
Store 740 in St Alban's Road, Watford, opened on 8 October 1938. Previously, these premises had accommodated Metropolitan 3d and 6d Stores Ltd, a short-lived firm which unashamedly copied Woolworth's business model. The shadow of Metropolitan's name can still be made out on the fascia, although the lettering has been removed. The name is still displayed over the entrance doors and the transom lights contain the letter 'M'. The store was soon rebranded as Woolworth's. [FWW01/01/0740/001]

Fig 4.4
Managerial portraits from
Twenty Years of Progress,
1928, including one of
Woolworth's 10 female
store managers.
[FWW01/05/01/25]

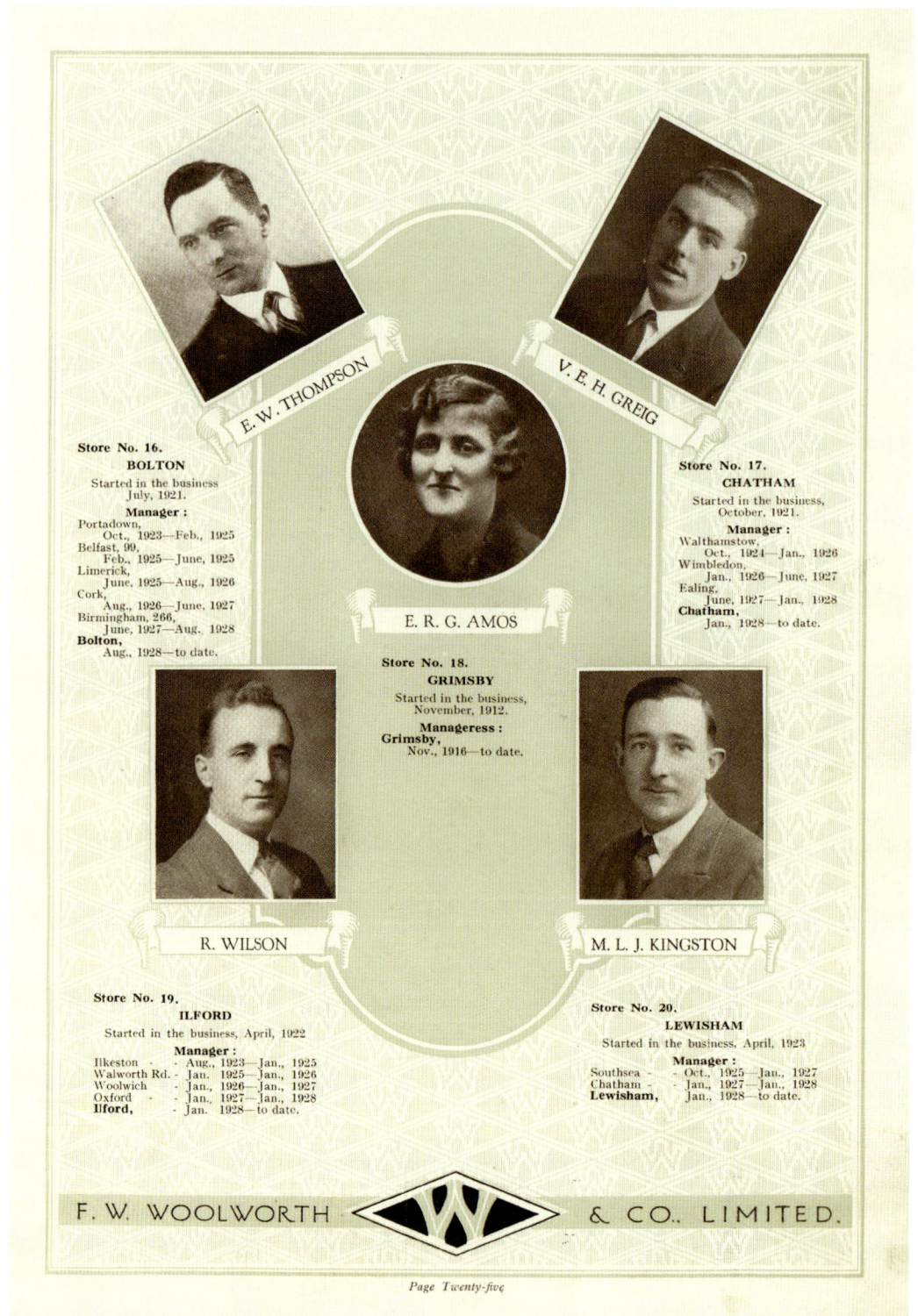

of the management team, from Executive Office down to store level. The absence of women from these galleries is striking. There were none whatsoever at managerial level in the Executive or district offices, but there were 10 female store managers in 1928 (Fig 4.4), 23 in 1934 and 63 in 1938. All of these women were identified as 'Miss', although some may have been married or widowed.

Most of the sales force – Woolworth's 'girls' (Fig 4.5) – were still young unmarried women. Full-timers worked long hours. Helen

Fig 4.5
Entitled 'As Others See Us', these carefully posed photographs of 1936 show a Woolworth's girl selling pans and on her break. Notice her uniform, with the 'diamond W' emblem. The pans and lids are priced separately, to stay within the 6d limit. From The New Bond, *1*, 5, May 1936, 114. [© Museum of London]

Dobson, who served on the sweet counter at Stockton from 1934 until her marriage in 1938, recollected:

> We were always kept on our toes serving. There was never any chatting or wasting time. The hours were Monday and Tuesday 9am until 7pm, Wednesday 9am until 8pm, Thursday 9am until 1pm (half day), Friday 9am until 8pm and Saturday 9am until 9pm. Friday and Saturday were our busiest evenings, as people would be going to the cinema or music hall and needed sweets ... I started with 18 shillings a week, but we had a rise every year. We had a grand staff of girls ... [16]

Although Helen Dobson had Sunday off, some branches in tourist areas, such as Blackpool, had permission from the local authority to open on Sundays throughout the summer. When Woolworth's was first established, the sales girls had worn their own clothes, with white pinafore-style aprons issued to those on the sweet counter. In the 1920s they were given plain maroon-coloured uniforms, while those on the confectionery counter continued to be distinguished by white overalls, with caps to keep their hair tidy. It is clear from memoirs that girls enjoyed the convivial experience of working in the stores, relishing the opportunity to chat and flirt with customers, but uniforms were universally despised, largely because they were inherited from former employees and seldom fitted. Pockets seem to have been removed from overalls at certain branches, to reduce pilfering. For the same reason sales assistants were not always allowed into the stockroom: once the reserve stock ('under-stock') stowed under the counter was depleted, they had to ring a bell for the stockman to come and replenish their displays. This might have applied particularly to sweets, biscuits and jewellery, which were locked away. Although women did work in stockrooms from time to time, this was a heavy

job. Goods were moved about in unwieldy wicker baskets fitted with castors and discarded packaging was formed into bales using powerful presses. Male staff were much better off financially than women, and enjoyed greater prospects of career progression. Stockroom men earned around £3 a week in the 1930s but, like learners, they could be posted from store to store at the company's whim, and a romantic liaison with a colleague might lead to instant dismissal.

Staff were often treated to a summer outing by charabanc. Reports of such trips were submitted by store 'correspondents' to the staff magazine, conveying the impression of a big, happy Woolworth's family. This magazine originated in 1933 as *Metropolitan News and Views*, published by the staff of the Metropolitan District Office. It was superseded in December 1935 – just a year after Marks & Spencer's launched its house magazine, *Sparks* – by *The New Bond*, which served the entire company until 1972, when it was taken over by *Woolworth News*. Group photographs of staff were often taken at the store or on high days and holidays. All in all, British staff were more content with their employment conditions than their American counterparts, who engaged in several sit-ins and sleep-ins between the wars, demanding higher pay and union recognition. They seem to have been particularly riled by the contrast between their own fortunes and that of Barbara Hutton, the Woolworth heiress.

The Woolworth heiress

Barbara Hutton (1912–79, Fig 4.6), Frank W Woolworth's granddaughter, had nothing whatsoever to do with the running of Woolworth's stores, yet everyone knew that she was a Woolworth heiress and her extravagant lifestyle brought glamour to the company in the middle of the 20th century.

Fig 4.6
A portrait of a pensive Barbara Hutton, taken in 1938 when she was 26 years old and married to her second husband, Count Reventlow. At this time she lived in her newly built neo-Georgian mansion, Winfield House, in London. [© William Hustler and Georgina Hustler/ National Portrait Gallery, London]

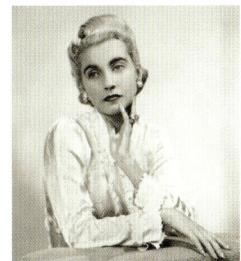

It also brought opprobrium. Barbara was seldom out of the gossip columns, and was often the subject of discussion and speculation on Woolworth's shop floor. On more than one occasion, in America, she was confronted by poorly paid Woolworth girls wielding placards that highlighted the gulf between their paltry pay and her inherited riches.

Following her mother's sudden death when she was a young child, Barbara lived with various relations or governesses. Her ostentatious debutante ball, held at the height of the Depression, delivered a taste of things to come. By 1933, when Barbara inherited her Woolworth millions, the sum left to her by her grandfather in 1919 had grown to $40,000,000. This was largely because her father, the businessman Franklyn Laws Hutton (d 1940), had had the foresight to sell her Woolworth shareholding and invest in gold just before the Wall Street Crash.

Barbara's seven marriages, mostly to Europeans with exotic, if slightly dubious, aristocratic titles, brought notoriety.[17] In 1936–7, while married to Count Reventlow, she built a new home in central London. Suitably secluded, it occupied a 12½ acre site on the north-west side of Regent's Park and was described as 'the largest residential property in London proper, except Buckingham Palace'.[18] The previous house on the site was St Dunstan's, a Regency villa designed by the architect Decimus Burton, used latterly as an institution for the blind. This was demolished and replaced by a red brick neo-Georgian mansion designed by the architect Leonard Rome Guthrie, of the firm Wimperis, Simpson & Guthrie. Barbara chose to name the house Winfield House, Winfield being her grandfather's middle name, and also the name of his summer house on Long Island. She moved in with Reventlow in 1937, staying on after their estrangement in 1938, but left for America on the outbreak of war in 1939.

The building programme

At the start of 1939, Stephenson invited his shareholders to 'conceive a shop with 90 miles of sales counter, a disproportionate mileage of display counter, and more than six miles of shop windows – this represents the selling space operated by the company at the close of last year'.[19] Woolworth's then had 737 stores. The decade had begun with around 375 branches, but plans to open at least one new store per week through 1939, bringing the total to over 800, were thwarted by the outbreak of war. In December 1939, just 759 Woolworth's stores were in operation. Nevertheless, by constantly ploughing profits into growth, the chain had doubled in size in ten years.

Phenomenal expansion – the creation of a 'long long chain' (Fig 4.7) – was achieved despite the fact that, by 1930, virtually every major town and city in Britain and Ireland already had a branch of Woolworth's. Underpinning the choice of new locations was a broad strategy, articulated in 1932 by Stephenson: 'In addition to the more thickly populated areas which we are not yet adequately serving, we have a big field before us in the smaller communities throughout the country, to which we are now turning our attention.'[20] Specifically, Woolworth's still had scope to generate growth by opening stores in the suburbs of large cities and in small towns with populations under 15,000.[21] As a result, most of the 380 or so new stores that opened in the course of the decade were of moderate size: no superstores were created from scratch, although Woolworth's continued to enlarge, rebuild or relocate many of its older premises.

Extensions could be carried out in various ways (Fig 4.8). A store might be elongated, often forming an 'L', with a façade on a secondary street. Some stores fronted three streets: the Y-shaped store in the seaside resort

Fig 4.7
'The long long chain': an illustration from The New Bond, *1, 1, December 1935, 3, accompanying an article on the history of the firm entitled 'The Story of a Wonderful Achievement'. Note the standardised store frontages and the chain strung with sixpences.*
[© Museum of London]

*Fig 4.8
This photograph of Store 367 in Upper Edmonton, north London, illustrates an unorthodox method of store expansion, involving departmentalisation in a series of small shops, in a manner more typical of co-operative societies. This was probably a temporary measure, pending redevelopment. The store was rebuilt in typical curtain-wall style in 1961.
[FWW01/01/0367/002]*

*Fig 4.9
Store 33, at Nos 29–31 High Street in Southend-on-Sea, opened in 1914. It was owned by Hillier and Parker and may have been designed originally by North & Robin. Around 1933–4 the premises next door were acquired and rebuilt in a matching style. This frontage lasted just five years before being replaced by a faience front (see Fig 4.30).
[FWW01/01/0033/002]*

Fig 4.10
Bruce Campbell Donaldson
(1896–1977), in a
photograph published in
Twenty Years of Progress
in 1928. Donaldson was
the construction supervisor
in Liverpool, with
responsibility for stores in
northern England, Wales,
Scotland and Ireland,
throughout the 1920s. He
took over as Woolworth's
Chief Architect following
William Priddle's death
in 1932, and held the post
until 1944.
[FWW01/05/01/13]

Fig 4.11 (right)
'Here's the Construction
Dept – that was!': a cartoon
published in The New Bond,
1, 12, December 1936, 338,
capturing the speed with
which Woolworth's
Construction Department
fitted out new stores.
[© Museum of London]

Fig 4.12 (far right)
On 6 March 1936 the
Liverpool District Office
moved to Martins Bank
Building, Water Street,
Liverpool (1932; Herbert
James Rowse). This
photograph, published in
The New Bond, 1, 12,
December 1936, 340–1,
shows the Construction
Department; led at the
time by William Leslie
Swinnerton, widely known
as 'Swinny'. The Department
moved to Armour House
on Lord Street in 1957,
by which time it controlled
244 stores.
[© Museum of London]

was extended in 1933–4 by duplicating the design of the old store (Fig 4.9). If this approach was out of the question, the entire site might be rebuilt in a more up-to-date style.

This building activity was overseen by Bruce Campbell Donaldson (Fig 4.10), who succeeded William Priddle as Woolworth's Chief Architect in 1932, moving from Liverpool to the Executive Office in London.[22] Priddle had died 'very suddenly' at the age of 47 on 31 January 1932, leaving a substantial estate of £19,590 11s 3d.[23] Beneath Donaldson in the Woolworth's hierarchy, the Construction Department (Figs 4.11 and 4.12) was represented by a superintendent in each of the district offices. London and Liverpool had been joined by a third regional office, Birmingham, in 1929. Donaldson's men were: William L Swinnerton in Liverpool (from 1932), Harold Winbourne in Birmingham (from 1929) and William A Sherrington in London (from 1929). A separate Real Estate Department continued to assume responsibility for identifying, acquiring and managing the property portfolio. Real estate managers are said to have paid retainer fees to estate agents to pass on information about prime sites that might become available through the expiry of leases or redevelopment.[24]

As before, steelwork was provided by Banister Walton, but from around 1930 floors – previously of wood – were of precast concrete units manufactured by Truscon (or, to give its full name, the Trussed Concrete Steel Company; Fig 4.13). This American firm had refined its reinforced concrete construction techniques in Detroit before setting up a factory at Trafford Park in 1907.[25] Steel ceilings were still manufactured by Steleonite, but towards the end of the decade the ornate Plastele pattern

of Clacton-on-Sea, for example, had entrance façades on Pier Avenue (1925), Jackson Street (1926) and West Avenue (1934), each one handled differently by Woolworth's architects. Matters were more complicated if a store was doubled or trebled in width by the acquisition of its next-door neighbour. Clearly, in this case, a uniform store front was desirable. Most simply, the acquisition could be refronted, if not completely rebuilt, to match the style of the existing Woolworth's store, even if this was rather dated. Thus the Southend-on-Sea branch

HERE'S THE CONSTRUCTION DEPT —

THAT WAS!

Construction Dept.

Architectural Design & Construction, May, 1939

TRUSCON
PRECAST
FLOORS HAVE BEEN USED IN
310 WOOLWORTH'S STORES

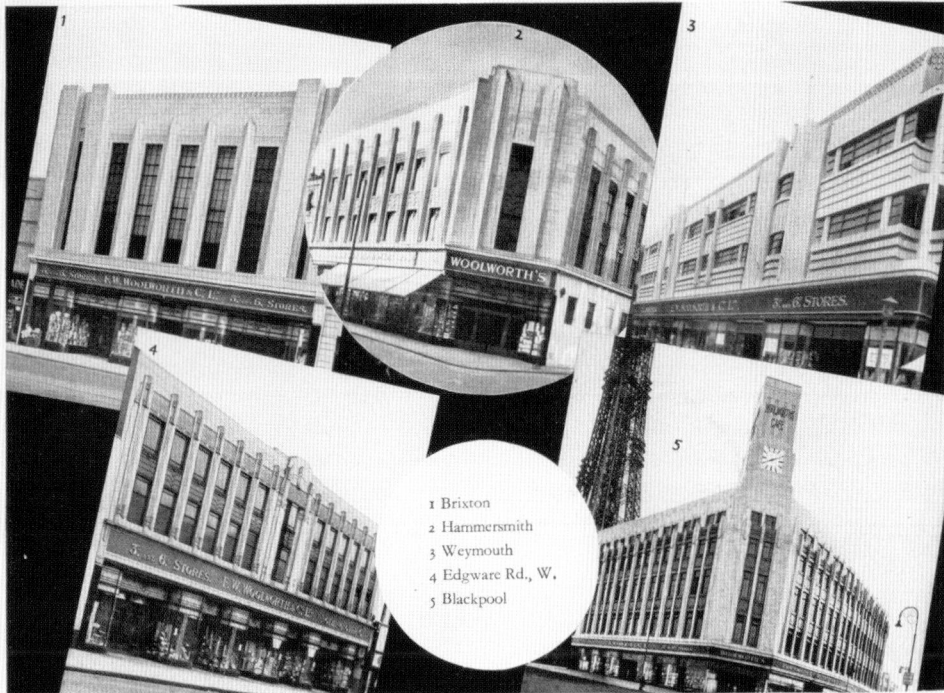

1 Brixton
2 Hammersmith
3 Weymouth
4 Edgware Rd., W.
5 Blackpool

Store after store, repeat after repeat—until nearly one-and-three-quarter-million square feet of Truscon Precast Floors have been used. In such definite terms does Mr. B. C. Donaldson, the Chief Architect to Messrs. F. W. Woolworth & Co. Ltd., express his opinion of our floor. Every requirement of floor construction for modern shops is met in the Truscon Precast Floor.

Our illustrated descriptive booklet will be sent on request

TRUSCON FLOORS
HORSEFERRY HOUSE, WESTMINSTER, LONDON, S.W.1
Telephone : VICtoria 4477 (12 lines)

Branch Offices at Manchester, Liverpool, Birmingham, Newcastle, Taunton, Cardiff, Glasgow.

TRUSCON
PRECAST
FLOORS

WHEN SPEEDY CONSTRUCTION IS AN IMPORTANT FACTOR, SPECIFY THE **TRUSCON PRECAST** FLOOR

4-427

viii

Fig 4.13
An advertisement for Truscon Precast Floors from Architectural Design & Construction *(May 1939, viii) illustrating Brixton, Hammersmith, Weymouth, Edgware Road and Blackpool, five of the most striking new Woolworth's buildings of the 1930s. Montague Burton wrote to his architect in August 1937, drawing attention to Woolworth's new buildings. Mentioning Blackpool, Newcastle, Sunderland, Nottingham, Leicester and Durham, he commented on the Woolworth's style: 'It looks very impressive, for it gives the impression of metropolitan immensity. I believe it is American sky-scraper architecture.'*[a] *[Reproduced by kind permission of the Syndics of Cambridge University Library]*

Fig 4.14
Store 464, No 24 Agincourt Square, Monmouth, opened for business on Saturday 9 April 1932. One of a handful of Woolworth's interwar shopfronts that have survived to the present day, this has been listed (Grade II, in 2009) by Cadw – the only listed Woolworth's in Wales. The extension to the right was added in 1964 and incorporated a garden centre from 1977. The photograph was taken in 1978.
[FWW01/01/0464/002]

was abandoned. Increasingly, brick-built façades were clad in faience, supplied by Shaws of Darwen. Shopfronts remained the responsibility of Curtis or Lindsey's.

Around a dozen Woolworth's shopfronts, all from standard-sized branches, have survived from the 1930s to the present day with many of their original features intact, minus their distinctive red and gold signboards. The most complete include Monmouth (1932, Fig 4.14), Ludlow (1933, Fig 4.15), Saffron Walden (1934, see Fig 4.76), Hertford (1934, see Fig 4.79), Leytonstone (1934), Frinton-on-Sea (c 1935–6), Bideford (1937) and Ilkeston (1938, Fig 4.16); others, such as North Shields (1930), Morpeth (1931), Huntingdon (1935)

and Ledbury (1937, see Figs 4.82 and 10.4) survive in a less complete condition, while just the consoles and pilasters remain from countless others. The design changed little over the decade. Most significantly, around 1936 semi-opaque patterned transom lights began to supersede the old-style pelmet cloths at the top of the main display windows. Several different designs were produced for the company by the London Sand Blast Co of Islington (Fig 4.17). The form of the entrance doors also changed, as the old-style curvilinear sills and pedimental transoms were abandoned in favour of a more modern design. Montague Burton, in 1937, noted that Woolworth's shopfronts had been 'improved' by introducing bronze door

Fig 4.15 (right)
Store 524, in Ludlow, opened in 1933 in an existing building, now occupied by Spar. The shopfront has survived, including the 'diamond W' mosaic on the lobby floor and the paired doors with shaped sills.
[AA009244]

Fig 4.16 (far right)
Store 141, Ilkeston: a detail of the shopfront showing the standardised pattern of the soffit, and the bronze window and door surrounds. See also Figs 4.26a and 4.29.
[AA99/07382]

Fig 4.17
Transom lights
manufactured by the
London Sand Blast Co began
to supersede Woolworth's
familiar floral pelmets in the
mid-1930s. These examples
are: a) a guilloche band
with an Easter frieze at
Knaresborough (Store 686,
1937); b) nested chevrons
and tasselled plaque –
which could be applied
with or without the 'W' –
imitating cloth pelmets at
Londonderry (Store 85,
c 1938); c) 'W' super-
imposed on horizontal lines
at Waltham Cross (Store
643, relocated in 1939);
d) a bespoke design for
Blackpool (Store 66, 1938).
The Londonderry design was
particularly common: an
example survives at Frinton-
on-Sea (Store 658,
c 1935–6, now Boots).
Post-war designs, however,
were closer in style to the
design at Waltham Cross.
[a] FWW01/01/0686/001;
b) FWW01/01/0085/001;
c) FWW01/01/0643/001;
d) AL2203/010/01]

frames and bronze lettering over the doors.[26] Unfortunately for modern-day researchers, Woolworth's never adopted Burton's useful habit of installing dated foundation stones on their new shopfronts.

Large stores

The preferred style for the frontages of important stores at the start of the decade was bold neo-Georgian, with giant pilasters, typified by Margate (Figs 4.18 and 4.19) or Woolwich. A similar style was favoured by both Marks and Spencer's and Burton's.[27] Woolworth's developed two prominent city-centre sites in close association with Burton's, which had previously been a partner in Liverpool (see p 40). After their neighbouring stores in Belfast burned down in 1928 (see Fig 3.49), the two companies collaborated to erect a composite building which displayed both of their names at the top of its Empire Stone façade (Fig 4.20). A few years later, in March 1932, the old prison site on English Street in Carlisle was sold for redevelopment to Woolworth's, Burton's and two other retailers on a 99-year lease (Fig 4.21). As in Belfast, the architecture of the new building more closely resembled Burton's house style than Woolworth's, and was probably the responsibility of their architect, Harry Wilson.[28] No comparable collaboration with any other national multiple has come to light, though Woolworth's sometimes leased a bay of its

Figs 4.18 and 4.19
Store 192 in the popular seaside resort of Margate. These two photographs show the corner site before and after redevelopment by Woolworth's c 1930. The 'after' photograph, from around 1960, shows displays of sunglasses, folding chairs and picnic-ware in the windows.
[FWW01/01/0192/001; FWW01/01/0192/002]

Fig 4.20
Store 59, Nos 1–15 High Street and Nos 2–10 Cornmarket, Belfast, was rebuilt following the disastrous fire of 1928 (see Fig 3.49). Woolworth's L-shaped store wrapped around Burton's corner site and had two façades. While Woolworth's preferred mid-block positions, sandwiched between other shops, Burton's deliberately sought prominent corner sites, making them ideal partners. This photograph was taken in September 1978.
[JLP01/10/05736]

Fig 4.21
Store 159, English Street, Carlisle: a red sandstone Woolworth's, photographed in 2001 and now B&M Bargains. The store was later extended to Victoria Viaduct (to the right). The shop on the corner was originally Burton's. In the 1930s both Burton's and Marks & Spencer's built a small number of stylish art deco store fronts clad completely in dark, emerald pearl granite, but this expensive idea was never taken up by Woolworth's.
[AA99/03525]

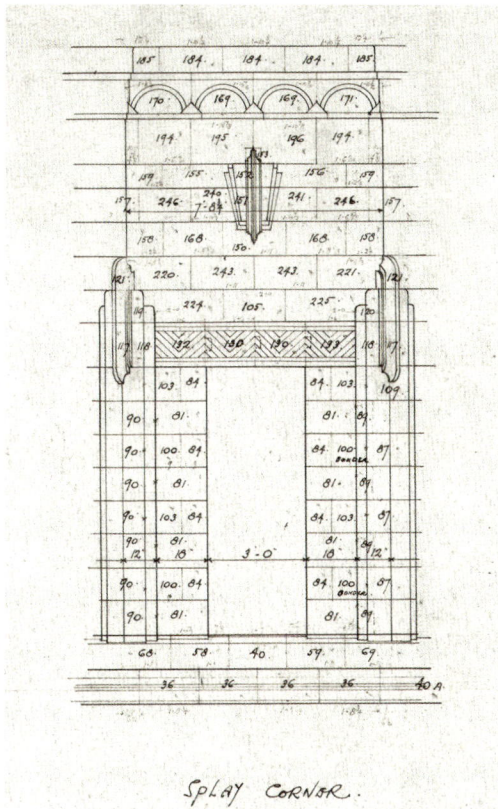

SPLAY CORNER.

own purpose-built premises to another chain store, often a multiple shoe shop, such as Easiephit at Wisbech and Cash & Co at Bury St Edmunds. It was probably thought that shoe shops nicely complemented Woolworth's, without presenting direct competition.

From around 1933, doubtless at Donaldson's behest, Woolworth's increasingly undertook the comprehensive reconstruction of extended frontages, encompassing both the old store and the new acquisition in an up-to-date art deco style, usually clad in faience tiles. These were among the most eye-catching and fashionable façades to be erected on British high streets in the 1930s, and unarguably marked the apogee of Woolworth's commercial and architectural confidence. Designed by Woolworth's and with tiles manufactured by Shaws of Darwen (Fig 4.22), these have been dubbed the 'cinema fronts' by some writers, and they certainly bore more than a passing resemblance to contemporary Odeons, many of which were also faced by Shaws.[29] Like Burton's contemporary faience fronts, these Woolworth's stores smacked of American popular culture, with overtones of Hollywood glamour. This was enhanced by the widespread application of red neonised lettering, not just

on fascias, but blazing from the top of elevations. The large red letters spelling 'WOOLWORTH' crowned the Brixton store until its closure in 2009 (Fig 4.23; *see also* the Lewisham store, Fig 4.36).

Inspiration for Donaldson's art deco fronts may well have come from the other side of the Atlantic, but their introduction pre-dated a major shift in architectural direction by the US parent company. This followed the abandonment of the fixed-price policy on 13 November 1935. Not only could the stores now sell a wider range of merchandise, they could sell more large-scale items than ever before. Suddenly, bigger stores were required. Under its new President, C W Deyo, US Woolworth launched a programme of expansion and modernisation, opening huge new stores in metropolitan locations: 'Emphasis shifted from the *number* of stores to stores of greater size, consistent with the expansion of merchandise lines and with the greater sales potential.'[30] New stores were often built in a vertical art deco style with pale façades, their jagged rooflines outlined against the sky (Fig 4.24). Some of these closely resembled contemporary British stores, and influence may have travelled in both directions.

Fig 4.22
A detail of a design by Shaws of Darwen, dated 4 May 1939, for the faience façade of Store 759 on the corner of Glasgow Road and Wallace Street, Clydebank. Numbers were cast into the individual faience slabs during the manufacturing process for easy assembly on site. The slabs were soaked, 'buttered' with a sand and cement mixture, then fixed to rough-struck brickwork with cramps at intervals. The corner turret here concealed a tank room at roof level. The rear of the store was damaged during the war but the frontage was spared. The branch closed on 31 December 1979. [FWW01/02/0759/001]

Fig 4.23
The new Store 7 at Nos 449–467 Brixton Road, Brixton, opened on 3 September 1936 (for the old store see Fig 2.16). In 1938 neon letters were installed at the top of the façade. These spelled out the old trading name of 'WOOLWORTH' to the end. By 10 April 2002, when this photograph was taken, the branch had adopted the 'Woolworths General Store' format: note the pharmacy sign. [AA032370]

Fig 4.24

The large new Woolworth store on Fifth Avenue, New York, around 1940. The generic resemblance to British stores of the late 1930s, such as Blackpool (see Fig 4.48) is obvious. This is one of a series of postcards illustrating American stores around the time of the Second World War.

[Author's collection]

LOOKING UP FIFTH AVENUE. NEW YORK CITY

32

K 4826

Fig 4.25 (below)

Store 41 in Hammersmith, west London, rebuilt in 1936, had plain moulded fins with curved tops, and a wave motif above the windows. The spandrel panels were of brown faience, with a nested chevron motif. The store – which closed on 16 March 1985 – occupied a corner site, with seven bays to King Street and five to Leamore Street. This drawing of the King Street elevation was made in winter 1935–6, when the building was being designed.

[FWW01/02/0041/002]

ELEVATION to KING STREET.

Donaldson's British façades were fashionable rather than 'Modern', in the strict architectural sense of the word. Their strong vertical emphasis was achieved through the use of tall, narrow glazing units with metal frames, sandwiched between boldly projecting piers or fins which soared above the heads of the windows (Fig 4.25). The inherent horizontality of intervening floor levels was suppressed by dark spandrel (infill) panels, either of metal (cast with a geometric design) or of bronze-coloured faience (sometimes decorated with nested 'V's or fluting). Visually, the darkness of the glazing units contrasted starkly with their pale, stone-coloured surrounds. Over this basic template, a wide range of decorative motifs could be applied, including fluting, scrolls, cable, guilloche and chevron (Fig 4.26). Such ornamentation was of Classical origin, but primarily geometric in nature. This was the hallmark of the art deco aesthetic (Fig 4.27), which had rapidly gained popularity in Britain following the *Exposition des arts décoratifs* held in Paris in 1925, and which borrowed widely from the cultures of ancient civilisations, from the Egyptians to the Aztecs, as well as from the Classical past and recent art movements such as Cubism. In terms of the zeitgeist, this style is often portrayed as the architectural equivalent of jazz music: just as youthful and daring, and perhaps a little vulgar.

The commonest variant among Woolworth's faience fronts can perhaps be regarded as the default pattern. It involved clustered fins that rose above the tops of the windows. Between their ringed tops (bundled like fasces) were rectangular panels, a narrow band of guilloche, and a broad frieze, S-shaped in profile and decorated with vertical fluting. This basic design could be adapted to stores with proportions as diverse as those of West Bromwich (1936), Lowestoft (1939, Fig 4.28) and Ilkeston (1938, Fig 4.29). For taller stores like Dudley (1935) the design could be

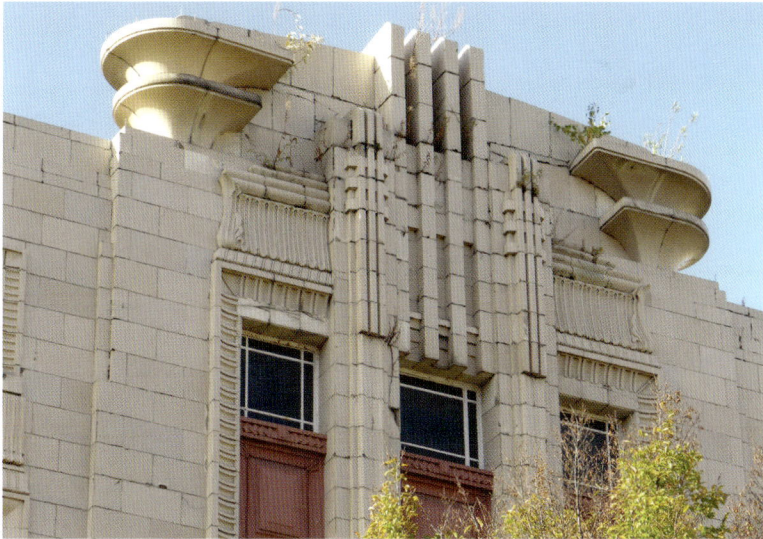

Fig 4.26
Details of Woolworth's
1930s faience fronts:
a, top left) Store 141,
Ilkeston, photographed
1999; b, top right) Store 2,
Preston, photographed
1999; c, middle left) Store
36, Nottingham,
photographed 2013;
d, middle right and
e, bottom left) Store 144,
Sunderland, photographed
2014; f, bottom right)
Store 27, Newcastle,
photographed 2014.
[a) AA99/07385; b)
AA99/08313; c, d and e)
Ron Baxter; f) Author]

Fig 4.27
Store 46 in Walsall seems to have been the earliest frontage in the art deco style to be designed by Woolworth's staff architects – possibly by B C Donaldson or Harold Winbourne – incorporating an angular version of the lion-head logo (see Fig 3.16d).[b] From 1941, until it moved to new quarters in Dudley, Woolworth's Birmingham District Office occupied the upper floors.
[Ron Baxter]

Fig 4.28
The short-lived Store 113 at Lowestoft was built in 1939 and bombed a year later. This basic design was used for many stores, including Bury St Edmunds, Ipswich, Malvern, Mansfield, Northampton, Peterborough and Swindon.
[FWW01/01/0113/002]

Fig 4.29
Store 141, No 102 Bath
Street, Ilkeston, opened
7 April 1938. This is one
of just a handful of
Woolworth's stores from
the 1930s to survive
intact, complete with
their shopfronts.
[AA99/07379]

elaborated, with projecting end bays. Because of their greater length, the stores in Preston (1935, *see* Fig 4.26b), Hanley (*c* 1937) and on Edgware Road, London (1939), rather than being book-ended by tower-like bays, were given strong centrepieces.[31] At both Preston and Hanley the fluted frieze bulged like a canopy over the central bay and was flanked by ornate pendants, the overall effect resembling a primitive headdress. The approach was similar at Southend-on-Sea (1938–9, Fig 4.30), where the fluting to the lateral bays was heavily stylised. A glazed green pantile roof, containing an attic lit by square dormers, lent Southend a Hispanic character. This feature reappeared atop several other stores, such as Edgware Road and Weymouth (*c* 1938, *see* Fig 4.44).

Other designs or approaches adopted by Donaldson and his team – especially Swinnerton's department in Liverpool – were applied to smaller clusters of stores. Newcastle (1936, Fig 4.31 and *see* Figs 4.26f), Doncaster (1938) and Dundee (1939–40), for example, all featured triple groups of windows. Douglas (*c* 1935), on the Isle of Man, was similar,

but faced in stone rather than faience. At Sunderland (*c* 1936–7, Fig 4.32), Dunfermline (1937) and Rochdale (1938, Fig 4.33) the windows had decorative stepped heads in a Mesoamerican style. One of the last large stores to open before the war, Morecambe (1939, Fig 4.34), was glazed with glass bricks. The sheer variety of these frontages illustrates the ingenuity of Woolworth's architects and reveals the tremendous output sustained by Shaws of Darwen – who undertook similar work for many other big-name clients in these pre-war years.

Despite retaining a 'deco' character, not all faience fronts were heavily decorated. Some, especially those designed in the south by Sherrington's team, were remarkably chaste, having the merest hint of ornamentation, often discretely edging curved fins or adorning slender friezes that ran between windows. These designs were often the most robust in architectural terms, with salient end pavilions bracketing the central bays. An early example was the store on George Street in Luton, which opened after rebuilding on 17 June 1933. Three later suburban London stores – the

Fig 4.30 (right)
Store 33 at Southend-on-Sea was rebuilt with a faience front in 1938–9. This crowded street view was taken in August 1939, on the eve of war (compare Fig 4.9). [FWW01/01/0033/001]

Fig 4.31 (far right)
Store 27, Nos 15–21 Northumberland Street, Newcastle, photographed in 2014. Built in 1936, this was sold by Woolworth Holdings in 1985 to Shearwater Estates, who had pre-let it to Next; it later became a Virgin Megastore and is now Sports Direct. [Author]

Fig 4.32 (right)
The new Store 144 in Sunderland of c 1936–7 was a particularly large building, 10 bays long and 4 storeys high. This photograph, probably taken in September 1940, shows how shop windows were often covered during the war – in this case using wooden boards – to minimise injuries from flying glass if a bomb hit. Woolworth's neighbours have not taken the same precaution, though Hope Bros displays a sign guiding people to the shelter at the rear of their shop. Store 144 closed in 2004. [FWW01/01/0144/001]

Fig 4.33 (far right)
Store 274 in Rochdale. During the construction of this store in 1938, the Construction Department General Foreman, Mr A Bendall, was killed in an accident. His obituary stated that he had joined Woolworth's in 1921 and had been foreman for the erection of no fewer than 30 new stores and 16 extensions and alterations.[c] [FWW01/01/0274/001]

relocated Brixton store (1936, *see* Fig 4.23), Ilford (1938) and Lewisham (1937, Figs 4.35 and 4.36) – fall into this category, as do many others, including Maidstone (1937, Fig 4.37) and Chatham (1937, Fig 4.38). The old building on Glasgow's Sauchiehall Street was simply reclad in tiles in 1935–6, to similar effect.

Recladding added a touch of style, allowing the store to compete with Marks & Spencer's striking new premises next door.[32]

The fronts of most of the art deco stores had an inherent verticality, but some, such as Nottingham (1937, Fig 4.39), introduced sleek curves associated more often with

THE ARCHITECTURAL REVIEW, September 1939

GLAS-CRETE CONSTRUCTION

Cristol Window Construction

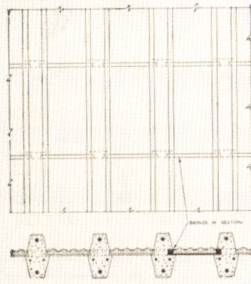

PLAN & ELEVATION OF CONSTRUCTION
PATENT No. 468091

LETS

DAYLIGHT IN

AT

MESSRS. F. W. WOOLWORTH'S NEW
PREMISES, MORECAMBE

This type of window consists of a series of vertical reinforced concrete mullions grooved and slotted to receive bronze H members, which in turn carry the high relief glass units. Mullions are spaced up to 2 ft. centres when glazing is carried out in sheet glass. This construction permits windows to be built to any desired height, as the weight of each glass is carried on the H members, which in turn transmit it to the mullions. This is necessary in order to avoid ultimate fracture of the lower glasses.

J. A. KING AND COMPANY LIMITED
181 QUEEN VICTORIA STREET, LONDON, E.C.4
TELEPHONE: CENTRAL 5866 (6 LINES)   TELEGRAMS: KINOVIQUE, CENT, LONDON

lxxx

Fig 4.34
This advertisement from
The Architectural Review,
September 1939, lxxx, shows
the frontage of Woolworth's
new seaside branch at
Morecambe, Store 408. The
upper-floor windows were
originally filled with ribbed
glass bricks ('glas-crete') but
were reglazed in later years.
[Reproduced by kind
permission of the Syndics
of Cambridge University
Library]

Figs 4.35 and 4.36
Store 20, Lewisham, south
London, photographed
before and after rebuilding
in 1937. A lamp post and
Cooper's tailoring business
remain untouched by the
upheaval. In the view of
1937 vans belonging to
Pearce Signs and Dickerson
Ltd, linoleum suppliers,
are strategically placed for
the photographer. Pearce
probably installed the
illuminated sign at the top
of the façade: this may have
been the first of many neon
installations carried out
by Pearce for Woolworth's.
Dickerson's no doubt
provided floor coverings,
perhaps in the cafeteria,
since these were often laid
with linoleum.
[FWW01/01/0020/001;
FWW01/01/0020/002]

Fig 4.37
Store 177, Maidstone,
photographed on 8 June
1937. The Union Jack
flags on the car and atop
the building were probably
left over from the
coronation celebrations
of the previous month.
[FWW01/01/0177/001]

the contemporary 'moderne', or 'streamline moderne', idiom. This had a predominantly horizontal emphasis that imparted an aerodynamic quality to structures. In the mid-1930s a small number of Woolworth's buildings, perhaps influenced distantly by the elegant German stores of Erich Mendelsohn, embraced the horizontal moderne approach. The mid-1930s stores at Bournemouth (Fig 4.40), Brighton and Worthing all fell into this category, suggesting this style might have been associated primarily with seaside towns following the completion of Mendelsohn and Chermayeff's sleek De La Warr Pavilion at Bexhill (1935). However, Woolworth's inland Watford store (Fig 4.41) was of the same type, puncturing this notion. These stores were rendered, painted white, and had minimal fluted decoration. The Blackburn store (Fig 4.42) was bolder, with projecting transoms and fins. Extensions at Brixton (Coldharbour Lane, 1937) and Wimbledon (1936, Fig 4.43) combined exposed

Fig 4.38
Store 17, Chatham: an
architectural perspective of
the store, which was rebuilt
around 1937, drawn by
the well-known architect
and draughtsman Cyril
Arthur Farey (1888–1954).
This was based on working
drawings provided by
William A Sherrington of
Woolworth's Construction
Department.
[FWW01/01/0017/001]

Fig 4.39
Store 36 on Lister Gate in
Nottingham, built in 1937,
had one of Woolworth's
most extravagant faience
fronts, displaying a bravura
combination of art deco and
streamline forms. This store
was much enlarged in 1961
but was sold by Kingfisher
in 1984, and is now
occupied by Marks &
Spencer's. Although it does
not retain its original
shopfront, this is the only
purpose-built Woolworth's
store in England to be listed.
The photograph was taken
in 1999.
[AA99/08294]

Fig 4.40
Store 54 at Bournemouth was extended and rebuilt in a moderne style in the mid-1930s. The part to the left of the kink in the frontage represents the store shown in Fig 2.31. The building was damaged during the war. [FWW01/01/0054/002]

Fig 4.41
The rebuilt Store 68 in Watford, next to Bottom Bros butchers, who seem to be receiving a consignment of pies from Doubleday's. Note the neon signs projecting from Woolworth's shopfront. This photograph was taken shortly after the rebuilding work was completed, c 1936. [FWW01/01/0068/003]

Fig 4.42
The style of Store 235 in Blackburn – seen here from the rear – was very unusual, with a strong horizontal emphasis and heavy transoms. Close up, however, signature Woolworth's detailing can be spotted in the chevron pattern on the window sills and lintels, in the stubby fins, and in the stylised cornice moulding. The building has now been incorporated into The Mall Blackburn.
[FWW01/01/0235/001]

Fig 4.43
Store 21 in Wimbledon, on the corner of Broadway and Gladstone Road, was one of very few stores designed by Woolworth's with exposed brickwork in a moderne style: this photograph was taken on 17 June 1936. In 1981 the building was destroyed by a fire that claimed a fireman's life; it was quickly rebuilt. The replacement was clad in dark red brick, with vertical window panels and an attic floor to the front, disguised as a roof; it is now home to T K Maxx.
[FWW01/01/0021/001]

Fig 4.44 (opposite)
Store 139 in Weymouth rivalled Nottingham for sheer style. It was heavily rebuilt in 1985 because water ingress had caused damage to the façade.
[FWW01/01/0139/002]

brick cladding with moderne styling, including a continuous horizontal band produced by an ashlar overhang above the upper-floor windows. The most splendid of all Woolworth's moderne creations, however, was undoubtedly Weymouth (Fig 4.44): its deeply channelled faience facings and stretched window bays were counter-cut by broad clusters of vertical fluting and topped by a gleaming green roof. The store unfortunately had to be rebuilt in 1985 after water entered through cracks in the faience and rusted the steelwork.[33] Whereas a bid to list this building was rejected at the time, the store in Nottingham was subsequently designated for its architectural merit and is widely regarded as an art deco classic. Had the Weymouth store survived a little longer, it would surely have attained the same status.

Store 66, Promenade, Blackpool

Beyond doubt, the most magnificent British Woolworth's store of the late 1930s was Store 66, which occupied a prime retail position on Blackpool Promenade. Standing next door to the famous Tower and close to Central Pier, it was a magnet for tourists. In 1986 the son of W L Swinnerton, the construction supervisor responsible for the building project, attempted to have the store listed.[34] He evidently considered Blackpool to be the most important of the 300 or so projects for which his father had been responsible in a career with Woolworth's that spanned over 30 years. Unfortunately, his attempt to obtain recognition for this achievement failed.

Fig 4.45
Store 66, Blackpool. This photograph of the Bank Hey Street entrance was taken between 1926 and 1930, when a second floor was added. The Promenade shopfront was similar in style.
[FWW01/01/0066/001]

The store first opened on the site of the Royal Market, beside the Royal Hotel, in April 1916, and Woolworth's had purchased the island block and expanded the premises by 1926 (Fig 4.45).[35] It proved a popular store – in 1937 The Spectator observed: 'A fraction only of the people who come to Blackpool enter the sea. Many day excursionists come straight off their trains, cross the street, and wander through the wonderful Woolworth's until the pubs open, then go there.'[36]

The Royal Hotel continued trading until 1936, when the decision was taken to replace all of the buildings on the block with a massive landmark store (Figs 4.46–4.48): Woolworth's remained open while this work was carried out in carefully planned phases. The new store – which some claimed was the largest Woolworth's in the world – reached completion in early July 1938.

The new building was the supreme example of Woolworth's soaring art deco style, clad in stone-coloured faience tiles by Shaws of Darwen, with bronze-coloured faience spandrels between the windows.[37] It filled an irregularly shaped (roughly triangular) site on the Promenade (west), hemmed in by Heywood Street (north), Bank Hey Street (east) and Adelaide Street (south). The Heywood Street frontage, forming the rear of the store, was of utilitarian buff brick laid in stretcher bond, with rendered concrete bands and glass bricks to the kitchen windows. The remainder incorporated a continuous shop frontage, 385ft 9ins in length. The shopfront itself was more elaborate than Woolworth's standard version (Fig 4.49). The main façades rose four storeys; above this, the fourth floor was set back by 3ft. Perched on its flat roof, on the Heywood Street side – where it was barely visible from the main streets – was the fifth-floor bakery (Fig 4.50). This, in turn, was topped by water tanks.

The main architectural feature of the store was its square tower, in reality a ventilation shaft, on the splayed corner of Adelaide Street (see Fig 4.48). This rose 132ft 9ins above pavement level and was topped by a clock with three illuminated dials (9ft by 9ft), with the fresh air intake on the fourth (rooftop) side. Above this, a red neon sign advertised 'WOOLWORTHS CAFÉ': the 3ft-high letters were cast in brown terracotta with 18mm neon tubes attached. This did not, as some writers have suggested, indicate the existence of a rooftop café, but signalled to afar the presence

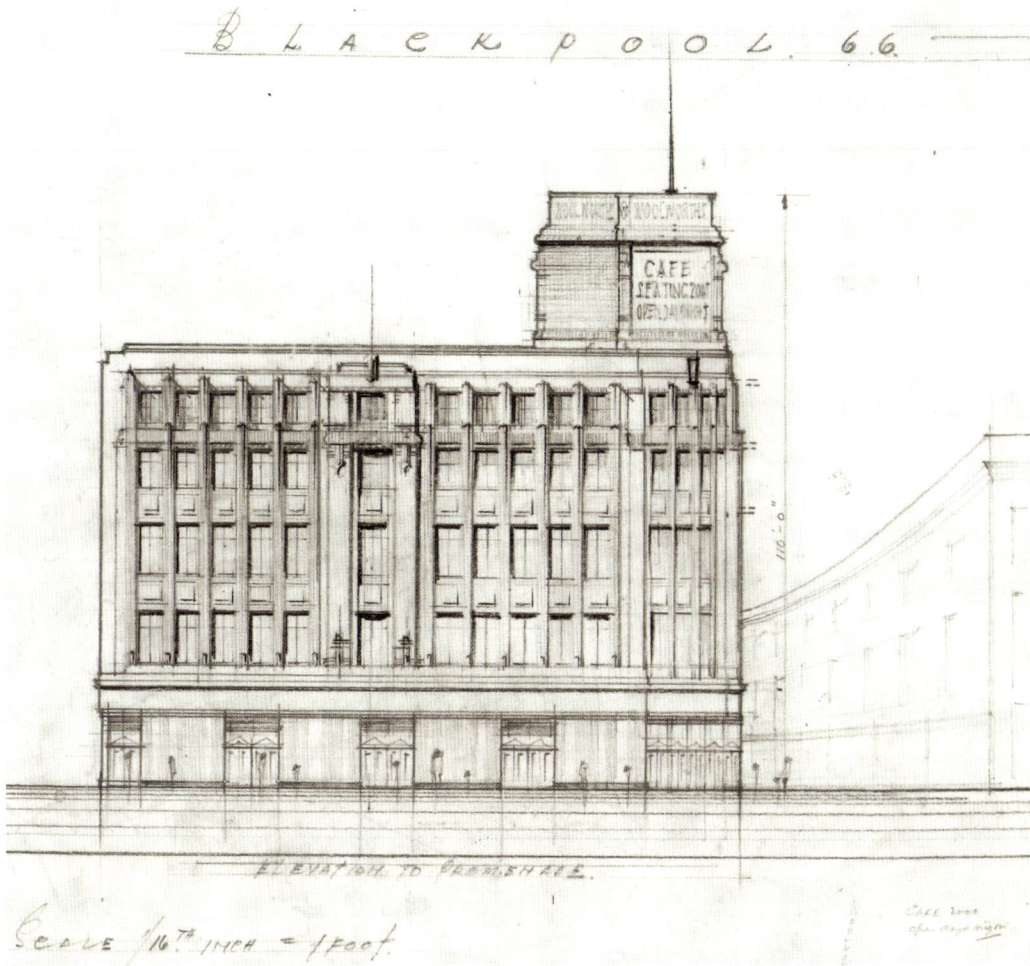

Fig 4.46
An undated design
drawing of Blackpool's
new store, c 1936–7.
[FWW01/02/0066/001]

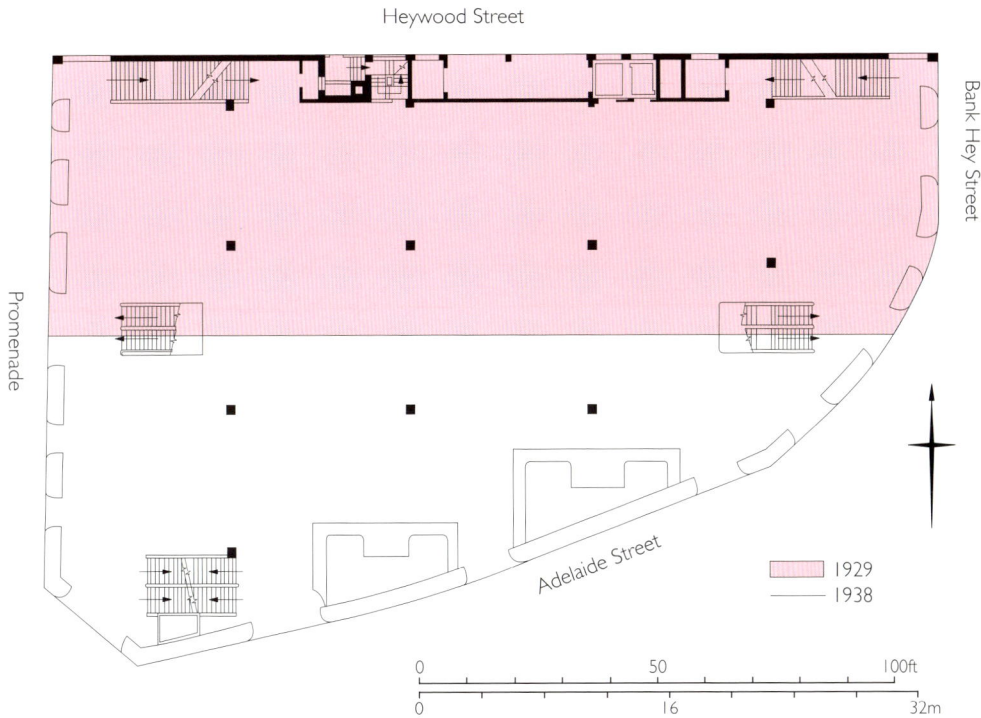

BLACKPOOL 66.

ELEVATION TO PROMENADE.

SCALE 1/16TH INCH = 1 FOOT.

Heywood Street

Promenade

Bank Hey Street

Adelaide Street

1929
1938

0   50   100ft
0   16   32m

Fig 4.47
The site of Woolworth's
premises in Blackpool,
showing its extent in
1929 and the outline
of the new store of 1938.
[Based on Architectural
Design & Construction,
May 1938, 189, and
a plan of 1929 in Historic
England Archive]

89

Fig 4.48
The new Blackpool store
opened in 1938. Its tower,
topped by a flagpole,
marked the junction of
Adelaide Street and the
tourist-thronged Promenade
and became a prominent
feature in postcards of
Blackpool Tower. The top of
the tower contained a fan
and motor which drew fresh
air down to the basement,
where the sales floor was
lined with large ventilation
panels covered in bronze
wire mesh and chevron
grilles. These, together with
the mullions and transoms,
were manufactured by
Walter MacFarlane & Co.[d]
The wave motif on the
exterior of the tower
recurred on other seaside
stores, such as Worthing.
The building was
refurbished in 1981 at great
expense: air conditioning
was installed and the bronze
windows replaced. Just two
years later, it was sold.
[FWW01/01/0066/002]

of the café inside the store. The main entrance, at the base of the tower, had a pair of revolving doorways separated by a slim display case. Like the sign on the tower, the lettering on the fascias was neonised, and burned red at night.

With the internal layout in mind, Banister Walton's engineers designed steelwork with an unusually wide span. Counters ran longitudinally between the Promenade and Bank Hey Street, the 7ft-wide aisles or gangways corresponding to the main entrances. The floor was adjusted to correspond to every

entrance, without the need of steps, despite the sloping site.[38] Sales areas were restricted to the basement and ground floor (Figs 4.51–4.54), and comprised 33,984 sq ft. Despite the illusion that everything was shiny and new, old counters and other fittings were reused whenever possible. Floors were still constructed of pitch pine, 'secret nailed' to precast Truscon units.

The stockrooms on the third and fourth floors, and the staff rooms on the fourth floor, were served by two staircases and a battery of six lifts entered from Heywood Street. The girls were allocated a sick room, a purse room and a cloakroom, and there were separate dining rooms for café girls and store girls. In addition, staff could use the flat roof, protected by a 5ft parapet, for recreational purposes. Customers were provided with numerous staircases, some of them rather grand – lined with Trani marble or Vitrolite – but there were no public lifts or escalators. Escalators had been installed in Selfridge's bargain basement in the late 1920s, and were just coming into more widespread use in major British department stores, such as D H Evans on Oxford Street in London. A correspondent to *The New Bond* reported from New York in 1938 that the new Woolworth 'Super Store' on Fifth Avenue (*see* Fig 4.24) had escalators.[39]

Discrete counters retailed food and refreshments. In the basement there was a fully refrigerated delicatessen counter with a reused white Vitrolite front. Next to this, a counter with an old mahogany front sold cakes and pastries. Both were backed by mirrors, which helped to make the basement look bigger and brighter. On the ground floor, a refreshment counter sold hot drinks and pastries; an ice-cream and mineral counter dispensed ice-creams and cold drinks, and a milk bar specialised in 'milk cocktails' (milk shakes), offered in flavours such as 'Egg Flip', 'Silver Lady' (peppermint flavoured) and 'Sunset Ray'. In all three cases, the white Vitrolite counter fronts were made out of existing fittings. Opposite the milk bar, a mineral bar (Fig 4.55) sold iced fruit drinks, including 'Khula Krush'. This was less stylish, however, having an old mahogany counter front.

The most impressive aspect of the new Blackpool store was its array of cafeterias, with walls finished in pastel green and primrose Vitrolite, a black skirting to box in the heating pipes, gold or peach coloured mirrors, and floors laid with chequered linoleum in 2ft

Fig 4.49
One of the standard
Promenade entrances to
the Blackpool store, with
the plate glass reflecting
a parked car and people
leaning on the rails of the
Promenade, enjoying the sea
air. Both windows exhibit 6d
goods and the opening hours
are advertised in the window
to the right. On weekdays
the store was open for
business from 9 o'clock each
morning until 9pm at night;
Saturday opening extended
to 10.30pm, but there was
more limited Sunday
opening, from 10.30am
until 7pm.
[AL2203/012/01]

Fig 4.50
Blackpool's rooftop bakery
was faced in Ruabon buff
brick and the windows held
textured glazing called
'pinhead Morocco glass'.
It was equipped with a
shower bath for bakery
staff. The teak benches
are a reminder that the flat
asphalted roof was available
to staff for recreational
purposes. Note Blackpool
Tower in the background.
[AL2203/076/01]

Fig 4.51
A panoramic view of
Blackpool's ground floor,
looking east from the
Promenade.
[AL2203/026/01]

Fig 4.52
A panoramic view of
Blackpool's basement or
lower sales floor. The
counters, reused from the
previous store, were
reconfigured into
Woolworth's new open-
ended, 'simplified' type. The
sales floor was lit by electric
lights (each 200 watts)
with moonstone shades on
chromium-plated rods; the
usual emergency gas lighting
was dispensed with in favour
of a 'Keep-Alight' system,
with an emergency battery
system for key lighting
positions. To help customers
– and staff – navigate the
store, the departmental
names and numbers were
displayed on hanging signs.
[AL2203/017/01]

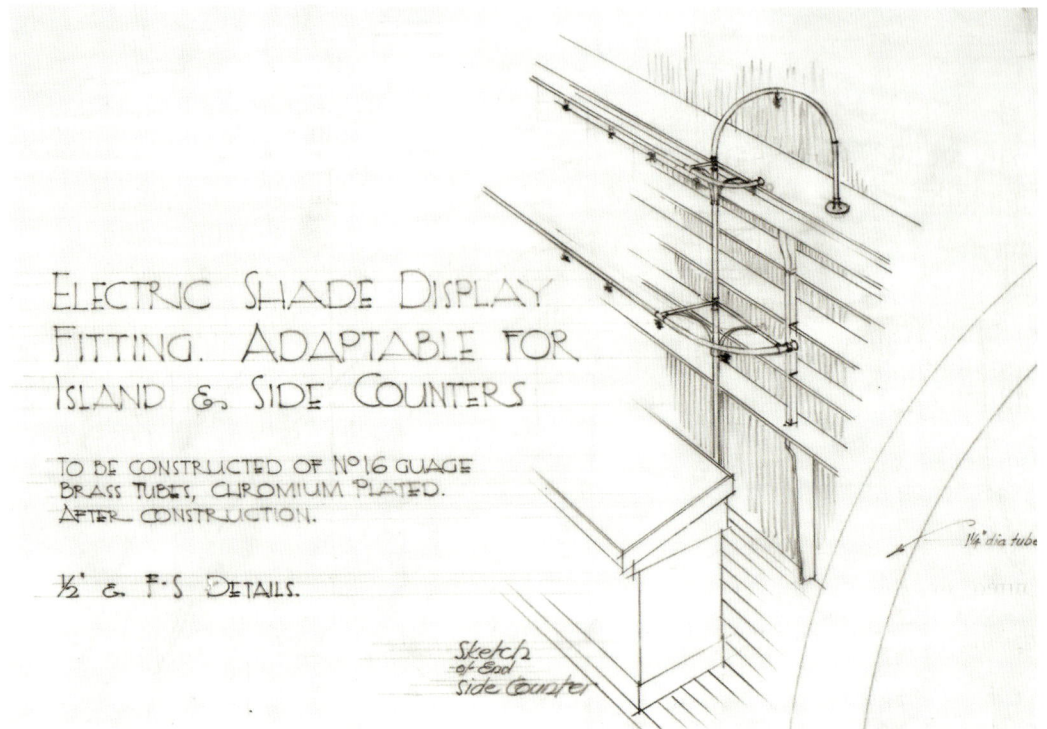

ELECTRIC SHADE DISPLAY
FITTING. ADAPTABLE FOR
ISLAND & SIDE COUNTERS

TO BE CONSTRUCTED OF Nº16 GUAGE
BRASS TUBES, CHROMIUM PLATED.
AFTER CONSTRUCTION.

½" & F·S DETAILS.

Sketch
of 6od
Side Counter

1¼" dia tube

Figs 4.53 and 4.54
Specialist fittings were
designed for particular
counters at the Blackpool
store. Here we see the design
for the Electric Shade
Display Fitting (sketch and
plan, dated 24 October
1938) and the end result.
Similar lighting displays
appeared in Woolworth's
stores into the 1950s.
[FWW01/02/0066/003;
AL2203/019/01]

squares, in two shades of mottled green with black borders.[40] The first floor was divided into two large cafeterias (Promenade Café and Bank Hey Café) by a double self-service counter, fitted by Ash's of Blackfriars, a company which had installed counters in many earlier Woolworth's cafés (Figs 4.56 and 4.57). With 275 tables, these cafés could seat 1,052 people. The second-floor Heywood Café could seat 627 customers at 157 tables. The remainder of the second floor was taken up by extensive kitchens and public lavatories. The kitchen was concealed behind a curved glass brick wall within the café servery. It was equipped with two automatic potato peelers, a great many deep fat fryers for fish and chips, four refrigeration rooms, a dishwashing room and a still room with a bread-slicing and buttering machine, capable of producing 55 slices per minute. Food was despatched to the first-floor cafeteria by seven 'subveyors' – an American invention of c 1920 – made by W & C Pantin Ltd.

As was the habit of the time, the cubicles in the gents and ladies lavatories at Blackpool required a penny in the slot to open the doors. These were quite possibly among the largest public lavatories in the town.

Standard stores

The brick-fronted house style established for standard-sized stores in the late 1920s was retained by Donaldson after Priddle's death and produced in large numbers (Figs 4.58–4.64). Architectural detailing, however, could vary. At Wilmslow (1933), for example, the central window had a tympanum laid with herringbone brickwork, while at both Morley (c 1934) and Armagh (1935) an open parapet contained a cluster of decorative horizontal rods. By the mid-1930s the standard approach was being superseded by the art deco style.

Red brick remained Woolworth's default material for small stores, but other materials were used increasingly as the art deco style took hold. A rusticated front at Dovercourt (1934, see Fig 8.20) was rendered. Many stores, mostly in northern towns, were faced in well-cut blocks of locally sourced stone. Variants adorned with Classical or art deco

motifs included Helensburgh (1934), which was decorated with paterae (discs); Rawtenstall (1935, Fig 4.65), with husks on the window jambs and a prow motif on the parapet, and Gosforth (1938, Fig 4.66), with a band of chevron ornament – which is, after all, a continuous row of Ws – running along the tops of the windows, between hefty mullions, and with a blank tablet in the parapet. Similar fronts in Conwy in Caernarfonshire (1936) and in Prestwick in Ayrshire (1937) were executed in dark red sandstone. Otley (1939), also of ashlar, is a particularly fine example of an art deco treatment on a relatively small scale (Fig 4.67).

Stores on corner sites, never Woolworth's preference, needed special consideration (Figs 4.68–4.71). Architecturally, the easiest way to achieve a satisfactory corner was to create a splay. For emphasis, this was often topped by a high parapet or turret, which might contain a water tank, perhaps with a flagpole.

Fig 4.58
Store 470, Aylesbury, photographed on inspection day, Friday 29 April 1932. The brickwork of Woolworth's façades was always of better quality than that on side and rear elevations, which were usually of cheap Fletton brick. Woolworth's quit this building and moved into a new superstore in January 1969.
[FWW01/01/0470/001]

Figs 4.59 and 4.60
Store 599, Chertsey:
a typical store of 1934,
pictured in the mid-1950s
when it still had the old cloth
pelmets and a sign for
the abandoned 3d and
6d price offer. The detail of
the shopfront, with
shoppers, was taken
on 31 December 1955.
[Popperfoto/Getty Images;
FWW01/01/0599/001]

Figs 4.61 and 4.62
Store 583, Feltham,
in south-west London,
shown before and after its
extension (the two bays to
the right) in 1939. In Fig
4.61, probably taken around
the time of opening in winter
1934–5, note the Christmas
decorations and the Peerless
weighing machine. The later
photograph was taken on
20 November 1940 at 11am
(for detail, see fig 5.10).
This was one of five stores
closed by Woolworth
Holdings on 29 January
1983, the others being
Richmond (Store 23),
Ilford (Store 19), Oxford
(Store 189) and Brentwood
(Store 451).
[FWW01/01/0583/001;
FWW01/01/0583/002]

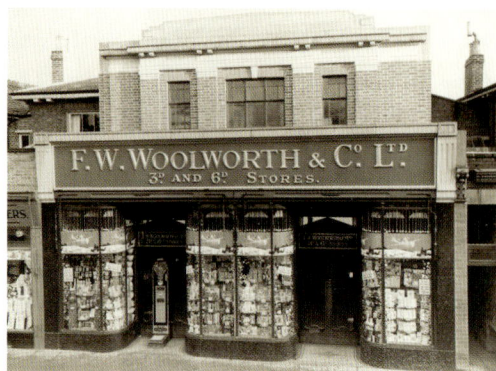

Figs 4.63
Store 614, No 21 Cromwell
Street, Stornoway, Isle of
Lewis, Scotland, in 1958.
This small branch, one of the
most northerly in the chain,
opened on 31 May 1935. On
the first morning of trading
the only visitors were a group
of herring girls, having a
critical look around but not
buying. In the afternoon,
to the relief of the sales
assistants, Stornoway
housewives turned out in
force.ˢ Standing in 'The
Narrows', in the heart of
Stornoway's then-bustling
town centre, Woolies quickly
became a focal point for the
islanders' social and
commercial life. It remained
successful to the end, being
extended in 1957 and
relocating to larger premises
at No 23 Cromwell Street in
the 1980s (designated Store
1211). After closure, on 27
December 2008, an ersatz
Woolies, 'Wee W', opened
down the street, in the charge
of Woolworth's former
manager. This closed in 2013.
[FWW01/01/0614/001]

Fig 4.64 (left)
Store 672 in New Malden, in south-west London. This shows the store shortly after opening on 30 November 1936. Two window dressers are busy in the left-hand window. Creasing tiles were used for quoining at several branches around 1936, as seen here. The shop unit to the right had been let to Boots the Chemist, which had yet to carry out its shopfitting. In later years, Boots' site was taken over by Woolworth's and rebuilt as a mirror-image of the original 1936 building, doubling the premises
[FWW01/01/0672/001]

Fig 4.65 (far left)
Store 607, Nos 49–51 Bank Street, Rawtenstall, built in 1935 and photographed in 1971. This was faced in local stone: smooth ashlar on the façade and rock-faced to the side. Similar stores included Clitheroe (Store 626), Cowdenbeath (Store 642) and Denbigh (Store 664).
[FWW01/01/0607/001]

Fig 4.66
Store 716 in Gosforth, near Newcastle-on-Tyne, opened in 1938. Other northern stores built to this common design included Sandbach (Store 635), St Andrews (Store 650), Airdrie (Store 675), Knaresborough (Store 686), Ilkley (Store 739) and Rothesay (Store 755). Bathgate (Store 753) was similar.
[FWW01/01/0716/001]

Fig 4.67
Store 754, Nos 38–40 Kirkgate, Otley, opened on 12 May 1939. The stone façade – has darkened, matching other buildings on the street.
[FWW01/01/0754/001]

Fig 4.68 (above)
Store 389, Nos 153–157
High Street, Erdington,
Birmingham, built in 1930
and extended in 1934. This
strongly resembled the
contemporary Bedford store
(compare Fig 4.69).
[FWW01/01/0389/001]

Fig 4.69 (right)
Store 184 in Bedford opened
in 1925 but quickly became
too small. Extensions opened
on 6 June 1930 and 16
September 1933, covering
Nos 7–11 Midland Road, as
shown here in a photograph
taken in 2009, when the
branch was branded as
'Woolworths Kids Store'.
A rear extension was added
in 1961.
[Ron Baxter]

*Figs 4.70 and 4.71
Harrogate: the corner
of Cambridge Street
and Cambridge Place,
before it was occupied by
Woolworth's Store 131 in the
1920s, and in a photograph
taken on 16 June 2000.
[FWW01/01/0131/001;
AA002967]*

Figs 4.72 and 4.73 Woolworth's updated the traditional Scottish high street of Dumbarton by rebuilding Store 122 which stood right next door to the Earl of Glencairn's Greit House of 1623. The Greit House's ground-floor arches were formed around 1924, after it had been acquired by the town council. By the late 1930s, this important historic building was incongruously sandwiched between new Woolworth's and Burton's stores, both in an art deco style; Fig 4.73 (far right) shows Woolworth's in 1971. [FWW01/01/0122/001; FWW01/01/0122/002]

Fig 4.74 (below) Woolworth's planned to erect a new building, Store 377, on Godalming High Street in autumn 1929. After receiving suggestions, shown here, from the architect A R Powys of SPAB, construction supervisor A Barton agreed to arrange the window heads at ceiling height, raise the parapet 4ft above roof level, and add brick arches over the window openings. Despite SPAB's best efforts, however, Woolworth's insisted on erecting its standard shopfront. [Image courtesy of the Society for the Protection of Ancient Buildings]

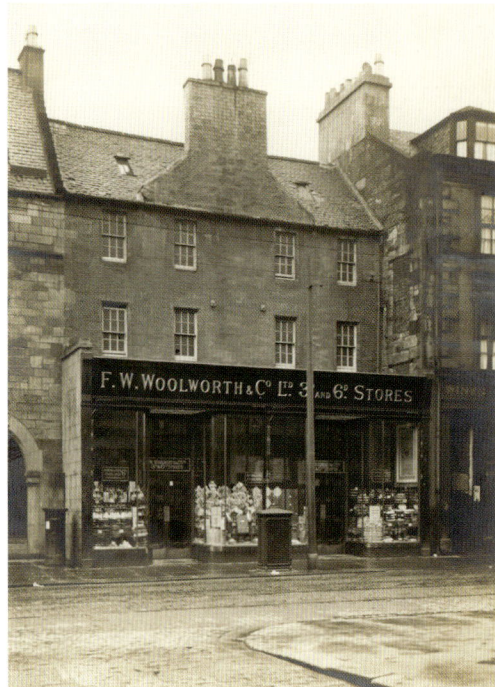

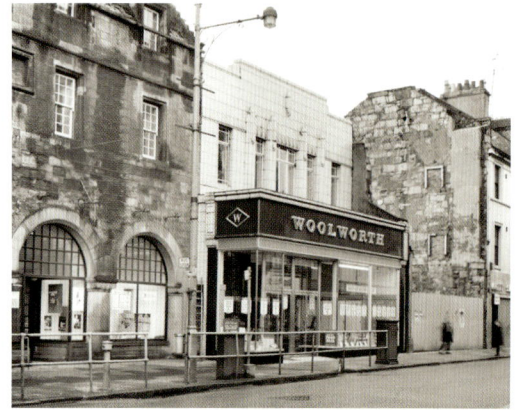

Woolworth's did not always go to the expense of erecting full architectural elevations to both main and side streets; often the stonework barely turned the corner before giving way to plain brickwork. This was the case at both Holderness Road, Hull (1938) and Bury Old Road, Cheetham Hill, Manchester (1938), and many of the larger faience-fronted stores.

One of the smallest stores to be fronted in faience was probably that on Dumbarton High Street, next door to the Glencairn Greit House (Figs 4.72 and 4.73). That this was permitted bears testament to the clout wielded by Woolworth's in such towns. Of course, Woolworth's always had to ensure that its architectural designs complied with building regulations, especially with regard to fire precaution measures and sanitary provision. But local conservation groups were becoming increasingly active, and occasionally the company had to deal with objections regarding the loss of old buildings and the impact of new stores on the historic streetscape.

When Woolworth's decided to build on the site of two old properties in Godalming in 1929, the West Surrey Society enlisted the support of the Society for the Protection of Ancient Buildings (SPAB), who suggested modifications (Fig 4.74) to Woolworth's construction supervisor, A Barton. As a result, the windows and parapet were altered, but Woolworth's would not budge regarding the size or position of its fascia.[41] Similarly, in 1936 the Hampstead Heath and Old Hampstead Protection Society intervened when Woolworth's proposed to replace two characterful but higgledy-piggledy old buildings at Nos 68–69 Hampstead High Street with a new store.[42] On the Society's behalf, the architect Maxwell Ayrton held a meeting with Woolworth's architect, probably Donaldson, and 'was able to secure a considerable modification of the proposed elevation'.[43] What

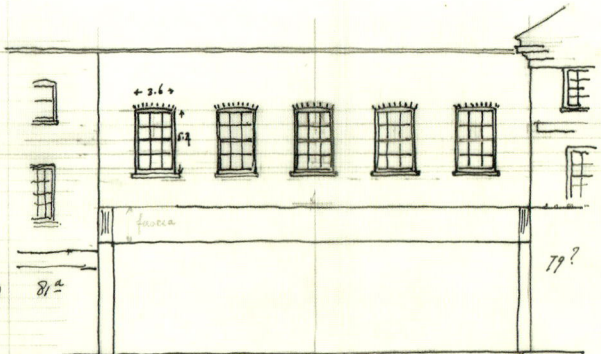

was erected was a convincing pastiche of a Georgian house, complete with rubbed brick dressings, sash windows and a pitched roof (Fig 4.75). The occurrence of similar Georgian-style stores – quite different from Woolworth's usual off-the-shelf façades – in places like the affluent market town of Saffron Walden (1934, Fig 4.76) or Camberley in Surrey (1936) suggests similar interventions elsewhere.

The biggest conservation battle involving Woolworth's took place in Chippenham, Wiltshire. SPAB, the Council for the Protection of Rural England (CPRE), local groups and individuals all weighed in to try to prevent the demolition of the 16th-century White's House at Nos 24–25 High Street. This had a particularly fine 18th-century frontage, attributed to the architect John Wood the Younger, which lent great distinction to the street (Fig 4.77).[44] On this occasion Woolworth's, perhaps having learned a lesson at Hampstead, refused to assume any responsibility: the company had

Fig 4.75
Store 681 at Nos 68–69 Hampstead High Street. Though it looks unlikely at first glance, this was purpose-built by Woolworth's in 1936. Behind the traditional frontage was hidden the usual steel-framed, flat-roofed store, and a closer look reveals that the well-designed sash windows were fitted with hammered glass. This is now occupied by Waterstones and the only hints of Woolworth's occupation – as is so often the case – are the end consoles.
[FWW01/01/0681/001]

Fig 4.76
Store 548 opened in the genteel Essex town of Saffron Walden, south of Cambridge, on 29 June 1934. One of the most complete Woolworth's stores to survive from the 1930s, it retains its original shopfront and 'tin' (Steleonite) ceiling. The doors themselves, however, are of post-war type. The Georgian-style brickwork is less authentic in its detail than Hampstead: note the soldier courses over the windows.
[DP088154]

Figs 4.77 and 4.78
The splendid 18th-century frontage of White's House (Fig 4.77, right), Chippenham, was dismantled in 1932 and re-erected in Bath. Woolworth's Store 493, in the standard house style, filled half of the gap it left and opened in April 1933 (Fig 4.78, below). It was extended and rebuilt in the 1970s (see Fig 8.14). [Image courtesy of the Society for the Protection of Ancient Buildings; FWW01/01/0493/001]

agreed to take a long lease on a vacant site which comprised just part of the plot containing White's House; demolition was the job of the lessor. When the façade was taken down in December 1932, the contractors sold it for re-erection at No 1 Sion Hill in Bath, where, in 1934, it became the end wall of an art gallery at the home of Ernest Cook, grandson of the pioneering travel agent Thomas Cook. Half of the gap left on Chippenham's High Street was filled by a standard Woolworth's store (Fig 4.78). Albert Reginald Powys, Secretary of SPAB, reportedly hung a large picture of White's House over the fireplace in his office, to remind him 'of an outstanding failure and as a spur to further unrelenting effort'.[45] As later related in the architectural press: 'Woolworths broached the sense of place by the characteristic modern device of bringing in a design which was deliberately standardised – the same here as in Penge or Buxton.'[46] Strictly speaking, this was unfair. The shopfronts were unarguably standardised, but otherwise these three stores were very different; Buxton was not even purpose-built. But the statement was typical of sweeping charges levelled at multiple retailers like Woolworth's.

After its experiences in places like Godalming and Chippenham, Woolworth's took steps to appease the conservation lobby. In 1937, for example, *The New Bond* reported that a 17th-century building standing on a site earmarked for redevelopment by Woolworth's in Stamford had been preserved by Dr John Kirk for the York Museum.[47] Pre-empting opposition may also have encouraged Woolworth's increasing use of an anodyne Georgian style in the 1930s (Fig 4.79). In particular, this may have attempted to deflect criticism and snobbery in middle-class towns with fine historic cores. Few of these buildings were as pure in their interpretation of 18th-century architecture as Hampstead. Usually of red brick, Woolworth's neo-Georgian

Fig 4.79
Store 590, Maidenhead Street, Hertford. This well-preserved red-brick Woolworth's was built in 1934 on the site of the Maidenhead Inn. The style is neo-Georgian, with casements rather than sashes. The photograph was taken on 15 December 2000, after the store had adopted the 'Woolworths Local' format. [BB016857]

Fig 4.80 (above)
Store 564 on Northdown Road in Cliftonville, at that time the fashionable quarter of the popular seaside town of Margate in Kent. The fluted motif in the centre resembles a sunburst: popular in the 1930s for front doors and gates, especially by the seaside. A similar motif can be seen on the façade of Epsom (see Fig 4.88). [FWW01/01/0564/001]

Fig 4.81
Store 680, Hove. When the store was extended to the left at a later date, two bays at the end of the new building accommodated Kelly & Son's butcher's shop, seen here far left. [FWW01/01/0680/001]

façades had small-paned sash or casement windows, flat window heads with stone keystones, and panelled parapets. Further Classical touches might include rusticated quoining, tripartite glazing, pulvinated (convex) lintels, pediments and even tympana. Occasionally, Woolworth's architects could not resist adding a modernising, deco touch (Fig 4.80).

One particular neo-Georgian variant gained ground towards the end of the decade. Its debut may have been at Banbury (1930–1), where a central window with a pulvinated lintel and pedimental head also featured on the National Provincial Bank next door. This type of window became a signature feature of Woolworth's neo-Georgian stores, including Swadlincote (1934), Hove (1937, Fig 4.81), Ledbury (1937, Fig 4.82), Pembroke Dock (1939, Fig 4.83), Diss (1939) and Clifton (1939, Fig 4.84). This design was so highly favoured by 1939, it appears to have usurped Woolworth's standard house design. It might have become ubiquitous, had hostilities not put paid to Woolworth's expansion.

Fig 4.82 (above)
Store 696, Ledbury,
opened in 1937 and was
photographed in 2000.
The central display window
was removed in 1987
as part of a refit opened
by Miss Corbett, who had
been appointed the store's
first manager 50 years
earlier. For the later use
of the store, see Fig 10.4.
[AA009148]

Fig 4.83 (left)
Store 741, Pembroke Dock,
opened in February 1939.
By this date the Royal Naval
Dockyard had closed, but a
new RAF base was giving the
town a fresh lease of life.
Appropriately, Woolworth's
was located on the main
commercial street in town:
Dimond Street.
[Author's collection]

Fig 4.84
Store 757, Whiteladies
Road, Clifton, Bristol.
One of the very last stores
to be built by Woolworth's
before the war, this is now
a Sainsbury's Local.
[FWW01/01/0757/001]

Conversions and parades

While most new branches of the 1930s were purpose-built by or for Woolworth's, some, as in previous years, were installed in older buildings that were adapted for the purpose. Among the company's most impressive conversions at this time was the former North of Scotland Bank in Wick, Caithness (1933, Fig 4.85).

As the 1930s progressed, a growing number of Woolworth's stores entered units in shopping parades. These long, uniform developments hugged the streetline and accommodated near-continuous rows of separate shops on their ground floors, with flats or maisonettes above, and rear servicing. Suburban parades had existed since the 19th century and were initially occupied mainly by independent retailers, alongside services such as tea shops and dry cleaners. From the 1920s, however, parades came to be dominated by national multiples such as Woolworth's, Sainsbury's, Tesco and Boots. Parades were erected in particularly large numbers around London as its suburbs burgeoned, with an estimated 600,000 houses added to its periphery between 1929 and 1939 alone. New shopping developments were

strategically positioned, with easy access to transport systems such as bus stops or tube stations. They were usually planned – if not completed – before the surrounding housing was occupied.

Sainsbury's built shopping parades through its own development company, Cheyne

Fig 4.85
Store 495, Nos 82–86
High Street, Wick,
Caithness. This store, in the
north-east extremity of the
Scottish mainland, occupied
the former premises of the
North of Scotland Bank.
The building was designed
in 1886 by the architect
Alexander Marshall
Mackenzie (1848–1933).
Of imposing grey Aberdeen
granite, it sported a
Classical pediment carried
by four giant Ionic pilasters.
Woolworth's took over the
premises, and transformed
the ground floor, in 1933.
Now occupied by The
Original Factory Shop, the
building is Grade B listed.
[FWW01/01/0495/001]

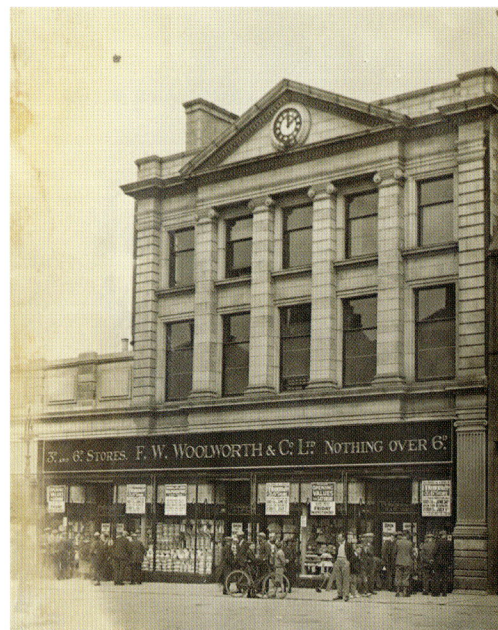

Investments. Woolworth's may have pursued this policy on occasion,[48] but generally had a different strategy. To secure the optimum position within a parade, and influence the form and appearance of its own unit as much as possible, Woolworth's collaborated closely with property developers and their agents. As well as Hillier, Parker, May & Rowden, these included Covent Garden Properties, Second Covent Garden Properties and Central Commercial Properties, firms which routinely employed their own staff architects. One of the first ventures of this kind to be entered by Woolworth's was a parade on Station Road, Harrow, north London, designed in 1929 by North, Robin & Wilsdon.[49] But by the late 1930s Woolworth's usual partner was Herman Edward Lotery (1902–87), a young entrepreneur whose company, Greater London Properties Ltd, specialised in suburban parades. Lotery worked with the agents Warwick Estates, just three firms of general contractors and the architects Marshall & Tweedy, who were allocated space in his offices at No 22 Conduit Street despite having their own premises on New Cavendish Street.[50] He simplified the development process in a manner similar to Woolworth's, by standardising architectural design and construction. In 1938, perhaps alarmed by recent events in Europe and foreseeing that war would curb his British enterprise, Lotery diversified into the development of suburban shopping centres in America, providing a new store for Woolworth in Linden, New Jersey, in 1939–40, designed by Philip Ives but possibly with some input from Charles Marshall.[51] After commuting regularly across the Atlantic for a couple of years, Lotery became a US citizen and never returned to live in England.

The first Woolworth's stores in suburban parades were built in the firm's standard house style, despite the disruptive impact this had on the uniformity of shopping schemes. The store slotted into the parade designed by North, Robin & Wilsdon in Harrow in 1929 exemplifies this approach. In contrast, many of Woolworth's units in Lotery's parades conformed outwardly to his house style, while providing customised accommodation behind the façade. Lotery is estimated to have built 80 parades (equating to 1,005 shop units) around London between 1930 and 1938, all of them three storeys high, of dark red

Fig 4.86
Store 692, in a typical suburban London shopping parade in Eastcote, in 1937. The shop unit to the left was in temporary use as a garage. Finlay's tobacconists occupied the unit to the right. Woolworth's was modernised in 1969 and is currently a Tesco Express. [FWW01/01/0692/001]

Fig 4.87
The original Store 643 in Waltham Cross, Hertfordshire, had been purpose-built by Woolworth's, but in 1939 the company relocated to this parade (compare Fig 4.86). The photograph, with ration posters in the window, dates from November 1940.
[FWW01/01/0643/001]

Fig 4.88
Due to congestion in Epsom, Surrey, it was decided to widen part of the High Street (A24) by knocking down the buildings on the north side, and setting back the street line. The old buildings remained standing until the new parades were completed. Woolworth's was one of the first occupants of the new scheme, opening Store 682 on 28 May 1937: note the bunting, celebrating the Coronation of King George VI. This illustrates Woolworth's new red-and-white striped 'Continental' sun blinds, manufactured by J Dean of Putney.
[FWW01/01/0682/001]

particularly successful commercial formula, beneficial to all parties. On occasion, however, Lotery conceded to Woolworth's preference for a two-storey building. Aesthetically the result could be odd, for example at Whitton (1937), which was given a blind parapet of almost full storey height in an attempt to make it sit comfortably within a standard Lotery parade.[52]

Woolworth's always managed to secure premises that were wider and deeper than standard parade shops. Negotiations took place while designs were still on the drawing board, ensuring that units earmarked for the company included ample stockrooms, sometimes in the basement rather than on the first floor, and upper-floor staff rooms. Woolworth's often had a distinctive frontage, even if this did not form a centrepiece to the parade (Fig 4.88). No doubt developers were eager to accommodate Woolworth's demands, since the firm served as such a strong magnet for other commercial tenants, guaranteeing the success of any new parade. As Lotery himself claimed: 'Once a chain store has signed its lease, most of the other stores rent themselves.'[53]

In one rare instance, Woolworth's took a unit in a local authority building. This was the Leytonstone Branch Library, designed by J Ambrose Dartnall for Leytonstone Borough Council on the corner of High Road and Church Lane, and now a listed building. The

brick with herringbone aprons beneath the windows and a modicum of Classical styling including distinctive pilaster capitals with upright foliage. Very similar designs were trotted out, from Eastcote (1937, Fig 4.86) and the relocated Waltham Cross store (1939, Fig 4.87) in the north, to Tolworth (1936) and Purley (1938) in the south, and Barkingside (1937) in the east. This was evidently a

layout suggests that Woolworth's had input at design stage, influencing the form of the development at an early stage. On the ground floor, an L-shaped Woolworth's with two façades wrapped around a corner electricity showroom; above the Church Lane entrance were the usual staff rooms, but the rest of the first floor was taken up by the library. Woolworth's rent here was £2,250 per annum.[54] Argos, the current tenant of the former Woolworth's premises, has retained the Church Lane shopfront of 1934; the remarkable art deco interior of the library also survives.

Interiors and merchandise

Woolworth's interiors changed little before the late 1930s, but new materials were introduced into important new stores. These included Vitrolite (opaque coloured glass made by Pilkington's) and Vitraflex (small rectangles of mirror glass, used to encase structural columns in frontages, Fig 4.89). By 1939 the floral-patterned 'tin' ceilings were being superseded by smooth plasterwork. Linoleum was used in cafés, but pitch pine floors continued to be laid in sale rooms. These were treated regularly with oil (supplied to stores by the Atlas Lubricating Co of Liverpool), which was liberally applied from a bucket and spread with a mop. On occasion customers slipped on the greasy surface, and some tried to sue Woolworth's for compensation for injuries.[55] Felspar was spread on floors after oiling, to make them less slippery.

Inside Woolworth's superstores, the name and number of each department was displayed on a hanging sign over the counter (Fig 4.90). These changed over the years: '33', for example, being 'lighting' in 1938 and 'tin and enamelware' in 1950. A new 'open-ended simplified type' of island counter arrangement was introduced around 1935. This involved four separate counters, two long and two short, positioned to form an oblong without touching one another, thus creating four entries into the central sales area. The earlier horseshoe counters, with their single entry points, were less flexible but probably more secure. Sometimes, old counters were reused to create 'open-end' arrangements,

Fig 4.89
A detail from 1938 of a show window at Store 66 in Blackpool, with a Vitraflex-clad column and toiletries display, including 'Stablond' and 'ShaveX'.
[AL2203/014/01]

Fig 4.90
These special light fittings
were installed on jewellery
counters in several
superstores, including Store
66 in Blackpool (pictured
here in 1938). Note the
new-style wall plaques.
[AL2203/028/01]

for example in the basement at Blackpool (*see* Fig 4.52). No matter how modern a store, the counters were still of mahogany, or pretend mahogany, with moulded fronts. An ingenious design from 1938 survives for a 'revolving cash register stand' for the store at Crook, and a similar stand can be seen in a photograph probably showing the Gorleston-on-Sea store in 1933 (Figs 4.91 and 4.92).[56]

Stephenson reassured his shareholders and customers in 1933 that over 90 per cent of the volume of Woolworth's sales represented goods of British manufacture.[57] Branding and wrapping were more prevalent than before, but most goods were still sold loose. New products appeared. Bakelite, for example, brought many items, previously made of expensive materials, within Woolworth's price range.[58] Among the lines of merchandise particularly associated with stores of the 1930s were gramophone records. Although sheet music had been sold since 1909, records were not introduced until after Fred Woolworth's death in 1923. The stores stocked Crystalate-produced records on the Victory and Eclipse labels from 1927, and then on the Crown label in the 1930s.[59] These were abandoned in 1937, when they became too expensive.

Also fondly remembered were biscuits, mostly supplied by Hughes & Sons of Birmingham. They were displayed in square silver boxes, sold loose, and weighed to the customer's requirement; broken biscuits were half price. Tinned fruit was another popular line, though some stores sold fresh as well as canned foods. In most towns, long before the invention of the garden centre, Woolworth's was the obvious place to go for seeds and spring bulbs. Additionally, much reading material could be found in 'Woolies', with movies, the wild west and romance all providing fodder for magazines. Cloth-bound classic novels had been sold in American Woolworth stores from the early 1920s for 10¢; in Britain, Allen Lane began to sell his 6d Penguin paperback books through Woolworth's in 1935, and sixpenny romances remained just as popular. Outdoor Girl cosmetics were introduced 1931. Ladybird

Fig 4.91
A rather clumsy sketch
for a 'revolving cash register
stand' for Store 529 at
Crook, County Durham,
dated 1938. It is annotated
'girl av. height 5' 6"'.
Compare with Fig 4.92.
[FWW01/02/0529/001]

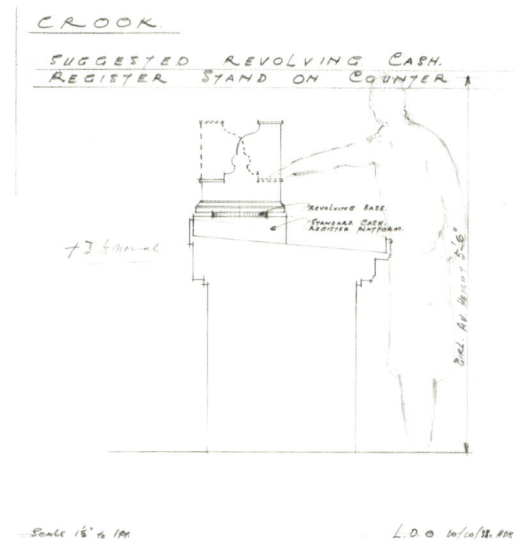

Fig 4.92
The unidentified interior of a small store, photographed before opening on Friday 4 August, as announced on the doors. The unusual occurrence of three entrance doors, and the slight kink in the floor plan, indicates that this is probably No 4 Lowestoft Road, Gorleston-on-Sea, which opened as Store 518 in 1933 (when 4 August fell on a Friday). Note the revolving cash register stand. Precociously, a sign on the far wall, laden with china, reads 'Self Service'.
[FWW01/01/0175/001]

clothing (specifically 'Directoire Knickers') made by Pasold Ltd in Langley, Slough, was first stocked in 1932. Blue-packaged 'Evening in Paris' (or 'Soir de Paris') perfume – launched by Bourjois in 1929 – is still remembered: some shoppers recall the stores smelling distinctively, even sickeningly, of cheap perfume and sweets.

Special merchandise was brought in for national celebrations such as the Silver Jubilee (Fig 4.93) and Coronation (Fig 4.94), as well as for Easter and Christmas.

Confectionery, like toiletries, was positioned close to the main entrance. Florence Harrison started working at the sweet counter in

Fig 4.93
Store 261 in Tunbridge Wells. Many Woolworth's stores were decorated to celebrate the Silver Jubilee of King George V and Queen Mary in 1935. Counters would have been laden with souvenirs.
[FWW01/01/0261/001]

Fig 4.94
Store 128 at Nos 64–66
Above Bar, Southampton,
dressed for the Coronation
of George VI in 1937. This
store opened on the ground
floor of Clark's College in
1923 and was rebuilt on the
same site in 1935–6. It was
one of a small number of
Woolworth's stores to be
clad in very shiny, mottled
oblong tiles, laid in a
rectilinear fashion (soldier
stack bond), manufactured
by Shaws of Darwen. None
of these is known to have
survived, but they seem to
have resembled the modular
tiled fronts that were
designed for Marks &
Spencer's in 1934 by the
architect Robert Lutyens.
The Southampton store
was destroyed by bombing
during the Second World
War (see Fig 5.20).

Similar tiling at Store
26, Wood Green, in north
London also dated from
1935–6, but was stripped
from the façade in the
early 1950s.
[FWW01/01/0128/004]

Sunderland's Woolworth's in 1931 and remembered:

> We sold buttered brazils, chocolate-covered dates, Pontefract cakes, marshmallows, assorted toffees, mint imperials, marzipan teacakes, orange and lemon slices, nougat, Fry's chocolate cream bars and all kinds of liquorice, the pipes were particularly popular. One end of the counter was devoted to salted nuts and raisins. Everything had to be weighed out on small brass scales using weights and most people bought in 2oz or 4oz quantities.[60]

By the end of the decade weights were no longer needed: sweet counters were equipped with distinctive silver-coloured self-indicating counter-balance scales, with a removable pan to scoop up the loose sweets, which were then tipped into a paper bag, its corners deftly twisted by the confectionery girls.

Woolworth's largest restaurants were 'designed on the American cafeteria self-service principle' from the early 1930s.[61] As long ago as May 1916 Frank Woolworth had described, at some length, his first experience of a self-service cafeteria during a business trip to California. In one of his regular letters to managers he wrote: 'These cafeterias are very popular, not only in Los Angeles, but all over California, and are a new method of running a restaurant that some eastern restaurants might do well to copy.'[62] As well as adopting self-service, after the First World War the largest American stores were equipped with luncheonette counters, lined with red leatherette stools. In the early 1930s these classic features of the American stores began to appear in Britain, where they were known as 'quick lunch bars' (Figs 4.95 and 4.96).

One of the first British stores to have both a self-service cafeteria and a quick lunch bar was Nos 150–154 Oxford Street, London, designed by Elcock & Sutcliffe. This opened for inspection on 13 April 1932: a Wednesday rather than the usual Friday. The arrangement was ingenious, with catering functions stacked one above the other on three floors, connected by subveyors: dishwashing (basement); lunch bar (ground floor) and kitchen and bakery (first floor). Woolworth's rarely placed advertisements in the press, but made an exception in this case. A two-page spread in the *Daily Mail* heralded Woolworth's 'newest and largest' store, and drew attention to the British-

made products available at its counters.[63] The principal draw, however, was undoubtedly the cafeteria and lunch bar, which could seat around 500 people. The food was 'the purest obtainable – home killed meat only – pure butter and lard – no substitutes'. The advert listed 28 'Other Woolworth's Cafes, Cafeterias, Lunch Bars', and flagged up the existence of 'Tea and Snack Bars' at a further 97 stores. So approximately a quarter of the stores in the chain provided refreshments for customers at this time.

A surviving menu from Nos 150–154 Oxford Street, dated 17 August 1937, reveals that a cooked breakfast could be had for 6d between 9am and 11am, 'special complete' teas were served for 6d from 3pm, and on each floor was a sandwich bar selling sandwiches and rolls, glasses of milk and bottled mineral water.[64] The luncheon menu was headed 'no gratuities by request', since all of Woolworth's cafés operated a 'no tips' policy. It offered an extensive choice of meals priced at either 3d or 6d, with drinks for 2d. Cakes, pastries, meats and cheeses could also be purchased at a delicatessen counter.

Store 10 in Bristol, a very large branch with around 300 staff, soon acquired a self-service cafeteria on an even greater scale than Nos 150–154 Oxford Street. Around 1931, a tailor's

"Woolworth's Quick Luncheon Counters" at Blackpool, Liverpool, Glasgow, Edinburgh, Birmingham.

Fig 4.95
Store 1, Liverpool: the quick lunch counter. As this undated 1930s postcard reveals, there were similar quick lunch counters – modelled on their American equivalents – in the Blackpool, Glasgow, Edinburgh and Birmingham stores. [Author's collection]

Fig 4.96
A plan of the quick lunch bar of Store 41, Hammersmith, designed in 1935 with 124 seats. The counters in front of the lunch bar (bottom of the plan) are of the company's new open-ended type. [FWW01/02/0041/003]

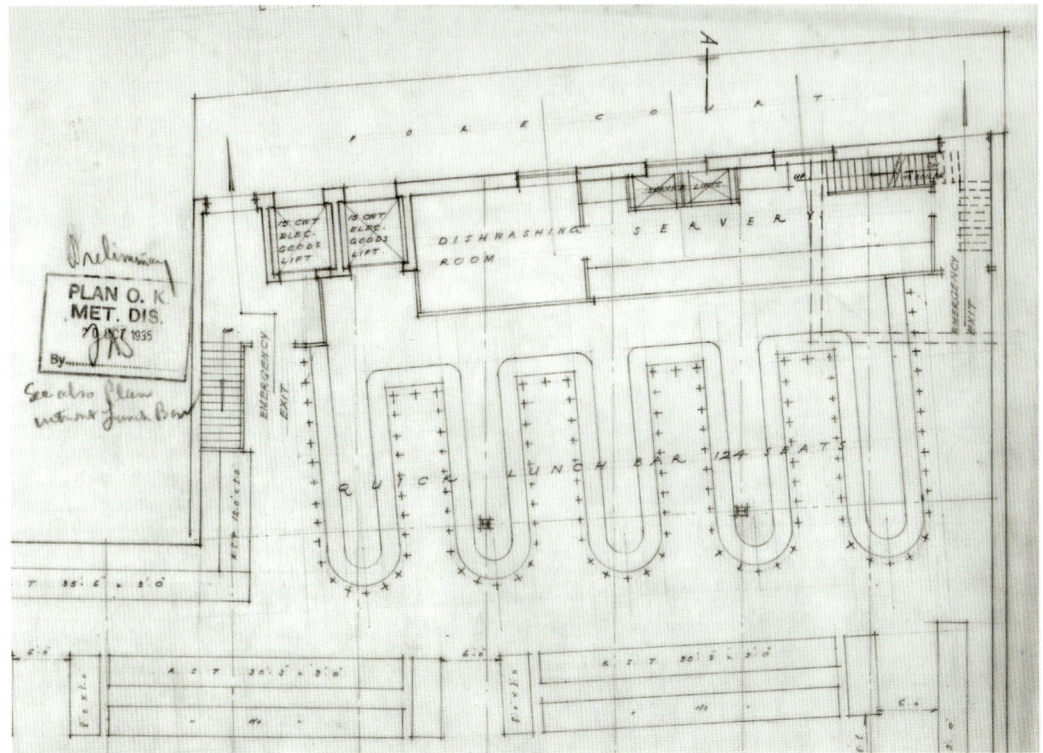

Fig 4.97
Around 32 stores offered a 'Souvenir Menu' to mark the Silver Jubilee of 1935. This example was issued in the cafeteria at Castle Street, Bristol (Store 10; see Fig 2.17). As well as a wide variety of dishes, such as roast pork and hot waffles, it offered a range of drinks including Ovaltine and Orlem. Also available were 'cigarettes (popular brands) and matches'. [Author's collection]

F. W. WOOLWORTH & CO. LTD.

CASTLE STREET, BRISTOL

CAFETERIA (Self-Service Cafe)

Chops and Steaks to order .. 6d. each.

FRIDAY, MAY 10th.
LUNCHEON MENU

Grape Fruit .. 3d.   Iced Milk Flip .. 3d.

SOUPS.
Clear Julienne .. .. 3d.   Thick Vegetable .. 3d.
(including Bread Roll)

FISH.
Baked Stuffed Cod .. .. 6d.
Fish Cake and Chips .. .. 6d.
Fried Fillet of Sole .. .. 6d.
Fried Plaice .. .. 6d.

ENTREE.
Steak and Kidney Pudding .. .. .. 6d.
Saute of Veal and Baked Beans .. .. 6d.
Grilled Pork Sausages and Chips .. 6d.
Hot Meat Pie and Chips .. .. .. 6d.
Cambridge Cutlet and Tomatoes .. 6d.

JOINTS.
Roast English Leg of Pork, Seasoning & Apple Sauce .. 6d.
Roast English Beef and Yorkshire Pudding .. 6d.

VEGETABLES.
Young Carrots & Cream Sauce 3d.   Braised Onions .. 3d.
Potatoes—Roast, Mashed, Chipped or New .. 3d.
Spring Cabbage .. .. 3d.   Green Peas .. 3d.

SWEETS.
Vanilla Ice & Chocolate Sauce 3d.   Stewed Figs & Custard 3d.
Baked Jam Roll & Custard 3d.   Stmd. Mxd. Fruit Pud. Custd. 3d.
Red Currant Pie and Custard 3d.   Jelly and Cream .. 3d.
Tapioca Pudding .. 3d.   Fruit Flan and Cream 3d.
Bread and Butter Pudding 3d.   Fruit Salad and Cream 6d.
Fruit Trifle and Cream 6d.

COLD BUFFET.
Cold Spring Chicken .. 6d.   Crab or Lobster Salads 6d.
Cold Roast Joints .. 6d.   Green Salads (various) 3d.
Ham or Tongue .. 6d.   Cold Severn Salmon .. 6d.

CIGARETTES (POPULAR BRANDS) AND MATCHES

NO GRATUITIES BY REQUEST

TEA MENU

Service at Tables if required.

BEVERAGES.
Tea, per pot per person .. 3d.   Milk, per bottle .. 2d.
Tea, per cup .. 2d.   Ovaltine, per glass .. 3d.
Horlick Plain or Chocolate 3d.   Orlem, Iced .. 2d.
Made with Milk, 1d. extra   Minerals .. 2d.
Coffee, with Cream .. 2d.   Bovril, per cup .. 3d.

FISH.
Fried Hake Cutlet .. 6d.   Fried Cod and Chips 6d.
Fish Cake and Chips .. 6d.   Fried Dab or Plaice .. 6d.

GRILLS.
Grilled Tomatoes .. 3d.   Grilled Bacon or Ham .. 6d.
Grilled Pork Sausage & Mash 6d.   Fried Onions .. 3d.
Grilled Steaks .. 6d.   Baked Beans 3d.

SAVOURIES.
Hot Meat Pie and Chips .. 6d.   Baked Beans on Toast 3d.
Fried Egg and Chips .. 6d.   Welsh Rarebit .. 3d.
Poached Egg on Toast .. 6d.   Sardines on Toast 3d.

SUNDRIES.
Bread and Butter—   Jubilee Fruit Cake 2d.
White or Hovis .. 2d.   Cream Pastries .. 2d.
Toasted Buttered Scone .. 2d.   Roll and Butter .. 2d.
Toasted Buttered Tea Cakes 2d. each

SWEETS.
Fruit Jelly and Cream .. 3d.   Trifle and Cream 3d. and 6d.
Fruit Flan and Cream .. 3d.   Hot Waffles with Jam,
Fruit Salad and Cream .. 6d.   Syrup or Butter 3d.
Fruit Pie and Custard .. 3d.   Stewed Prunes & Custard 3d.
Delicious Cream Ices .. 3d. and 6d.
Ice Cream Sundaes .. 6d.

Suggestions for the Improvement of our Service will be appreciated by the Management.

shop at No 64 Castle Street had been bought out, giving Woolworth's a clear run of Nos 63, 64 and 65. The store was extended and remodelled with 'A new Cafeteria or Self-Service Restaurant with seating for 1,000 persons' (Fig 4.97).[65] As on Oxford Street, much was made of the hygienic electric plant, 'considered the most modern of its kind in existence', although some other branches, like London Road, Liverpool, continued to use gas cookers (Fig 4.98). All of Woolworth's eateries were, of course, put in the shade by the extraordinary double cafeteria in the new Blackpool store of 1938 (see Fig 4.57). Here the cafeteria assumed equal, if not greater, importance to the sales floors themselves. By this date Woolworth's had one of the largest chains of restaurants in Britain, let alone the country's leading chain of shops.

5

Woolworth's at war, 1939–1945

Wartime challenges

As Britain accelerated its preparations for war in the late 1930s, Woolworth's took measures of its own: staff received gas-mask training; air-raid shelters were excavated, some public shelters were created within the stores and counters were stocked with necessities for the anticipated bombing raids and blackouts (Figs 5.1–5.4). In vulnerable cities, store windows were neatly taped to minimise injuries from flying shards of glass in the event of a hit (Fig 5.5).

For nearly a year after war was declared on 3 September 1939, new Woolworth's stores continued to open. These included Uckfield (1 March 1940, Fig 5.6) and Porthcawl (28 June 1940). But after Store 768 opened in Crawley on 26 July 1940 (Fig 5.7), new openings stopped. Store 769 at Newry in Northern Ireland was mothballed until 1946, and Store 770 in Drogheda, Republic of Ireland – the next number in the sequence – did not open until 20 January 1950. Weybridge (1939;

A J Fowles for The Oak Property Company, Fig 5.8) was retained as an emergency bunker for the Executive Office and only opened as a store in 1946.

The outbreak of war affected every Woolworth's store in Great Britain, but had a lesser impact on the 20 stores in Eire, which remained neutral throughout the conflict. The Dublin Buying Office (a subsidiary of the Liverpool District Office) had been granted extra responsibilities in the build-up to war, and became practically autonomous. Elsewhere, trading was subject to British wartime regulations, including rationing. Clothes were rationed from June 1941 (Fig 5.9), tea from July 1940 (Fig 5.10) and sweets from July 1942 (see Fig 6.4). Customers could buy these goods only with coupons, which were cancelled by the shopkeeper when a transaction took place. Notices in Woolworth's windows advertised useful products such as Cuthbert's seeds, which had been sold through Woolworth's since 1937 and now, at 2d per packet, contributed to the 'Dig for Victory' campaign.

Repeating the experience of 1914–18, many of the factories producing Woolworth's stock were turned over to war work. Others suffered from shortages of raw materials, fuel and labour, not to mention structural damage caused by bombing raids. Under such difficult conditions prices rose and Woolworth's was compelled to abandon the long-cherished upper price limit of 6d (Fig 5.11). The familiar signs reading '3D. and 6D. Stores' were taken down. On fascias, the name 'F. W. Woolworth & Co. Ltd.' was reset centrally, sometimes flanked by 'diamond W' plaques. After the war the company tried to maintain an upper limit of 5s, but so many exceptions had to be made that the notion of fixed-price retailing was dropped altogether, as it had been in the US in 1935. Without this tight restraint, merchandising

". . . And as our obstinate artist thinks these instructions would be carried out!"

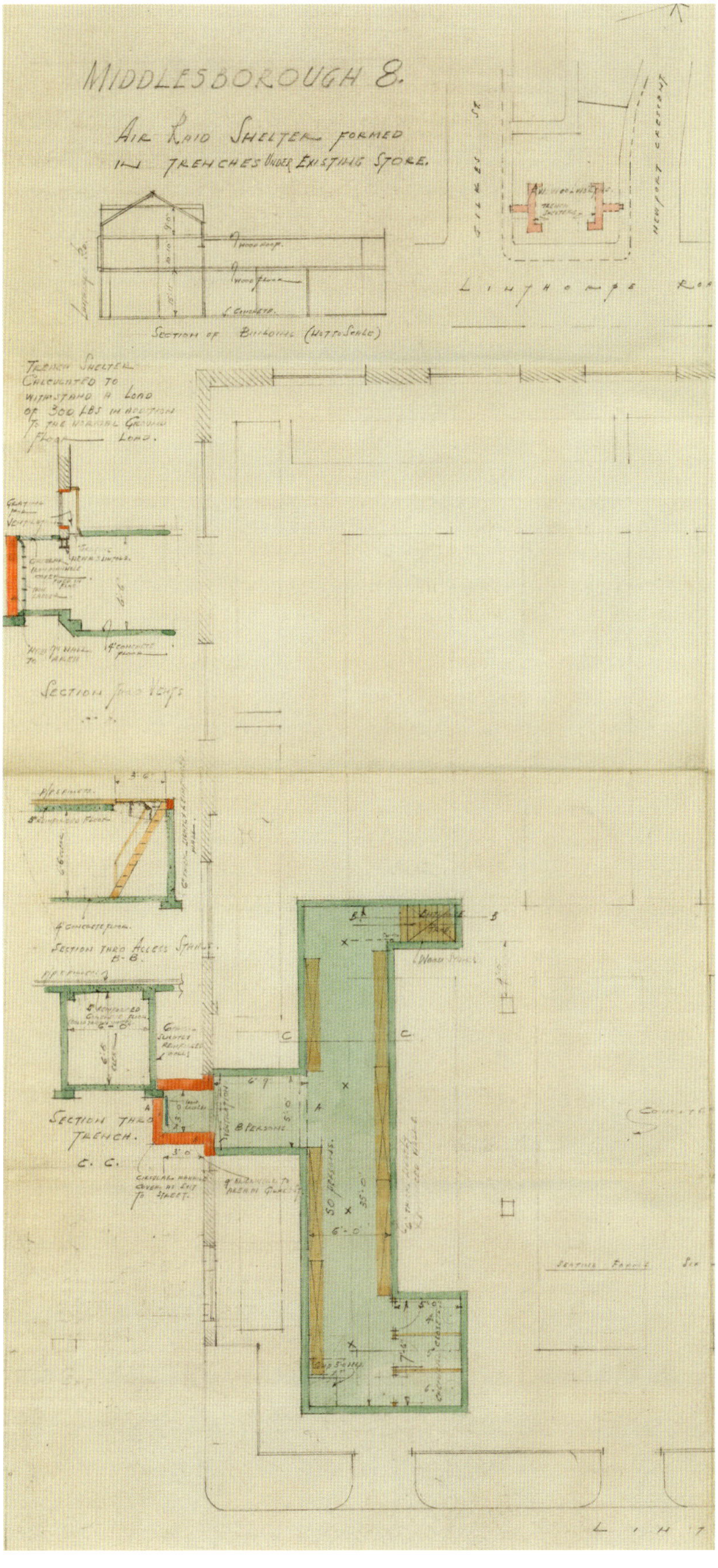

Fig 5.2
An architect's drawing,
dated October 1939,
showing the 'trench
shelters' planned for
Store 8 on Linthorpe Road,
Middlesbrough, which
had 116 members of staff.
This was one of two shelters
with reinforced concrete
roofs, each capable of
accommodating 58
people. Note the three
'chemical closets'.
[FWW01/02/0008/001]

Woolworth's "Serve" Defence to the Masses

Fig 5.3
'Woolworth's "Serve" Defence to the Masses': a cartoon from The New Bond, *2*, 9, September 1937, 337. [FWW01/04/02/337]

began to lose its focus. Woolworth's rivals were in a similar position; fixed-price retailing seemed to have failed, and the concept was sidelined for the next 30 years.

Many store managers and stockroom men joined the armed forces: special 'Forces Souvenir' editions of The New Bond published their names and photographs. In all, around 2,000 members of staff served in the war. Taking their place, pensioners came out of retirement and women were given promotion on a temporary basis. Although people returned to their jobs at the end of the war, they lost

several years of their company pension, an innovation introduced as recently as 1939.

Woolworth's Chairman, William L Stephenson, served from July 1940 in the Ministry of Aircraft Production as Director-General of Equipment. Wishing to contribute to the war effort, and procure goodwill for Woolworth's, the company decided to buy a fighting aircraft by subscription. Marks & Spencer's had a similar idea, funding a Spitfire named The Marksman in 1941.[1] Woolworth's went one better, raising £10,000 (£4,933 from staff and £5,067 from the company) for two

Fig 5.4
Store 750 at No 10 Varley Parade, The Hyde, Colindale, north London, photographed on 19 November 1939 at 2.30pm. The design is unusual, with simplified Ionic pilasters and porthole windows. This is now a Wetherspoons pub, 'The Moon under Water'. During the war the receiving and packing area next to the basement stockroom was partitioned off as a public shelter. [FWW01/01/0750/001]

3D AND 6D STORES   F. W. WOOLWORTH & Cº LTD   3D AND 6D STORES

Fig 5.5 (far left)
The frontage of Store 129
in Leyton High Road, east
London, prepared for war.
The glass is neatly taped
for safety. This photograph
was taken just weeks
into the war, at midday
on 27 October 1939.
The L-shaped store survived
the blitz with both of its
1930s frontages intact.
[FWW01/01/0129/002]

Fig 5.6 (left)
Store 765 in Uckfield
opened on 1 March 1940.
Like Colindale (see Fig 5.4),
this was a modern rendition
of Classical architecture,
with porthole windows.
[FWW01/01/0765/001]

Fig 5.7
Store 768 in Crawley High
Street, which opened on
26 July 1940, was probably
the last new Woolworth's
store to open during the war.
No more new branches
would open until 1946,
although many existing
stores had to move to
different – often unsuitable
– premises when they were
bombed out. The store
shown here was superseded
by a new self-service store on
Queen's Square in 1957.
[FWW01/01/0768/001]

Fig 5.8
Store 760 in Weybridge
(by A J Fowles of Knight &
Co for The Oak Property Co)
was completed before the
war but retained as an
emergency bunker for
Woolworth's Executive
Office in case New Bond
House had to be evacuated.
The balcony resembled that
at Crawley (see Fig 5.7).
The store eventually opened
on 11 October 1946, and
this photograph was taken
after it had been trading
for a month.
[FWW01/01/0760/001]

Fig 5.9
A woman buys underwear
with her clothes ration
book at the counter of
an unidentified English
Woolworth's store on
3 June 1941.
[Davis/Getty Images]

Fig 5.10
A detail of Store 583, Feltham, south-west London (see Fig 4.62). It was November 1940 and rationing had started: a notice advertises a reduced price for tea – a most precious and scarce commodity – and reminds customers to bring their coupons. From July 1940, people were allowed to buy just 2oz of tea each per week, and tea leaves were often reused several times. Tea continued to be rationed until 1952. [FWW01/01/0583/002]

Supermarine Spitfires named *Nix over Six Primus* and *Nix over Six Secundus. Primus* survived the war but *Secundus* crash-landed during a training exercise in 1941 and was broken up for spare parts. Barbara Hutton also contributed to the war, donating money to the Red Cross to buy ten ambulances. Her London home, Winfield House, was commandeered for use by an RAF barrage balloon unit. In 1946 she gifted it to the US State Department, as a house for the American Ambassador.

Casualties of war

In total, 26 Woolworth's stores were completely destroyed in the course of the war, while another 326 were damaged (Fig 5.12). Some of these stores continued to operate in a salvageable section of the original building (Figs 5.13–5.16). Others had to move into temporary premises, where trading resumed on a greatly reduced scale (Figs 5.17–5.21). Other multiples were similarly affected: BHS, for example, saw 8 of its 58 stores destroyed, while 16 of Marks & Spencer's 234 stores were lost and more than 100 damaged.

The greatest loss of life experienced by Woolworth's during the war took place when Store 362 on New Cross Road, south London, was hit by a V-2 rocket at lunchtime on 25 November 1944. The store was filled with Saturday morning shoppers, attracted by a rare delivery of saucepans. The V-2 was Germany's latest weapon: it could not be intercepted by traditional air defence measures and its silent arrival gave people no time to seek shelter. The V-2 that struck Woolworth's in New Cross was the 251st to target London and had one of the deadliest outcomes: 160 people, customers and staff alike, were killed, while 103 were seriously

Fig 5.11
Shoppers in Store 111, Broad Street, Reading, towards the end of the war. The 6d price limit had been abandoned. Goods in the foreground are priced at 1s. The Reading store was one of the large new faience-fronted stores built by the company during the late 1930s: note the new style of 'diamond W' plaque on the wall, the chevron frieze and the plain Steleonite tiles. This building closed for redevelopment in 1989. [© Imperial War Museums (D 253460)]

*Fig 5.12 (opposite)
Store 173 opened in a
new building designed by
Constantine & Vernon on
High Holborn, on the corner
of Grey's Inn Road, London,
in 1924.ᵃ Its shopfront
was interrupted by the
entrance to the upper-floor
showrooms and offices of
Morton Sundour Fabric Ltd
(a Carlisle firm) and W T
Copeland & Sons, Spode
china. This photograph
was taken in the immediate
aftermath of bombing:
probably the daylight raid
of 8 October 1940. Glass
from shattered windows
and rubble from the attic
storey are scattered over
the pavement. Copeland's
offices took the brunt of the
hit. Sundour's, on the lower
floors, had been vacated and
were 'to let' at the time of
the impact. A new store with
a curtain-wall façade was
erected here after the war;
it closed in 1984 and the site
was redeveloped yet again.
[FWW01/01/0173/001]*

*Figs 5.13 and 5.14
Store 302 at Nos 7–11
Chrisp Street, Poplar,
opened in 1928 and had
an unusual shopfront with
square windows. By 1939
the premises had been
extended to the right, in a
matching style (Fig 5.13).
Remarkably, the shopfront
survived the heavy
bombardment of the area,
which lay close to London's
docks, but the upper storey
must have been damaged
and (one presumes)
dismantled for safety.
Woolworth's remained here
through the early 1950s
(Fig 5.14) rather than
moving to the nearby
precinct that formed part
of the 'Living Architecture
Exhibition', built as part
of the Festival of Britain
in 1951. This photograph
was taken in 1954.
[FWW01/01/0302/002;
FWW01/01/0302/001]*

injured. The nearby premises of Pearce Signs, which manufactured many neon signs for Woolworth's in peacetime, became a temporary mortuary. To put this tragedy in perspective, across the entire Woolworth's organisation, around 145 members of staff were killed in the course of the war. Due to wartime reporting restrictions, details of the New Cross attack could not be published until April 1945, when it topped the list of 'worst incidents'.[2]

*Figs 5.15 and 5.16
Store 14 in Swansea,
photographed c 1939–40,
before it was bombed, and
after, in 1949. It occupied
the former Hotel Cameron,
which had been bought
freehold by Woolworth's in
1928. A window in Fig 5.15
is stacked with tinned foods
and displays a sign reading
'Food Reserves – Store for
Emergencies'. The fascia
and lettering were replaced
after the 3d and 6d fixed
price was abandoned.
A new store was built here
in 1958–9 (see Fig 6.38).
[FWW01/01/0014/002;
FWW01/01/0014/001]*

Figs 5.17 and 5.18
After being bombed on 22–23 April 1941, Store 69 in Devonport, a district of Plymouth, moved into a temporary shop on the Royal Hotel site. The first of these photographs pictures the shop on the eve of opening on Friday 24 October 1941. Note the single, makeshift display window. By the time the second photograph was taken for the Picture Post on 15 May 1954, the ruins to the rear had been cleared and the shopfront tidied up. Despite the date ascribed to the photograph, Easter eggs are on display. It was 1960 before the store moved into new premises.
[FWW01/01/0069/001; Charles Hewitt/Getty Images]

Fig 5.19 (right)
Woolworth's outlet in Plymouth's Pannier Market opened in October 1941, six months after Store 56 was bombed – in the same raid as Devonport (see Figs 5.17 and 5.18). It was photographed by Norman Smith for the Ministry of Information. [© Imperial War Museums (D 16666)]

Fig 5.20 (far right)
This unprepossessing temporary store, Store 128 in Southampton, was described by former stockroom manager Harold Gilham as 'a hastily built, single-storey concrete block, a long, narrow "shed" in the middle of a bomb-site with no other buildings around. It was constructed over the cellar of the original pre-war building. The labyrinth of cellars was below ground, dimly lit, with no windows, and fitted out with alleyways and shelves to make a stockroom. Access to the stockroom from the street was down a slope at the rear of the building with a single flight of stairs going up into the shop.'[b] For the pre-war store, see Fig 4.94. [FWW01/01/0128/003]

Woolworth's lost several stores temporarily during the war. Five were wholly requisitioned by the government and many others were part-requisitioned. For example, for several months in 1943, leading up to the D-Day landings, the top-floor stockroom of the Dudley store accommodated American airmen.[3] More ominously, when the Channel Islands were occupied by Germany in July 1940, the stores on Guernsey and Jersey were cut adrift.

Before long they ran out of merchandise, staff members were laid off and trading became sporadic. Just three months after the islands were liberated in May 1945, the stores were refurbished and reopened by the company. In Germany itself, 70 Woolworth Company stores were destroyed in 1939–45; additionally, the state-of-the-art Woolworth warehouse at Sonneberg was bombed by USAF Bomber Command.

Fig 5.21
The temporary premises of Store 113 in Lowestoft. For the pre-war store, see Fig 4.28. [FWW01/01/0113/001]

6

Catching up, 1945–1960

Post-war challenges

Emerging from wartime conditions, Woolworth's had to navigate a rapidly changing world with a new management team at the helm. Stephenson retired as Chairman in 1948. His successors were Benjamin E Uffindell (1948–51), Stanley Victor Swash (1951–5) and Reginald John Berridge (1955–61). Each of these men had climbed through the company hierarchy and was imbued with its founding ethos. Nevertheless, as will be seen, they had to respond to growing pressure from American executives to make radical changes to the traditional Woolworth's formula.

While management was still overwhelmingly male, the sales staff remained universally female (Fig 6.1). At the end of the 1950s, just 35 out of 1,000 stores had female managers –

remarkably, fewer than in 1938. The entrenched patriarchal structure of the company is evident from the briefest perusal of the progress reports of 1950 and 1959, which featured conventional photographic portraits of Woolworth's clean-shaven and suited managers and buyers. These contrast sharply with the lively house journal, *The New Bond*. Each edition included a beauty competition, with a portrait of the winner adorning the cover. Undeniably the magazine conveyed a sense of fun and comradeship, featuring weddings, long-service presentations, sporting events, summer outings and carnival queens, but it engaged only rarely with corporate matters, career opportunities or the finer points of salesmanship.

Woolworth's employed around 60,000 people in the mid-1950s, twice as many as Marks & Spencer's.[1] This figure probably

Fig 6.1
In the 1950s the core staff of a typical Woolworth's store – in this case Store 163 in Chester – included the store manager, the deputy manager, the staff supervisors, the sales assistants and a couple of stockmen. As ever, a stint in the stockroom was the starting point for management trainees, who usually joined the company in their early 20s and could make a rapid ascent. [Chester History & Heritage & the Cheshire Imagebank]

Fig 6.2
In 1944 Harold Winbourne
replaced B C Donaldson as
Woolworth's Chief Architect.
He was in charge of the
regional construction
supervisors: W A
Sherrington (retired 1962)
in the Metropolitan District
Office; W L Swinnerton
(retired 1959) in Liverpool;
and W A Draysey (retired
c 1968) in Birmingham.
In 1954 they were joined
by H W Schofield (retired
1960) in the newly formed
Kensington District Office,
which took responsibility for
a swathe of stores running
diagonally across England
from East Anglia to
Cornwall. This portrait is
from Forty-two Years of
Progress, 1909–1950.
[Author's collection]

Fig 6.3
A crowd of shoppers in an
unidentified Woolworth's
superstore, photographed
on 1 November 1955 by
Charles Hewitt for Picture
Post. Jean Croft, who
began to work as a sales
assistant in 1961, recalled:
'Sometimes when the store
was busy, it was difficult
to remember who had
been waiting to be served
the longest. Often, irate
customers would tap
repeatedly on the glass,
shouting "Miss, Miss,
I was here first"; it could
be very annoying.'[a]
[Charles Hewitt/Getty
Images]

included large numbers of part-time and seasonal staff, such as schoolgirls who worked on Saturdays. Group photographs of the late 1940s and early 1950s show the sales assistants wearing neat maroon uniforms with a pleated skirt, belted at the waist. Those working in the grocery and confectionery departments, as ever, stood out from the crowd with their hygienic white overalls and headbands adorned with the 'diamond W'. In 1957 nylon uniforms were introduced: turquoise for sales assistants (button-through dresses for full-timers; shapeless wrap-around overalls for part-timers) and royal blue for supervisors (as can be seen in Fig 6.1, though black and white).[2] Such details often help to date store photographs.

Many of the young women smiling out from the pages of The New Bond fully intended to quit Woolworth's as soon as they married, but some took advantage of centralised training courses, such as a window trimming school established in 1947. Limited promotion was possible: a girl might take charge of a department, become a staff supervisor or a cashier, but her career path was quite separate from that of the management trainees. In the late 1940s wages started at around £2 per week but varied according to age and length of service, as well as the size and location of a branch. Working hours for full-timers dropped to around 42 per week, but it was not until 1965 that Woolworth's introduced a five-day week for all its shop assistants. Staff received two weeks paid holiday per annum, rising to three after 10 years of service.

Woolworth's Chief Architect from February 1944 was Harold Winbourne (Fig 6.2), the former construction supervisor for the Birmingham District who had joined the company in 1922. His predecessor, B C Donaldson, was put in charge of 'repairs and maintenance' until his resignation on 31 August 1951.[3] Donaldson had experienced an episode of bankruptcy in 1939,[4] and his problems evidently persisted. In 1943 he was summoned by the Surrey Public Assistance Committee for failing to pay his wife's hospital fees, despite earning a salary, as Woolworth's Chief Architect, of £3,000 per annum.[5] His new position suggests that he had been sidelined, especially since his salary was reportedly less than Winbourne's in the 1940s.[6] But Donaldson's post also reflected the fact that no new buildings were being erected, and repair and maintenance consequently assumed disproportionate importance.

The colossal task facing Winbourne's team, from the late 1940s until the mid-1950s, was physical reconstruction. Stores destroyed or damaged by bombing had to be rebuilt, while unscathed branches looked bedraggled after six years of war and were in desperate need of basic maintenance. But proceeding to deal with Woolworth's catalogue of works was no straightforward matter. Nationally, all building activity was subject to stringent controls: construction could not proceed without a licence, ensuring that labour and materials were focused on national priorities, such as replacing blitzed housing and building factories to feed the government's export drive. Without a licence, no more than £10 per annum – increased to £100 in 1948 – could be spent on any individual store. Even the demolition of a redundant air-raid shelter, and reinstatement of the space, required a licence.

Woolworth's, like all retailers, struggled within these constraints, managing to open new branches only by lowering its normal standards. Nevertheless, suspicions were voiced in some quarters that the company received preferential treatment. In Parliament, an MP queried how Woolworth's and Marks & Spencer's managed to obtain timber for their shop floors.[7] More specifically, in 1952 Harold Macmillan, then Minister for Housing, was interrogated about the granting of a licence to rebuild Woolworth's store on Deansgate, Manchester, at a cost of £130,000: 'Is the Minister aware ... that this very unnecessary building is gobbling up steel in Lancashire at a time when new industrial buildings in Lancashire are being held up through the shortage of steel ... ? Will he not see that this building is stopped at once?'[8] Once building licences were abolished, in November 1954, Woolworth's was poised to cover lost ground

by implementing an ambitious expansion programme.

It was one thing to rebuild and repair stores, quite another to restock counters (Fig 6.3). Woolworth's suppliers could not resume normal service overnight. Moreover, clothing was rationed until 1949, tea until 1952, sweets until 1953 (Fig 6.4) and some other foodstuffs until 1954. On the other hand, certain lines which had been difficult to source during the war, such as nylons (*see* Fig 6.21) and gramophone records, crept back onto counters alongside new items including ballpoint pens (1947), Airfix kits (1949) and home ('Toni') perm kits (1949). In 1951 Woolworth's counters were heavily stocked with souvenirs of the Festival of Britain, and in 1953 with Coronation memorabilia (Fig 6.5), their windows dressed according to instructions

Fig 6.4
A sweet counter in Store 463 on Oxford Street, London, with catarrh pastilles, mint imperials and liquorice allsorts to the fore. Sweets and chocolate were rationed from 1942 until February 1953, with a brief respite in 1949. This photograph was taken in December 1949, after rationing had resumed. Notices explain that 2oz of chocolate and sugar confectionery required 2 points.
[FWW01/01/0463/004]

Fig 6.5
A brochure of 1953, listing
Coronation decorations
and memorabilia available
from Woolworth's stores.
[Author's collection]

COAT OF ARMS

COAT OF ARMS No. 506/C.
Embossed Coat of Arms in gilt foil finish on heavy millboard. Design includes the Lion and Unicorn supporting a centre shield inscribed "Honi Soit Qui Mal y Pense." Supporting ribbon design below bears the phrase "Dieu et mon Droit." A striking Coronation decoration measuring 12" by 9".

Price **9d.** each

COAT OF ARMS No. 510/C.
Similar in design to the Arms illustrated above. This piece is carried out in bright gilt foil on millboard and measures 19" by 13".

Price **1/6** each

EMBOSSED LETTERS

LETTER 'E.' No. 501/C.
To form part of the letters 'E.R.' Elizabeth Regina. Attractively embossed gilt foil on millboard. Letter measures 6" by 4".

LETTER 'R.' No. 502/C. To complete the 'E.R.' symbol, embossed gilt foil letter also measures 6" by 4".

Price **3d.** each letter

LETTER 'E.' No. 504/C. As illustrated above. Gilt foil finish on millboard. Letter measures 9" by 7".
LETTER 'R'. No. 505/C. To match letter 'E' above. Gilt foil finish on millboard. Letter measures 9" by 7".

Price **6d.** each letter

LETTER 'E' No. 508/C. Embossed gilt foil on millboard. Bright studded relief design on body of letter which measures 11" by 9".
LETTER 'R.' No. 509/C. Carried out in same design and material as above letter. Measures 11" by 9".

Price **9d.** each letter

CROWNS

CROWN No. 500/C.
Embossed metal foil Crown on millboard base. Measurements 6" by 5¼". Attractive gilt finish to realistic Crown design.

Price **3d.** each

CROWN No. 503/C. Same Crown design as illustrated above carried out on millboard. Measures 9" by 9". Bright gilt foil finish.

Price **6d.** each

CROWN No. 507/C. A large impressive Crown in gilt foil, realistic embossed design on millboard measuring 11" by 11".

Price **9d.** each

The CORONATION OF HER MAJESTY QUEEN ELIZABETH II. 1953

Catalogue of FLAGS SHIELDS PENNANTS SOUVENIRS DECORATIONS

Obtainable from your local branch of F. W. WOOLWORTH AND CO. LIMITED

issued from head office. A year later, the Chairman boasted about a particular best-seller, a brass curtain rail on roller runners (no doubt the 'Ezeglide', manufactured by Harrison [Birmingham] Ltd, see Fig 7.27), saying: 'We sold ... enough mileage of this rail to extend a peaceful curtain from London to Berlin and back again.'[9] In 1957 Woolworth's began to stock the popular, and today hugely collectable, Homemaker china range, designed by Enid Seeney for Ridgeway. Far and away the most significant merchandising developments of the 1950s, however, were Woolworth's incursions into supermarket-style food sales and the burgeoning do-it-yourself market. Gardening also assumed a new importance (Fig 6.6).

Fig 6.6
Woolworth's maintained a strong reputation for horticultural supplies in the 1950s. This gardening brochure advertised goods at the firm's higher post-war prices: the abandonment of the 6d limit greatly increased the range of goods that could be sold. [Author's collection]

Reconstruction, c 1945–1955

The rebuilding of post-war Britain took place in an atmosphere of austerity, and the style of architecture most suited to the zeitgeist was appropriately sober. Commercial buildings usually had steel frames and their elevations, heavily laden with Scandinavian influence, were modern and astylar. When it came to the provision of upper-floor windows, they generally adhered to one of three different approaches. Some displayed regular rows of fully framed square openings, seemingly punched through walls; others – like giant TV sets – had a framed central panel of curtain walling (sometimes balanced by hole-in-the-wall windows, or portholes, to either side), or even full curtain walling, bled to the edges of the façade. Pitched roofs were avoided. Flat canopies interposed between plate-glass shopfronts and more solid upper storeys made a positive contribution to the horizontal layering of façades, as well as sheltering shoppers. Architectural ornamentation had little place in this aesthetic, but the spandrel panels of curtain walling presented an opportunity to interject elements of colour or texture. Panels were often of slate (most popularly, green-hued Westmorland), of glass mosaic tiles or opaque sheets of coloured glass. Another commonly used material was vertical hardwood boarding, which could be applied to façades, fascias or merely the edges of canopies.

Woolworth's post-war stores have to be judged in this context. The jazzy art deco designs of the late 1930s looked old fashioned, even vulgar, by the early 1950s, just as the heavy scrolls and curlicues of Edwardian frontages had looked dated after the First World War. No attempts were made to revive the faience fronts, though faint hints of moderne glamour lingered: for example, in the 'egg shell finished serpentino' mullions on the façade of the Bristol store, and the sweeping chrome rails of cafeteria staircases and mezzanine galleries (*see* Fig 6.17).

New designs did little to promote the character of Woolworth's brand. Many of the superstores rebuilt under licence in the early 1950s had handsome, well-proportioned façades; they were admirably suited to their purpose, but were not significantly – and, perhaps, not sufficiently – differentiated from buildings erected by other retailers at the same time. Standard-sized stores, built from 1953 onwards, had innocuous fenestration: often a row of square windows, either set individually or grouped collectively within a thin salient frame. These rarely caught the eye. Architecturally, on the high street, this was an age of utility and uniformity, and Woolworth's

Fig 6.7
Store 779, Haslemere, 1952. This tasteful branch did not even have a Woolworth's fascia. Instead lettering was affixed to the tile hanging. Most new premises of the early 1950s were superseded once building restrictions were lifted, but the Haslemere store lasted to the bitter end, in 2008. It clearly suited the locality. Perhaps encouraged by this, Woolworth's went on to build a vernacular-style store in Leatherhead in 1955.[b]
[FWW01/01/0779/001]

had to comply with guidelines laid down by the architects and planners of local authorities and development corporations. In comparison with the 1930s, it took considerably longer to conclude negotiations and win approval for new schemes. Company architects like Winbourne lost much of the freedom they had enjoyed before the war, and their buildings, consequently, lost some of their brio.

Fig 6.8
Store 792 in Wymondham opened in 1953. Note the Coronation decorations in the window.
[FWW01/01/0792/001]

Between 1945 and the beginning of 1954 Woolworth's managed to add 60 stores to its portfolio, bringing the total to 825. However, with building licences in force, most new branches had to be set up in converted buildings (Figs 6.7–6.10). Restrictions meant that structures received little modification, and existing shopfronts could not be replaced. In the event, all kinds of buildings were adapted, including many of the theatres and cinemas that were falling into disuse at the time. These included the Carlton in Wickford, the Coliseum in Cleethorpes and the Empire in Eastwood. Other types of building also offered vast, open-plan interiors well suited to Woolworth's. The Swanage store opened in 1952 in the Central Garage, while Govan's store took up residence in a Congregational church and Atherton's store occupied a billiard hall. Several suburban branches moved into 1930s parades which had been left incomplete at the outbreak of war. The largest branch created anew at this time was probably Store 800. This opened in September 1953 in Parnell House, next to the Apollo Theatre, opposite Victoria Station in London. It extended into a very modern tower-and-podium development to the south in 1965, and had one of the longest frontages in the chain.

One or two new branches occupied rudimentary single-storey units that must have

Fig 6.9
Store 795 in Totton, Southampton, occupied an Edwardian shop when it first opened in 1953. These customers had queued to be among the first inside. [FWW01/01/0795/002]

Fig 6.10
On 6 November 1953, Store 818 in Bulwell, near Nottingham, opened in the former Olympia Theatre, built in 1915. This was one of many new branches to occupy disused theatres and cinemas in the early 1950s. It was rebuilt in 1969–70. [FWW01/01/0818/001]

been erected under licence: these included Woolston in Southampton (1951, Fig 6.11) and Bletchley (c 1953), the latter evidently a prefabricated hut, perhaps a reused wartime building. For the store on Westmuir Street, Parkhead, Glasgow, it was proposed to adapt an ex-government stock Nissen hut, with scaffold poles forming an armature for the shopfront. The building currently on the site ('The Old Woolies Discount Store') followed a design that had been prepared in 1939.[10] Evidently this project was abandoned at the outbreak of war and completed, in stone rather than faience, after restrictions were lifted in 1954. Licensing ensured that the initial rebuilding phase of most stores assumed the form of a single-storey sales floor, with the superstructure being added later (Figs 6.12 and 6.13). Complete new buildings were exceptional: that at Debden (1953) occupied a parade serving a large London County Council housing estate built on the northern edge of London between 1947 and 1952, while Galway (1953), in the Republic of Ireland, lay beyond the reach of the British licensing authorities.[11] Numbers of new buildings, and shopfronts in Woolworth's house style, increased noticeably in the course

of 1954, suggesting that restrictions were relaxing, prior to being dropped altogether.

In 1950 the first five replacements for blitzed stores opened at Lowestoft (19 May), South Shields (11 August), Portsmouth (26 October, see Figs 6.13 and 6.16), Norwich (3 November, see Fig 6.15a) and Plymouth (24 November, Fig 6.14). All of these towns had been particularly hard hit by German bombing. In each case, phased construction had to continue after the store became operational. Of the five, only Lowestoft had been completed by the end of 1950.[12] Plymouth was not finished until 1957.

The reopening of these Woolworth's stores stirred so much excitement that people queued all night to be first through the doors (Fig 6.15). *The Western Evening Herald* reported that the queue for the new Plymouth store started at 6 o'clock on the previous evening, with 18 people waiting all night in freezing temperatures.[13] It was noted that 'a kindly manager, Mr W Hutt, had provided biscuits and cigarettes, and Boy Scouts brought some hot cocoa'. Having chatted with people in the queue, the reporter established that most of the women wanted to buy nylons at 5s a pair (some of the younger women confessed that they had

Fig 6.11
Store 771, Woolston, near Southampton. This single-storey store opened on 19 October 1951. A policeman is stationed out front to maintain order.
[FWW01/01/0771/002]

Fig 6.12
Before the war Store 127
in East Ham, London,
had an impressive building,
with a faience front. This,
however, was bombed in
1943. Woolworth's leased
temporary premises until
1950, when a new sales
floor was built on a corner
site. It is shown here in a
photograph of 22 June
1950, with a small boy
admiring toy boats.
The superstructure was
added later.
[FWW01/01/0127/005]

Fig 6.13
The first rebuilt stores,
replacing ones lost in the
blitz, were erected under
licence in stages: the shop
floor was built first, then the
remainder of the building
was constructed above and
around it. This shows Store
35 in Portsmouth in 1950.
[FWW01/01/0035/001]

never owned a pair of nylons), but they were also lured by the prospect of tinned fruit and half tea sets (six settings).

These early post-war stores, designed by Winbourne with steel frames (still by Banister Walton) and concrete floors (still by Truscon), had much in common. Their façades, while not identical, had a generic similarity, with a flat roofline and framed curtain wall panels. In each case the shopfront was separated from the upper floors by a solid canopy. More individual features included a brise soleil that topped the frontage at Plymouth (*see* Fig 6.14), an idea later repeated elsewhere, for example in Corby (1954). To the rear of Portsmouth, as completed with two storeys in 1952, a glazed, curved wall corresponded to the restaurant (Fig 6.16). This was the Top Tray Bar, a modern

Fig 6.14
After trading from Plymouth Market (see Fig 5.19) for over six years, Store 56 moved into a new building on New George Street in November 1950. This was hailed in the local press as 'the first large shop in any reconstruction area in any blitzed city in Britain since the war'.[c] It was photographed shortly after reopening in 1950, with reconstruction continuing to either side of the store. [FWW01/01/0056/001]

Fig 6.15
The reopening of bombed Woolworth's stores in the early 1950s generated queues and crowds. These photographs show: a, middle left) Store 44, Norwich, in 1950; b, middle right) Store 50, Southsea, in 1951; and c, right) Store 10, Bristol, in 1952. [a) FWW01/01/0044/002; b) FWW01/01/0050/001; c) FWW01/01/0010/002]

Fig 6.16 (left)
Store 35, Portsmouth: the curved exterior of the Top Tray Bar restaurant in 1952. [FWW01/01/0035/002]

Fig 6.17 (below)
Store 10 on Broadmead, Bristol, was rebuilt in 1951–2. This view of the main sales floor before Christmas 1952, with jewellery displays in the foreground, shows Woolworth's new-style Formica counters with flush fronts and overhanging tops. A string of pearls cost 2s 9d and the carrier bags stowed behind the tills were 3½d each. The structural piers were clad in mirror glass to appear less conspicuous. Note the fluorescent strip lighting, suspended from the tiled ceiling on rods, and the chequered terrazzo flooring of the public gangways. Just visible in the background, to the left, is the cafeteria staircase. [FWW01/01/0010/003]

cafeteria on a mezzanine level with a railed gallery overlooking the principal sales floor. The same arrangement was adopted elsewhere through the 1950s, for example at Norwich, Bristol (Figs 6.17–6.19) and Oxford.

New sales floors were lit by long strips of fluorescent lights suspended from plain ceilings. One of the first installations, probably a trial for the new-build stores, was at Nos 150–154 Oxford Street, London, in 1949 (Figs 6.20 and 6.21). Floors were of terrazzo, laid in 1ft squares in pink and grey. The traditional counter layout was largely unchanged, but walnut-effect Formica replaced the old mahogany fronts. Plastic laminates were to take on a new importance for Woolworth's in the 1950s, for wall finishes as well as store fittings.

In 1951 the Chairman reserved particular praise for the self-service dining rooms, kitchens and lounges provided for staff in the new stores, including separate (very small) rooms for male staff.[14] An account of a typical old-style staff canteen had been published in the *Porth Leader and Gazette* in 1949. For just 5s a week, the 30 employees of Porth, in the Rhondda Valley, were supplied with tea and a buttered cob in the morning, a cooked dinner including a sweet and a cup of tea at lunchtime, and another cup of tea with a bun or a pastry in the afternoon. They were served in the upstairs canteen by Mrs Reid. The canteen itself was 'tastefully decorated in pastel shades of green and cream with bright pictures on the walls'.[15] The girls were allowed to smoke if they wished, but there was a fire extinguisher to

Fig 6.18 (above)
Bristol's mezzanine
cafeteria, in 1952. The
gallery overlooking the
ground-floor sales area is
to the left. On the menu was
grilled fillet steak for 1s 6d,
chipped potatoes for 5d and
Christmas pudding for 8d.
[FWW01/01/0010/004]

Fig 6.19 (right)
The ice-cream machine in
Bristol's cafeteria, in 1952.
Soft ice-cream had been
invented in America in the
1930s by introducing air
during the freezing process.
After the war, Lyons 'softa
freez' was served in
Woolworth's stores for 4d
per cone. The Bristol store
was demolished in the
1980s, making way for The
Galleries shopping centre.
[FWW01/01/0010/005]

Figs 6.20 and 6.21
In May 1949 the main sales areas of Store 463 at Nos 150–154 Oxford Street, London, were still lit in the usual manner, with pendant electric lights (Fig 6.20), supplemented by emergency gas lights. Between June and September 1949, fluorescent strip lighting was installed (Fig 6.21; see also Fig 6.4). Around Christmas time, photographs were taken showing the brilliantly lit interior, including the lingerie department with disembodied legs exhibiting newly available nylons. [FWW01/01/0463/001; FWW01/01/0463/006]

Figs 6.22 and 6.23
Store 869, St Ives,
Cambridgeshire, opened in
1955. This is a rare survival
of a mid-1950s Woolworth's
shopfront, complete with
monogrammed Carter's tiles
on the lobby floor. The fluted
decoration on the central
column and pilasters was
unusual for Woolworth's,
but the other elements
were standard at the time.
The photographs were
taken in March 2014.
[Both Ron Baxter]

hand 'in case a careless smoker starts a fire'. Having two sittings enabled the store to remain open through the lunch hour. Old-fashioned stores such as Porth seldom provided a separate staff lounge.

The shopfronts of the first wave of new-build stores in 1950–1 were more restrained than their pre-war counterparts, having shed the clutter of signs advertising the 3d and 6d prices. They retained the traditional alternation of display windows with lobby entrances, but the windows now had angled rather than curved corners, and the central one was elongated. Doors had shiny stainless steel surrounds and push plates. Internally illuminated fascias were of white glass, with red Perspex lettering flanked by the 'diamond W'. Transom lights were of Belgian white glass, with horizontal lines superimposed with the red 'diamond W' plaque (see Fig 6.12). Above the doors

was a transom strip, 7ins high, with the word 'Woolworth' in gilded lettering on a red backdrop. Similar lettering edged the canopies. As before, the 'diamond W' motif was also picked out in mosaic tiles, made by Carter's, on the lobby floors (see Fig 6.23). Set into the backs of the window enclosures, facing into the stores, were shallow, illuminated display units and doors, for use by window dressers, set with mirror glass.

Illuminated fascias were particularly suited to frontages shaded by canopies. Elsewhere, the standard post-war fascia was a wooden signboard, painted red and set with gilded wooden letters. Generally used for small, adapted premises, these appeared on some large stores without canopies, such as The Moor, Sheffield (1952). The fascia at Nos 23–27 Albion Street, Broadstairs, an old Home & Colonial shop converted by Woolworth's in

Fig 6.24
Floral pelmet cloths were
consigned to the past in the
course of the 1950s. They
were often replaced by
louvred pelmets, as at Store
162 in Kensington, London,
photographed some time
before it relocated in 1963.
(To compare the store's old
pelmet cloths, see Fig 3.22.)
[FWW01/01/0162/002]

Fig 6.25
Store 109 in Canterbury was bombed in 1941 and reopened on 25 July 1952. Without a canopy, the elevation appears top heavy. Despite its scale there was no curtain walling and the arrangement of the windows was unconventional – an inversion of traditional fenestration – with one large second-floor window above two small first-floor windows. A comparable topsy-turvy approach was adopted for Store 236, Hornsey, north London, which opened on 31 October 1957. This photograph was taken on 31 December 2008. [DP069302]

1952, seems to have been a one-off: it was of hardboard, painted with the simple word 'WOOLWORTH'. Starting with Bristol in 1952, 'San Stephano marble' or an equivalent stone was commonly set with gilded, red-rimmed, sans serif letters. This type of fascia was integral with the pilasters, without intervening consoles or trusses, creating a seamless surround. Smaller stores had humbler shopfronts. An example from 1955 survives at St Ives, Cambridgeshire. It is remarkably intact, complete with display windows, wooden doors and lobby floor; all that has changed is the signage (Figs 6.22 and 6.23). It was perhaps fortunate in this case that Woolworth's successor – West End DIY – had a name beginning with the letter 'W'. Oddly, St Ives had no transom lights or pelmets. Around this time many pre-war shopfronts were being updated with louvred pelmets – essentially short

Venetian blinds, which took the place of the old cloths (Fig 6.24).

Rapid progress was made with rebuilding bombed stores: notably with Southsea (1951, see Fig 6.15b), Bristol (1952, see Figs 6.15c and 6.17–6.19), Canterbury (1952, Fig 6.25), Coventry (1953, see Fig 6.28), Southampton (1953, Fig 6.26), Manchester (Deansgate; 1953) and New Cross (1953), the last replacing the store that had suffered such a deadly V-2 attack in 1944. Handsworth (1955) was one of Woolworth's first stores to have a full curtain wall (Fig 6.27). Store 337 on Commercial Road, east London, was abandoned and Store 313 at Elephant & Castle in south London did not reopen until 1965, when it became Store 1104. In the meantime, the original store numbers, 337 and 313, were reallocated to Tipperary and Arnold (a suburb of Nottingham), respectively.

Fig 6.26 (below far left)
Store 128, Southampton, opened in Coronation year, on 19 November 1953, replacing the temporary store shown in Fig 5.20. It was chastely decorated with three carved Tudor roses and was unusual in having regularly spaced upper-floor windows with traditional proportions rather than a central panel of curtain walling. The fascia – a type that remained standard for large stores through the 1950s – was of 'San Stephano marble' set with wooden gold and red lettering. [FWW01/01/0128/002]

Fig 6.27 (left)
Store 299, Handsworth, Birmingham, opened on 14 October 1955. This fashionable curtain wall façade was very different from its predecessor, an old terraced building on Soho Road which had been bombed in 1942. [FWW01/01/0299/001]

Lessons from America

British Woolworth's had been more profitable than American Woolworth for some time, and in its Golden Jubilee year, 1959, it delivered an extraordinary dividend of $14,000,000 to the parent company.[16] However, this gave British Woolworth's little leverage. It was submitted to relentless pressure to emulate American Woolworth, which was still the major shareholder and carried substantial weight in the London boardroom.

Increased interference from the US was especially problematic because the chasm between the British and American shopping experience had widened greatly since 1939. While British high streets had atrophied during the war, American retailing had evolved to serve a new generation of car-borne, fridge-owning consumers. By the mid-1950s self-service had become well-established and out-of-town shopping malls – covered, air-conditioned and surrounded by expansive car parks – were luring people away from city centres. Some observers believed that such developments were fundamentally unsuited to the British character and lifestyle, and would never succeed on this side of the Atlantic.

In Britain, the most advanced retail format of the time was the pedestrianised shopping precinct, something of European rather than American origin. Woolworth's was a pivotal presence in many of the country's earliest precinct developments, for example in the centres of Coventry (1953, Fig 6.28), which was being rebuilt after the blitz, and Stevenage (1958, Fig 6.29), one of the first new towns built principally for Londoners displaced by bombing or slum clearance. Like contemporary American malls, these urban centres responded to the rise of the motor car. They sought to create a safer and more pleasant experience for shoppers, while traffic was allowed to speed around their peripheries on dual-carriageway ring roads.

American Woolworth made its first forays into self-service in 1952. Embracing the format wholeheartedly, it had converted half of its stores by 1960. Self-service differed from the company's previous self-selection system, with customers now paying for goods at a single checkout rather than at individual counters. Set-up costs were high: special display fixtures – free-standing, low-level shelving units known as gondolas – replaced the old mahogany counters; merchandise had to be either pre-packaged or individually ticketed, and new cash desks were required. In the long term, however, self-service was cheaper to operate, since it required fewer staff and allowed for a quicker turnover of goods. In Britain, by the mid-1950s, only a handful of food

Fig 6.28
Store 123, Coventry.
After being devastated by bombing, Coventry's city centre was replanned with an extensive pedestrianised shopping precinct at its heart. This included a Woolworth's store in a prominent position, guarding the entrance to the Lower Precinct. The store opened in 1953, some time before the precinct itself reached completion.
[FWW01/01/0123/002]

retailers, including some co-operative societies and Sainsbury's, had adopted self-service. No 'variety' traders had yet taken this radical step.

Although they harboured grave doubts about self-service, Woolworth's managers were prevailed upon to invest in the format. In March 1955 the company opened its first self-service store in a very small converted building in Cobham, Surrey (Figs 6.30 and 6.31).[17] Many purpose-built self-service outlets followed (Figs 6.32 and 6.33). At Burgess Hill, the preliminary layout of the gondolas was changed in the course of 1955, following 'suggestions received from America': this resulted in more, shorter gondolas, and the inclusion of one old-style, open-ended counter arrangement, retained solely for the sale of sweets and nuts.[18] Seventeen stores operated self-service by the end of 1955, rising to 29 in 1956, 46 in 1957, 56 in 1958 and 62 in 1959: figures that suggest a dwindling confidence in the format.

Self-service stores were, naturally, organised quite differently from traditional branches.[19] 'Way in' and 'way out' signs attempted to control the route taken by shoppers, while illuminated signs guided them around the store. To the front were piles of wire baskets and checkouts with tills that could compute prices automatically. Goods were displayed on gondolas with tiers of shelving set on top of understock cupboards with sliding fronts. Innovations trialled at Didcot in 1956 included shelves rather than counters around the walls,

with special display fixtures for hanging merchandise such as handbags.[20] Items that had previously been sold loose and weighed for the customer, like sweets, were now pre-packaged. The large new Crawley store, completed in 1957, was one of the first to have 'low-boy' gondolas, with shelving to the floor, despite fears that customers would not be prepared to bend down.[21] Crawley also introduced refrigerated cabinets and tiered racks for birthday cards. As well as opening self-service stores, in 1958 Woolworth's trialled a mobile self-service shop, a Green Line bus converted by Eustace Partners, shopfitters and coachbuilders, and serving an area of Essex including Basildon and Canvey Island.[22] Customers, summoned by a four-note musical horn, entered by one door and left by another. Opposition from local traders ensured that this experiment was short-lived.

The first free-standing Woolworth's supermarket opened in Salisbury on 17

Fig 6.29
Store 1008, Stevenage, photographed on 5 May 2000. At this date it had an Operation Focus shopfront (see p 191) dating from the late 1980s, with peppermint blue door and window frames. The appearance of buildings in pedestrian precincts was laid down by local authority architects and planners, creating uniform shopping areas where retailers like Woolworth's had little say in the outward design of their stores.
[BB007086]

Figs 6.30 and 6.31
Store 871 in Cobham, Surrey, Woolworth's first experiment with self-service, opened in March 1955.
[FWW01/01/0871/001; Courtesy of woolworths museum.co.uk, © 3D and 6D Pictures Ltd]

Fig 6.32 (above)
Store 106, Hounslow, west
London. A checkout with
wire baskets can be seen
inside this Woolworth's
stand-alone self-service
supermarket. The building
had opened as a temporary
store on 20 October 1949,
with conventional service.
It may have become a self-
service supermarket when
a new Woolworth's store
opened at Nos 269–270
High Street in 1959. The
Kingsmere brand of food,
visible in the window, was
introduced to Woolworth's
in 1959.
[FWW01/01/0106/001]

Fig 6.33 (right)
The self-service Store
1039, in the affluent
Hertfordshire town of
Radlett, photographed
at 11.15am on 17 August
1960, the year it opened.
[FWW01/01/1039/001]

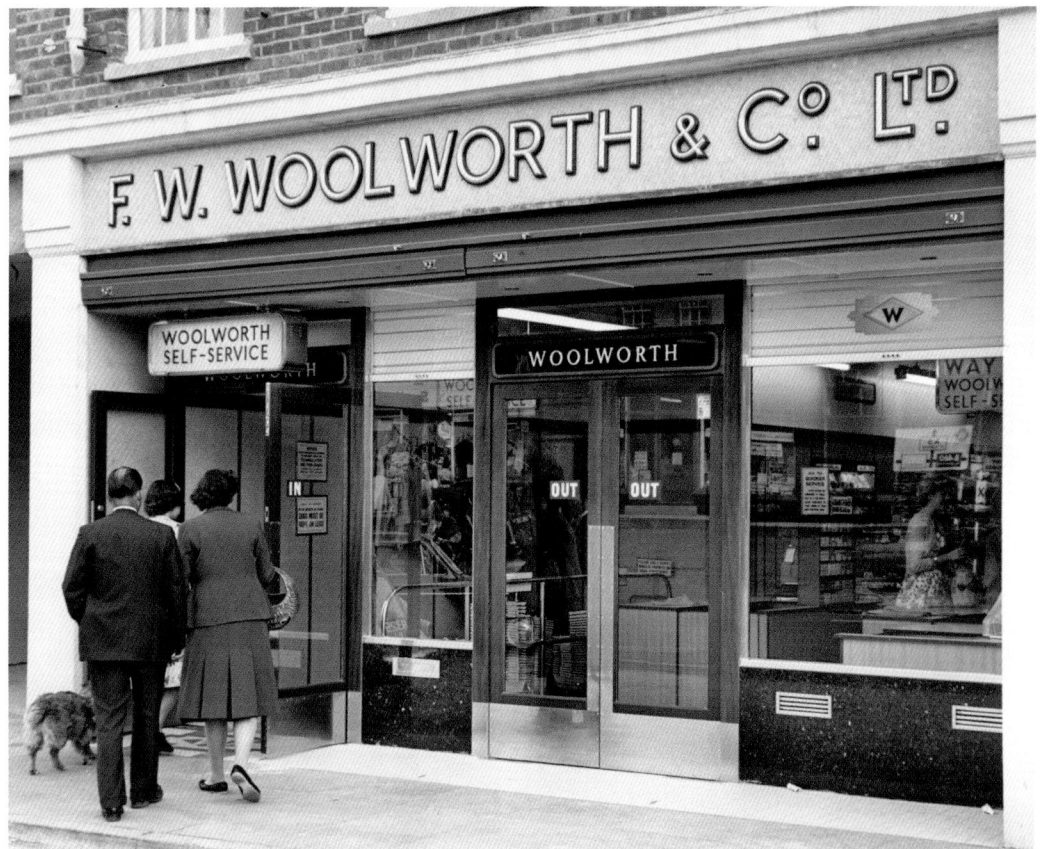

April 1958.[23] The opportunity arose after Woolworth's existing store relocated from Silver Street to the High Street. The old store on Silver Street (*see* Fig 3.44) was reinvented as Store 999, with a fascia reading 'Woolworth Food-Market'. Inside, ten 14ft gondolas were arranged in five parallel rows, supplemented by refrigerated units and cabinets for fresh meat. The first-floor stockroom was refitted with a cold store for meat, and food preparation rooms. A supermarket appears to have been created in a similar way at Hounslow, following relocation in 1959 (*see* Fig 6.32). The lasting solution for Woolworth's, however, was to incorporate a self-service 'Foodmarket' or 'Food Hall' within a conventional store. The test bed for this was Guildford, which relocated across the road from the old store in October 1958, to the site of the former Lion Hotel (Figs 6.34 and 6.35). Its frontage, by the town planner Thomas Sharp (1901–78), was 'specially designed ... as a gesture of local interest', including a striding lion rescued from the hotel pediment.[24] As well as having a Foodmarket, Guildford included the first example of a particular design of cafeteria, widely adopted by Woolworth's into the mid-1960s. Railed off from the sales floor, this had a diamond-pattern counter front and fixed seating, arranged in pairs on opposite sides of each table.[25] In these key respects, Guildford provided a template for the superstores of the next decade.

Woolworth's store managers disliked self-service. Customers complained and shrinkage (a euphemism for shoplifting and pilfering,

as well as damage and breakage) was high. Managers, whose salaries were adversely affected by shrinkage, had a chance to express their feelings on 2 March 1959, when Woolworth's Golden Jubilee was celebrated in London. This event was attended by all management personnel, with 1,200 delegates and guests. In his speech, the President of Woolworth, Robert C Kirkwood, explained how the American stores had adapted to modern conditions. When he urged the British company to follow their lead, this struck a sour note. Kirkwood received no applause from his disapproving audience. Nevertheless, in the annual report for 1959, R J Berridge sounded wearily resigned to the inevitability of self-service, stating: 'Whilst many shoppers do not take readily to this mode of selling, they seem to accept it after a while.'[26]

One more area where American influence was brought to bear was advertising. Except for publicity surrounding major store openings, advertising had been shunned by Woolworth's since the days of Frank W Woolworth, who regarded it as a needless waste of money. Actually, Woolworth's obtained a lot of free publicity, since it was often cited in its suppliers' advertisements. In 1958, however, American Woolworth launched its first major advertising campaign and this was followed in 1959 by the British company's first foray into television commercials, with the slogan 'Walk into Woolworth'. Accompanying this was a new symbol for Golden Jubilee year, the outline of a basket containing the letter 'W'.

Figs 6.34 and 6.35 Store 285, Guildford, relocated in 1958 to a new building. To the rear, on North Street, was a self-service 'Foodmarket' (Fig 6.35); note the new-style weighing machine, with its huge round face. The store closed in 1984 and was redeveloped as the White Lion Walk shopping precinct. The pre-1958 store is now occupied by W H Smith's. [FWW01/01/0285/001; FWW01/01/0285/002]

145

Modernisation and expansion, c 1955–59

Around 1956, with most of its bombed stores rebuilt or repaired, Woolworth's began to attend to its older city-centre superstores, rejuvenating some ambitious projects that had been shelved in 1939. One of the most publicised schemes was in Oxford, where the company faced a protracted planning battle. The store at Nos 8–10 Cornmarket (*see* Fig 3.10) no longer fulfilled requirements, and so the Clarendon Hotel at No 52 Cornmarket had been purchased from Trust Houses in December 1939, with the intention of erecting larger premises. This immediately sparked fears that the Clarendon's pleasant Georgian façade was doomed.[27] A correspondent to *The Times* opined that Woolworth's 'familiar red and gold band … may brighten an ugly street but disfigures a beautiful one'.[28] The architect Albert E Richardson (1880–1964) – writing as Vice-President of the Georgian Group – called upon Woolworth's to 'secure an elevation for their new store freed from ostentation and cheap vulgarity', attributes commonly associated by the intelligentsia with Woolworth's architectural efforts.[29]

In the event, the redevelopment of the Clarendon site was delayed by the war. While the building was requisitioned, the debate rumbled on, with Woolworth's continuing to reassure its critics that it was 'their endeavour at all times, as far as is reasonably possible, to meet the wishes of local authorities and bodies interested in the preservation of architectural features'.[30] Planning permission was refused in 1951, and in the course of an appeal hearing it was even suggested that the Minister might list the Clarendon for its 'historical and architectural merit'. Nevertheless, Woolworth's won on appeal to the Minister of Works. The company no doubt owed this victory to its representative, the distinguished architect and town planner Sir William G Holford (1907–75), who is said to have 'possessed an ability to build consensus opinion in order to resolve complex planning and civic design problems'.[31]

Once building licences were abolished, the Clarendon was flattened to make way for Woolworth's new store and upper-floor offices. The structure, which had early medieval origins, was recorded by archaeologists and historians as demolition and excavation progressed.[32] Eventually, 18 years after the purchase of the site, the new store was opened by the mayor on 18 October 1957. Holford's frontage (Fig 6.36) received praise from many quarters, including the architectural historian Nikolaus Pevsner, who declared it 'very tactfully and elegantly done'.[33] The inevitable curtain wall treatment was tempered by the careful selection of facing materials: Bladon and Clipsham stone, from Oxfordshire and Rutland respectively, set off by green-grey slate panels. Strips of darkness at ground and roof level were created by recessing the shopfront and adding a brise soleil. The 'familiar red and gold band', dreaded by Oxford's preservationists, was conspicuous by its absence. The store was notable for its large footwear department (fitted out like a shoe shop), record counter, tobacco kiosk and a delicatessen with a refrigerated display. The cafeteria – where pheasant and champagne were served on opening day – was one of the first to have a counter-front in Woolworth's distinctive diamond pattern, adopted at Guildford, Gravesend (Fig 6.37), Swansea and elsewhere.

Instead of a cafeteria, the almost contemporary neo-Georgian style store in York had a quick lunch bar, called a 'Diamond Bar', lined with 56 high stools.[34] The York store had been enlarged by taking over the picture house next door. Woolworth's Real Estate Department now frequently targeted former theatres and cinemas, as well as hotels, for redevelopment. The highest profile theatre acquisition was the Aldelphi Theatre on the Strand, London, but the London County Council Planning Committee would not permit Woolworth's to redevelop it as a store.[35] At Rotherham, on the other hand, Woolworth's demolished and redeveloped the Regent Theatre, while an extension at Burnley occupied the site of the Victoria Theatre.[36]

The introduction of toughened armour-plated glass in the 1950s allowed Woolworth's shopfronts to become more transparent. Solidly backed displays of merchandise shrank to the sides, while glass doors and 'clearview' windows multiplied, offering a tempting – yet secure – view of brightly lit store interiors. It was not unusual for a new shopfront to be equipped with banks of four or five pairs of glass doors. At both Middlesbrough (1958) and Swansea (1959, Figs 6.38 and 6.39) the central window was still used for display, but at Leeds (1959, Figs 6.40 and 6.41) it overlooked a

Fig 6.36 (opposite) Store 189, Oxford, as featured in The Builder, *10 January 1958, 65. With elevations designed by Sir William G Holford and Howard Mason,[d] and a recessed shopfront, this was one of Woolworth's most acclaimed architectural ventures of the 1950s. Like pre-war stores, it had steelwork by Banister Walton and precast concrete floors by Truscon. After the branch closed in 1983, it was remodelled as part of the Clarendon Centre. A flowing 'W' with the date 1957 can still be seen over the entrance to the upper-floor offices. [Reproduced by kind permission of the Syndics of Cambridge University Library]*

THE BUILDER   January 10 1958

STORE, Oxford

for F. W. Woolworth & Co., Ltd.

Designed by: Sir WILLIAM HOLFORD, MA, MTPI, FRIBA

HOWARD MASON, ARIBA, AMTPI, Assistant
in conjunction with the Architectural Dept. of
F. W. Woolworth & Co., Ltd.
H. WINBOURNE, FRIBA, Chief Architect,
H. W. SCHOFIELD, LRIBA, District Staff Architect,
R. W. TIETZE, Assistant

Main Contractors: THE CONSTRUCTION DEPARTMENT,
F. W. Woolworth & Co., Ltd.

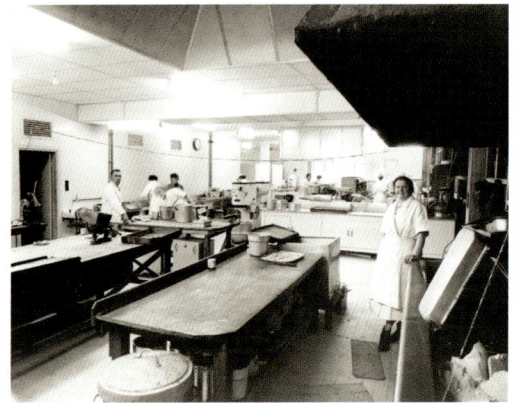

Figs 6.38 and 6.39
Store 14 at Nos 239–242 High Street, Swansea, photographed on a wet day before Christmas in 1959. Shoppers scurry across a pedestrian crossing while a man on a ladder cleans a window. The pre-war store (see Fig 5.15) was rebuilt in 1958–9, opening on 16 November 1959 with the mixed service typical of the time. The interior of the cafeteria kitchen appears in a rare behind-the-scenes photograph showing the 'Temporary Fish Frying Area', facing Welcome Lane (Fig 6.39). The store closed on 28 June 1986. [FWW01/01/0014/003 South Wales Evening Post; FWW01/01/0014/006 South Wales Evening Post]

double stair to the lower ground floor. Inside the Leeds store, a Waygood Otis escalator bore customers up to the first-floor Foodmarket. Escalators appeared in several of Woolworth's largest stores around this time.

In 1958 Woolworth's Chairman assured those stockholders whose local stores were still of pre-war vintage that 'the Company's development programme is proceeding with all speed'.[37] Old shopfronts were modernised by removing central display windows, with the consequence that structural columns were externalised (Fig 6.42). The interiors of old

stores were also changing (Fig 6.43). Floors, previously of pitch pine, were now of chequered terrazzo. Counters, often fitted by Harris & Sheldon, were of laminate rather than mahogany. Tin ceilings had been abandoned in favour of fire-resistant 'Asbestolux' tiles suspended on metal frames.[38] In 1958, the decision was taken to introduce fluorescent lighting more widely: it had been rolled out to 80 per cent of the stores by 1959, often necessitating the full rewiring of premises.[39] In 1964, Atlas boasted that its Atlantic fluorescent tubes had been installed in 800 Woolworth's

Fig 6.40
Store 5, on Briggate and
Central Road in Leeds, was
the principal superstore to
be completed in Woolworth's
Golden Jubilee Year, opening
on 26 February 1959.
Typically, the Portland stone
façade was dominated by a
central expanse of curtain
walling, of aluminium with
blue glass panels. While
most of the store had
conventional counter
service, the self-service
Foodmarket, with its
gondola units, can be
glimpsed through the first-
floor windows. Also on the
first floor was a 444-seater
cafeteria. A novel feature
of this store was a record
department with listening
booths. After Woolworth's
closed in 1987 the building
was occupied by Schofields
and Rackhams, before
being remodelled, in 1996,
by House of Fraser.
[FWW01/01/0005/003]

Fig 6.41
A detail of the crowded
frontage of the Leeds store
in 1959. Stairs to the lower
sales floor could be seen
through the central
'clearview' or 'view-through'
window. The glass is
plastered with
advertisements for bargains
in the Foodmarket,
including 'local chickens'.
Starting at Guildford, it was
normal for new superstores
to include a self-service food
hall alongside departments
with conventional service.
[FWW01/01/0005/002]

stores.[40] Woolworth's apparently borrowed money, for the first time in its history, to finance this project.[41]

In the five years from 1954 to 1959 Woolworth's spent £35 million on its properties.[42] Around 200 new stores were added to the portfolio, including Store 1000, which opened in Portslade in May 1958, and many existing stores were rebuilt or moved to better sites, including Great Yarmouth (Fig 6.44). Furthermore, in 1959, the Golden Jubilee year, the Executive Office relocated to new headquarters fronting Marylebone Road in central London (Fig 6.45). The building was topped by a colourful mosaic 'diamond W'. One of the main benefits of the site was car parking

Fig 6.42
The 1959 revamp of the shopfront of Store 366 at Nos 30–32 Dockhead Street, Saltcoats, in Ayrshire, was still surviving in 1981 (datable by the 'Crackdown' price cuts advertised in the window), complete with its typical 1950s wooden fascia and lettering. As happened so often, the central display window of 1929 had been removed, exposing a structural post, while the original side windows were retained.
[FWW01/01/0366/001]

Fig 6.43 (right)
Inside Store 291 in St Austell in 1958. Sweets were not yet sold on a 'pick 'n' mix' basis. Many standard stores built in the late 1920s and 1930s were modernised in this manner, with new counters, a flush ceiling, fluorescent lights and a chequer-pattern terrazzo floor.
[FWW01/01/0291/003]

Fig 6.44 (far right)
Store 134 in Great Yarmouth was built in 1959. The pale blue colour of the spandrel panels was widely favoured by Woolworth's.
[BB007125]

for visitors, something which had been lacking on New Bond Street. It would not be long before the largest stores, too, were being planned with parking spaces.

As well as rebuilding the chain on home ground in the 1950s, British Woolworth's established subsidiaries in the West Indies and in Southern Rhodesia.[43] When the first West Indian store opened in Kingston, Jamaica, in

November 1954, it was noted that 'the building and layout follow very much the traditional Woolworth pattern, with variations necessary to accord with the climatic conditions'.[44] This principally referred to the almost complete absence of windows and the open frontage, secured at night by roller shuttering. J1 in Kingston was followed by seven more stores in Jamaica (Fig 6.46), six in Trinidad (from

Fig 6.45
The company leased
Woolworth House at
Nos 242–246 Marylebone
Road from April 1959. This
office block was designed by
R Seifert & Partners and was
adorned with decorative
work by the sculptor
Bainbridge Copnall,
including an elaborate and
colourful mosaic 'diamond
W' in heraldic style at the
top of the façade, and
incised figures representing
sunrise and sunset.
[Author]

Fig 6.46
A sketch of Store J2 on
Slipe Road, Kingston,
Jamaica, built in 1956. The
foreign stores were very like
their British counterparts,
with many of the same
fixtures and fittings.
Compare with Fig 6.14.
[FWW01/02/00J2/001]

Figs 6.47
A drawing of Store R2
in Bulawayo, Southern
Rhodesia (Zimbabwe),
by architects Rinaldi,
Macdonald & Harvey,
dated 30 June 1958.
[FWW01/02/9998/002]

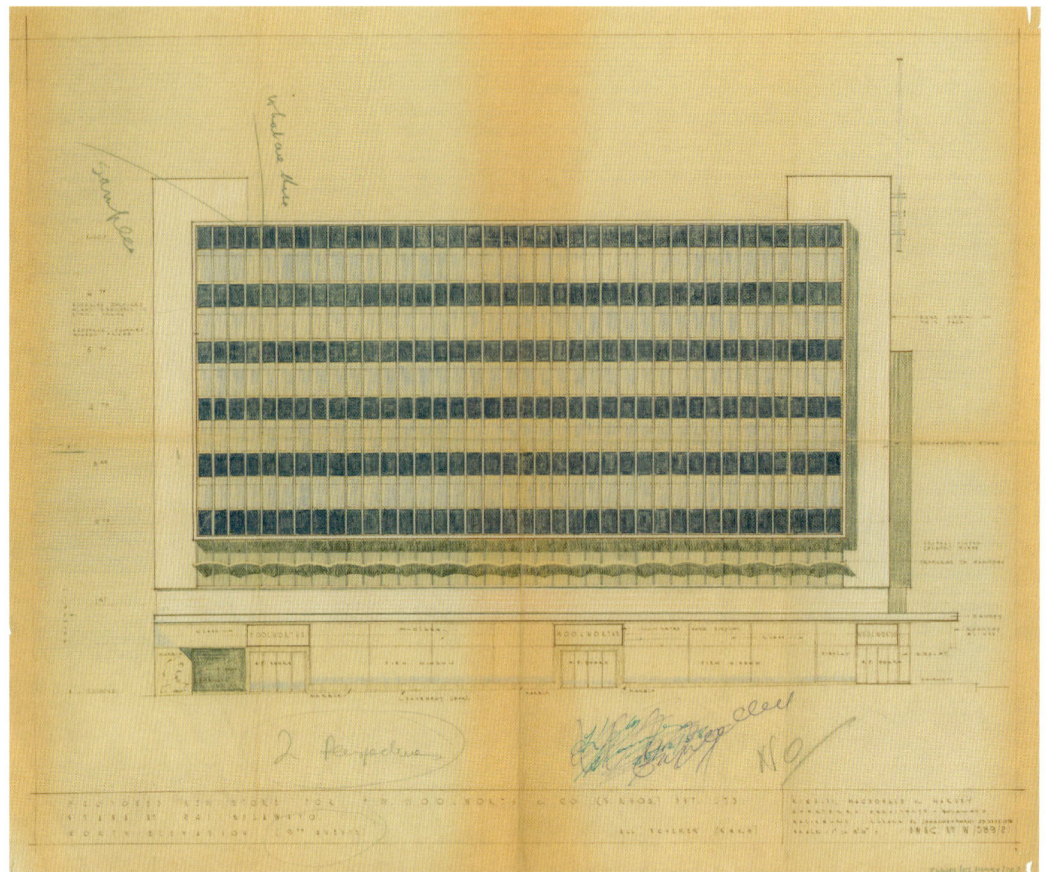

Figs 6.47
A drawing of Store R2
in Bulawayo, Southern
Rhodesia (Zimbabwe),
by architects Rinaldi,
Macdonald & Harvey,
dated 30 June 1958.
[FWW01/02/9998/002]

1955) and one in Barbados (1956). In each case, preliminary plans were drawn up by Woolworth's in Britain, and sent out to local architects – in the case of Kingston, Norman & Dawbarn – who produced the final designs and oversaw the building works. Shopfronts and fittings were despatched from Woolworth's usual suppliers, including John Curtis and Harris & Sheldon. Most of the merchandise was British, as, initially, were the managers. The first of the four stores in Southern Rhodesia (now Zimbabwe) opened in Salisbury (now Harare) in 1959, the second in Bulawayo in 1960. The Salisbury store, by architects Ross Mackenzie, Van Heerden & Hartford, had an elevation clad in honeycomb Italian ceramic tiles, and three air-conditioned sales floors. For Bulawayo (Fig 6.47), Winbourne's plans were developed locally by Rinaldi, Macdonald & Harvey. For one façade they adopted a 'louvred treatment' with vertical fins, supposedly in response to the hot climatic conditions. Fins were applied to the façades of a small number of British stores a decade later.

7

Retail revolution, 1960–1970

The American grip

Managers attending Woolworth's birthday celebrations in 1959 little imagined the profound changes they would face in the 1960s. Not only did American executives continue to press for the rollout of the disliked self-service format, but they encouraged British Woolworth's to move into shopping centres, to launch own-brand products, to diversify into specialised retail formats, to computerise and centralise stock control and, most radically and most expensively, to develop out-of-town stores called Woolco. At the same time, the high street superstores grew ever-larger, departmentalising on the pattern established in America in the late 1930s and accommodating bulky new lines such as furniture, carpets, wallpaper and white goods. As the Chairman stated in 1962: 'It is our belief that as far as possible the housewife likes to do all her shopping under one roof.'[1]

For most of the decade, the company was run by Fredrick Leslie Chaplin (Chairman, 1961–9). Woolworth's tradition of promoting managers from within its ranks was beginning to attract criticism, since it meant that the men sitting in the boardroom alongside Chaplin – for, indeed, they were still all men – were approaching the ends of their careers and, arguably, were less receptive to progressive ideas. Following Harold Winbourne's retirement in March 1960, Doug Hardy (Fig 7.1) took over as Woolworth's chief architect, staying in post until 1980.[2]

The adoption of self-service continued, but at a snail's pace. As late as 1968, it had been introduced to just 180 stores, mostly new outlets rather than conversions. When superstores were rebuilt or modernised they generally followed the Guildford model, retaining counter service (Fig 7.2), with a self-service Food Hall grafted on. It was the advent of decimalisation, and the need to replace the old National Cash Registers (see Chapter 8), that eventually forced the company to accelerate the self-service rollout, thus transforming the character of the store interiors, and probably also the allegiance of many Woolworth's customers, forever. Behaviour was more controlled in a self-service store, where customers had to follow a prescribed route, and opportunities for fun and chatter were limited.[3]

Woolworth's continued to open in developer-built precincts. In addition, units were taken in covered shopping centres, or malls, including the very first to open in a British city, the Bull Ring Centre in Birmingham (see pp 158–60). From the mid-1960s, malls became increasingly common as part of town centre 'comprehensive redevelopment' schemes or to serve new towns (Fig 7.3), and several earlier precincts were roofed over. Woolworth's invariably had a presence, ideally with entrances on more than one level of the mall, and also to the street.

One of the most prolific commercial developers of the 1960s and 1970s was Arndale Properties Trust. Founded in Bradford around 1950 by a successful baker, Arnold Hagenbach, and an estate agent, Sam Chippendale, Arndale was a combination of their names. Chippendale apparently had 'a friend at Woolworths who could guarantee that the chain would take a large unit in each development; with such a name on board others would follow'.[4] Woolworth's thus became an anchor tenant in many Arndale centres. The earliest – for example, in Jarrow (now the Viking Centre) in 1961 – were designed as precincts, and occupied peripheral locations.[5] But by the mid-1960s Arndale was opening covered shopping centres, for example at Cross Gates in Leeds. Arndale depended on the cooperation of local authorities, who had the power to implement far-reaching compulsory purchase orders. The city-centre Arndale centres of the 1970s, in

Fig 7.1
Doug W Hardy was Woolworth's architect through the 1960s and 1970s, a period of great change for his department. From 55 Years of Progress, 1909–1964, *16. [Author's collection]*

*Fig 7.2 (above)
Store 150, Nos 100–104
Kilburn High Road, north
London. A counter-service
store in full swing – with
girls serving loose biscuits
from square metal boxes –
photographed by Henry
Grant in 1965. Former
sales assistant Dorothy
Byers vividly remembered
the Woolworth's girls' sense
of ownership over their
counters, saying: 'We walked
up and down in the centre
of (the counters) feeling
like a captain on a boat.'*
[© Museum of London]

*Fig 7.3 (right)
Store 1084, in the new town
of Glenrothes in Fife, opened
in a glass-roofed shopping
development in 1963 and
had conventional counter
service. The fascia was
of a type of Formica known
as 'Beautyboard', one of
several laminates used by
Woolworth's in the 1960s.*
[FWW01/01/1084/001]

places such as Manchester and Luton, involved the clearance of hundreds, if not thousands, of old properties, and the elimination of entire streets and lanes. These monolithic developments assumed a colossal scale. They acquired a bad reputation, in terms of their architectural treatment and their approach to town planning, and few retain the name 'Arndale Centre' today. It is arguable whether Arndale would have enjoyed such commercial success without Woolworth's backing.

In 1962 a brand name was introduced for a wide range of products sold exclusively by Woolworth's, including foodstuffs (Fig 7.4) and stationery. The chosen name was 'Winfield' – Frank W Woolworth's middle name. This endured for 20 years but, unlike Marks & Spencer's 'St Michael' brand, it never acquired a reputation for quality. Another brand name of the 1960s, initially very popular but eventually derided, was 'Embassy' (Fig 7.5).[6] The singles and EPs sold between 1954 and 1965 on the Embassy label were cover versions of popular hits. From 1965, however, Woolworth's concentrated on original chart music, quickly becoming one of the principal music retailers in the country (Fig 7.6). Other popular lines included plastic flowers, cosmetics (with brands Outdoor Girl, Miners and, from 1967, Baby Doll) and, as ever, confectionery (including, since the 1930s, the Milady brand). Following experiments in self-service outlets it was discovered that pre-packaged sweets were less popular than the loose variety, and so 'pick 'n' mix' was adapted to Woolworth's traditional counter layout (Fig 7.7). DIY lines were still strong, especially the range of paints (branded as 'Household', and later as 'Cover-Plus') made for Woolworth's by Donald Macpherson & Co (*see* Fig 7.29).

Woolworth's had always been a general variety store, but in 1962 it launched one of its first specialist spin-off formats, a 'Cards and Gifts' shop close to the new store on High Street, Sutton, Surrey.[7] Diversifying on a greater scale, American Woolworth's had set up a free-standing garden centre in Santa Clara, California, with the intention of establishing another 20 by the end of 1960.[8] British Woolworth's, which had always been the place to go for seeds and bulbs, did not emulate this, but did open an experimental garden centre beside the Windsor store in May 1961. Created 'from a backyard', the space was surrounded by glass pergolas.[9] Like 'Cards and Gifts' in Sutton, this may not have been a runaway success since few dedicated Woolworth's garden centres were created prior to the 1970s.

Computerisation and centralised warehousing were adopted together in the mid-1960s, following the model of a distribution centre opened by American Woolworth in Chicago in 1963. The aim was to control the inventory stocked by the company and to

Fig 7.4 (left)
The peanut counter, in the revamped Store 51 in Huddersfield, photographed on 8 June 1967.
[JLP01/08/076469]

Fig 7.5 (below)
The gramophone section, tucked beneath the stairs in Store 103, Birmingham, in 1962. From 1954 'Embassy' was Woolworth's own-brand label for records: these were cover versions of popular songs recorded by session musicians. The Beatles hit 'She Loves You', for example, was recorded by a casually assembled group called The Typhoons. Oriole Records continued to produce Embassy recordings, exclusively for Woolworth's, until 1965.
[JLP01/08/063615]

Fig 7.6
Store 49, Leicester, reopened after rebuilding on 7 May 1965. The 'Record Corner' – tucked under the stairs as at Birmingham (see Fig 7.5) – stocked the Top 20 singles. Although Woolworth's already sold chart music and had provided listening booths since the late 1950s, more serious music departments opened from the mid-1960s. Between 1968 and 1985 branches large and small stocked LPs in the 'Top of the Pops' series, each 'volume' containing around a dozen cover versions of Top 40 hits. [Courtesy of woolworths museum.co.uk, © 3D and 6D Pictures Ltd]

reduce shipments to stores. Between 1965 and 1967 Woolworth's developed a 17-acre former factory site by the railway line at Royle Barn Road, Castleton, near Rochdale, creating a warehouse with adjoining offices and a computer centre. The warehouse had its own sidings and loading dock. Stock was organised into individual sections for each branch – initially, 50 stores, rising to 104 by 1970 – and was shifted about on pallets using electric fork-lift trucks.[10] In the adjoining computer centre (Fig 7.8), the warehouse transactions with the stores, and the stock records, were controlled through ICT 1903 and 1904 magnetic tape computers, running software developed in the US and used by American Woolworth. The offices included a training suite for would-be managers.

By the mid-1960s Woolworth's was approaching saturation point in Britain. Of the 100 new branches created between 1960 and 1970, only around 20 opened after 1965. By the end of the decade, with 1,130 outlets, Woolworth's had peaked. Some growth was still being generated by enlarging the superstores, really pushing their size beyond the viable limit, but company executives were persuaded that the best way to ensure future growth was to develop enormous retail outlets

for car-borne shoppers. They took the radical step, in 1967, of instigating one of Britain's earliest flirtations with American-style out-of-town shopping by opening the first Woolco store, a format that had been introduced several years earlier in America (see pp 170–72). Three Woolcos were in operation by 1970.

Woolco diverted attention from the high street chain, where growth was stalling. In 1968, in an ominous sign that the glory years were over, Marks & Spencer's overtook Woolworth's as Britain's leading retailer, in terms of both sales and profits.[11] Marks & Spencer's was now a very different concern, focusing on quality clothing and food. Inevitably, criticism was levelled at Woolworth's. It was condemned for its failure to move into mail order, deemed in 1967 'the most explosive growth field in retailing'.[12] Another gripe was its failure to generate capital from its property portfolio, then valued at £117 million. The Observer commented, 'It has not exploited this potential one bit, to the amazement of its High Street rivals.'[13] As the 1960s drew to a close the company was under tremendous pressure to deliver an outstanding performance for shareholders, and executives began to contemplate how they might take advantage of their property goldmine.

Fig 7.8 (below)
The computer room in Woolworth's new Castleton distribution centre in the late 1960s. [Courtesy of woolworths museum.co.uk, © 3D and 6D Pictures Ltd]

Store 103, Bull Ring Centre, Birmingham

The first British Woolworth's to open in a modern shopping centre formed a crucial part of Birmingham's Bull Ring Centre, designed by Sydney Greenwood and T J Hirst for the Laing Development Company. Greenwood worked on many of Laing's projects, including shopping centres in Shrewsbury and Southend. The Bull Ring was a landmark development, showing that British retailing was, at last, catching up with North America. The vast mall subsumed the old city markets, as well as the site of Woolworth's Store 103 (*see* Figs 3.19 and 3.20), between 1961 and 1964, at a cost of £8 million.

As part of the first phase of development, the northern half of Store 103 was demolished and rebuilt. Once this opened in September 1962, the remainder was flattened, and work resumed (compare Figs 7.9 and 7.10). Building in stages ensured that Woolworth's could continue trading throughout. The complex was all-but complete on 29 May 1964, when it was opened by the Duke of Edinburgh. Laing's claimed that the Bull Ring was 'the largest air-conditioned, multi-level shopping centre in Europe'.[14] It measured 350,000 sq ft, with Woolworth's alone occupying 95,000 sq ft. Of this, the sales floors took up 44,000 sq ft.[15] It was thus bigger than the Blackpool store.

When complete, Woolworth's had entrances to every level of the mall. It occupied four floors, connected by escalators and stairs (Fig 7.11). The stockrooms took up half of the lower floor as well as the entire basement. The ground floor, with its old-style personal service counters, was arranged around a vast square well, overlooking the lower sales floor and conveying a tremendous sense of space (Fig 7.12). The Guildford Bar cafeteria and the self-service Food Hall were on the first, or upper, floor (Fig 7.13).

A covered bridge with shops spanned Birmingham's new inner ring road, connecting the Bull Ring with New Street Station. By taking

Fig 7.9
The Bull Ring Centre in Birmingham, under construction on 14 September 1962, with half of Woolworth's old building still standing alongside the ultra-modern new Store 103 (compare Fig 3.20). This had taken just 10½ months to build.
[JLP01/08/063611]

Fig 7.10
The Bull Ring Centre,
Birmingham, at night in
1967, showing Woolworth's
Store 103. Cut off from the
town centre by the inner
ring road and reached via
insalubrious pedestrian
underpasses, the Bull Ring
became synonymous with
the worst aspects of post-war
urban redevelopment and
was completely rebuilt in
2003–4.
[JLP01/08/076229]

Fig 7.11
Escalators had featured
in Woolworth's superstores
since the mid-1950s:
this one led to the upper-
floor cafeteria in the
Bull Ring store.
[JLP01/08/063614]

this route, or an underpass, it was a relatively short – if unpleasant and circuitous – walk to the main shopping streets. The recently rebuilt Woolworth's store on New Street (*see* Fig 7.20) was, therefore, quite close to the branch in the Bull Ring Centre. No fewer than 28 Woolworth's stores lay within the boundaries of Birmingham by 1962.

In the course of their collaboration at the Bull Ring, Woolworth's architects seem to have established a good working relationship with Laing's, whose Construction Department was subsequently contracted to build several Woolworth's stores. These included Campbeltown, Shrewsbury (*see* Fig 7.21),

Huddersfield, Wrexham and Mere Green, Birmingham (*see* Fig 7.29).

High street stores in the 'swinging sixties'

Developers and retailers obtained permission for some astonishingly poor architectural designs in the 1960s. Too often, functionality and economy trounced aesthetic considerations, and cheap constructional systems were embraced with disregard for proportions, scale or context. Many architects seem to have had insufficient understanding of the modern

idiom within which their profession was now expected to work. Woolworth's was as much of a culprit as anyone else, and seems only rarely to have been reined in, as it had been in Oxford, by the growing conservation lobby (see p 146). Sadly, several of the company's new buildings were rather ordinary replacements for attractive old buildings, some being mediocre substitutes for older Woolworth's stores. Inevitably, as at the Bull Ring Centre, many of the new Woolworth's stores of the 'Swinging Sixties' formed part of multi-functional, and often multi-level, town-centre redevelopment schemes, with the company's construction superintendents having minimal input into their architectural framework. Ironically, some of the most successful store designs of the decade were those which met with the least architectural interference from outside forces: it appears to have been commercial developers who introduced the company to a second-rate brutalist approach, and the adoption of windowless fronts. One of the first of these was in Bracknell (Fig 7.14), which opened in 1960.

The range of stylistic options favoured for Woolworth's street elevations in the 1950s endured into the mid-1960s. Thus many stores had buff brick or Portland stone façades lit by tiers of small, square windows; others had a dominant curtain-wall panel in a projecting frame (Figs 7.15 and 7.16), while a few presented an all-encompassing grid of curtain walling (Figs 7.17 and 7.18). Again as in the 1950s, all sorts of materials were used for infill panels – mosaic, slate and coloured glass – with aluminium window frames.

The trend for see-through shopfronts, begun in the 1950s, continued (Fig 7.19). Shopfront surrounds were usually either red or pale grey, clad in either small square mosaic tiles or a polished stone (such as grey 'Merlin' or

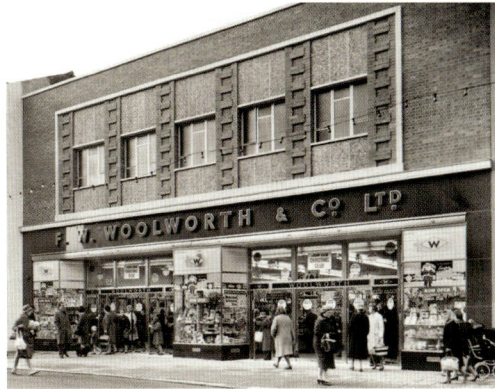

Fig 7.15
Store 18, at Nos 58–59 Freeman Street, Grimsby, was 'reskinned' in 1964, as this picture shows. Located near the docks, this branch was overshadowed by a new town-centre store (Store 981) which had opened in September 1957. In 1971 Store 981 was extended and converted to self-service, and Store 18 closed. Many towns with two branches lost one of their outlets in the 1970s. [FWW01/01/0018/001]

Fig 7.16
Store 25, Cardiff, was rebuilt and extended on the old site – Nos 50–54 Queen Street – reopening on 20 July 1960. The shopfront boasted a continuous row of eight doorways, interrupted by two structural piers, with small end display windows. The photograph shows the store during the National Eisteddfod of Wales, in August 1960, with the Welsh dragon taking pride of place. It closed in 1984, and the building is now occupied by BHS. [FWW01/01/0025/001]

Fig 7.17
Store 185, at Nos 147–148
Commercial Street,
Newport, Monmouthshire,
opened on 21 September
1962. Classed a superstore
(or, more correctly at this
date, 'Super Store'), it had a
Food Hall and a Guildford-
style cafeteria.
[FWW01/01/0185/001]

Fig 7.17
Store 185, at Nos 147–148
Commercial Street,
Newport, Monmouthshire,
opened on 21 September
1962. Classed a superstore
(or, more correctly at this
date, 'Super Store'), it had a
Food Hall and a Guildford-
style cafeteria.
[FWW01/01/0185/001]

red 'Balmoral' granite), though other materials were used, including relatively cheap Formica 'Beautyboard'. Until 1965 letters were of sans serif type, in gold with red outlines. Neonised letters were manufactured for Woolworth's by Pearce Signs: with names such as 'Ambassador', 'Regency', 'Embassy' and 'Kent', these were available in a range of sizes.

Woolworth's largest projects of the early 1960s were undoubtedly in central Birmingham, where the 13-storey Woolworth Building (Fig 7.20) was built between New Street and Stephenson Street, opening on 20 July 1961. Architecturally, the overly ambitious design by Cotton, Ballard & Blow (rather than Woolworth's own architects) was dictated by the diverse uses of the building, resulting in a lack of visual cohesion. Indeed, the author of the Pevsner Architectural Guide to Birmingham, published in 2005, went so far as to call it 'New Street's architectural disaster'.[16] Like its predecessor, much of the building

Fig 7.18
Store 88, Torquay, opened
on 11 June 1964 at a new
site, Nos 21–25 Union
Street. The New Bond
reported: 'To quote a
member of staff …
"Staffrooms are out of this
world." They are situated at
the top of the building and
comprise lounge, dining
room, kitchen, cloakroom,
toilets and sick bay.' Many
Woolworth's stores had
curtain walling with pale
blue panels – here they are
suspiciously bright and may
have been renewed since
their installation in 1964.
The photograph was taken
on 1 July 2009, several
months after closure.
[DP085600]

Fig 7.19
Store 166, Nos 7–15 Port
Street, Stirling: a typical
early 1960s shopfront, here
added to an older building,
a new location for
Woolworth's, which opened
on 8 November 1962. It had
a pale grey Saivo mosaic
fascia, red and gold
lettering, and a projecting
illuminated 'Woolworth'
sign. The mosaic also clad
the structural columns.
[FWW01/01/0166/001]

was taken up by office suites, rented out to tenants.

Woolworth's proclaimed 'store of the year' in 1965 was built on Castle Street in Shrewsbury (Fig 7.21).[17] It actually opened on 30 October 1964, replacing the picturesque Victorian Gothic Raven Hotel with a severe red-brick frontage of seven bays. To the rear, where the land fell away steeply, a spectacular curtain wall, 111ft high, screened eight floor levels, with a pedestrian walkway serving the store, together with neighbouring Littlewood's, and doubling as a canopy over a delivery yard (later, in 1985, infilled by a mall development). Inside, the store was vast, with three sales floors and a large restaurant. It was one of the first to have a soft furnishings department, selling fabrics such as Terylene and net curtaining. It was also one of the first with a photographic department supplied by Dixons.[18]

Soon after the Shrewsbury store opened, the standard sans serif lettering initially installed on its red granite fascia was replaced with Egyptian (or slab-serif) lettering, a blocky form of typography that had been fashionable since the mid-1950s, and was also used by Littlewood's. Similar typefaces had been used before by Woolworth's: the word 'WOOLWORTH' on the upper elevation of Bracknell, in 1960, being spelt out in illuminated and slightly italicised Egyptian-style letters (see Fig 7.14). Now named 'Shrewsbury' lettering, this was rolled out to many stores between 1965 and 1972 (Figs 7.22 and 7.23). Before long the full name of the company was

Fig 7.20
The Woolworth Building,
New Street, Birmingham,
occupied the site of
the Theatre Royal and
looked incongruous on a
thoroughfare that was lined
by tall, confident Victorian
and Edwardian buildings.
The sales floor of Store 266
was on the ground floor,
with the cafeteria above.[d]
As well as the now
obligatory Food Hall, the
store had a tobacco kiosk,
two listening booths for
gramophone records and a
heel bar. This was one of the
first properties to be sold by
Woolworth Holdings in
1982–3. It was subsequently
extensively refurbished, with
a glass-sided lift protruding
from the façade.
[FWW01/01/0266/002]

Fig 7.21
Store 312 in Shrewsbury,
erected by John Laing
(Construction) Ltd in
1964. The scale of the
new developments for
Woolworth's (right) and
Littlewood's (left) is
striking. The precast
Truscon floor units favoured
by Woolworth's since c 1930
(see Fig 4.13) can be seen.
[JLP01/08/066410]

Fig 7.22
Store 1126, Enniskillen,
Northern Ireland, in 1967.
This counter-service store
thrived despite stiff local
competition from the
Moore Brothers' flagship
Wellworth store.
[FWW01/01/1126/001]

Fig 7.23
Store 1107, Nos 33–39
Newry Street, Banbridge,
Northern Ireland, opened on
30 July 1965. The shopfront
had a red Saivo mosaic
fascia set with the firm's
chunky new 'Shrewsbury'
letters. It was photographed
at dusk to show the effect of
the illumination. This store
was damaged by a car bomb
on 1 August 1998.
[FWW01/01/1107/002]

dropped from new fascias and replaced with 'WOOLWORTH'. This had often been used in the past, but usually on upper elevations (*see* Fig 6.38, Swansea), projecting signs or narrow secondary entrances, rather than main fascia boards. It was adopted consistently, however, from 1968. Some instances of this design were ridiculously out of proportion (*see* Fig 2.28). Increasingly, 'WOOLWORTH' lettering was set directly on the building rather than on a fascia, and the conventional framework of the shopfront was abandoned.

Traditional architectural styles were still produced occasionally by Woolworth's

Fig 7.24
Store 163 at Nos 37 and 43 Eastgate, Chester. This shows the genuine timber-framed building taken over by Woolworth's in 1924 (left), and the extension in 'half-timbered English oak' of 1961 (right).[e] They were linked by a sales area to the rear of House of Bewlay and the Kardomah café. [FWW01/01/0163/001]

Fig 7.25 (below)
Store 452 opened in Hitchin in 1931 (see far left, now Boots). In August 1965 Woolworth's opened a new Georgian-style superstore to the other side of its neighbour, 'The Cock'. It occupied the site of Perks & Llewellyn chemists' shop, noted for lavender since 1823. The design, by the architect Herbert Kellett Ablett (1904–97), was carefully negotiated with the local authority. In 1985 this was transformed into the prototype 'Woolworths Weekend' (see Fig 9.4). [FWW01/01/0452/001]

architects, no doubt at the insistence of planning authorities in towns with highly valued historic environments. Historical scale, however, was often disregarded, and many of these stores stood out on fine-grained British high streets like the proverbial sore thumb. The timber-framed extension erected on Eastgate Street in Chester in 1958–61, for example, was admittedly referential to surrounding medieval buildings, but it had a mechanical quality, and the units of the boxy frame were oversized (Fig 7.24). In 1963 the store in Bath moved down Stall Street to a massive, stripped-Classical building erected on the site of St James's Church, which had been bombed in a Baedeker raid in 1942. Although faced in smooth ashlar like its Georgian neighbours, and with a set-back upper floor that could not be seen from the street, the sheer size of the new store, and especially its overly large quasi-sash windows, swamped its well-mannered surroundings. The new Alnwick store of 1968, though similar in style and materials, was much more convincing, being just five bays long, broadly respecting the widths and storey heights of its neighbours, and having a traditional pitched roof to the front. Newbury, rebuilt in 1962, was also sympathetic in design, with its two-tone brickwork and horned sashes. One of

Woolworth's most innovative neo-Georgian stores was erected two doors down from the original branch in Hitchin (1965; Fig 7.25).[19] Here the pitched roof was a mere frill over the brick façade: behind it the flat roof was used as a car park, accessed by a long two-way ramp at the rear of the store, set to one side of the unloading bay. As in Bath, the frontage was just slightly too large for the comfort of the street.[20]

Fig 7.26
Store 288 in Brighton:
the right-hand wing was
added to the former
Rosling's drapery store by
Woolworth's, who relocated
here in 1965. The facing
included hexagonal blocks,
creating an unusual
geometric surface pattern.
[FWW01/01/0288/001]

Fig 7.27
Store 23 opened on a new
site in Richmond, south
London, on 21 November
1963. Here we see the
interior, with an 'Ezeglide'
curtain rail display and a
rudimentary refreshments
bar – a descendant of the
counter shown in Fig 2.22.
[JLP01/08/067399]

One of the few Woolworth's stores of the 1960s to open in an old building was Store 288 in Brighton, which relocated to the former Rosling's drapery shop on London Road in 1965. This had been built in the mid-1930s in an art deco style, and Woolworth's added a new wing to balance the original design (Fig 7.26). A completely different example of reuse, in a more vernacular style, was Sherborne.[21] Uncharacteristically, this store relocated, in 1968, to a half-timbered former bakery with a red tiled roof. Even elements of an existing bronze shopfront were retained, complying with the wishes of the planning authority.

Woolworth's interiors changed little in the early-to-mid-1960s, retaining their beige laminate fittings, chequered terrazzo floors and tube lighting (Figs 7.27–7.29). Pale blue italicised Egyptian letters were set on side walls to signal the locations of different departments. Maintenance man Peter Taylor recollected that the interior of the Portsmouth store was painted every five years: ceilings in 'white satin-finish paint' and walls and pillars 'in a colour called "sales floor pink", applied by roller'.[22] The cafeterias were usually of the so-called Guildford (or 'G') type (Fig 7.30), often with wall decoration appropriate to the locality. Dragons and castles, for example, featured at Cardiff, and scenes of the city in 1731 at New Street, Birmingham. At Argyle Street in Glasgow, rebuilt after a fire in 1962, the floor

and ceiling were decorated in a plaid pattern. A glass screen in the mezzanine cafeteria in Chester bore the city's coat of arms. This cafeteria gave direct access to the city walls, and offered a view over the cathedral gardens

Fig 7.28
The interior of a typical self-service branch of Woolworth's in 1963. This is Store 1082, Lydney in Gloucestershire, which opened on 23 August 1963. The gondola display units still had cupboards with sliding doors in their bases. Often cut-down mahogany counters (known as 'Leeds counters') were used instead of brand new units. [FWW01/01/1082/003]

Fig 7.29
Store 1133 in Mere Green, a suburb of Sutton Coldfield, was built for Woolworth's by Laing's and opened on 31 October 1969. Woolworth's had sold a large range of do-it-yourself items since the early 1950s: here we see the paint display. The high gondolas can be compared with the earlier design at Lydney (see Fig 7.28). [JLP01/08/085108]

Fig 7.30
The 396-seat Guildford-type cafeteria in Store 49, Leicester, dated from 1965. It was decorated with scenes of old Leicester and of hunting, 'most appropriate in this hunting county'.[f] [Courtesy of woolworths museum.co.uk, © 3D and 6D Pictures Ltd]

(see Fig 6.1). Some stores continued to have a 'Diamond Bar' rather than a cafeteria (Fig 7.31).

So many of Woolworth's stores of the late 1960s were 'built propositions' – with shells provided by the developers of large schemes – that it is hard to distinguish the company's own architectural preferences. By and large, curtain walling was falling out of fashion and Woolworth's reverted to elevations with a vertical emphasis, faintly echoing the approach of the 1930s, while favouring small windows. The Regent Street façade of the new Wrexham store, which opened in 1970, had a row of 19 close-set, frameless windows with oblong proportions (Fig 7.32). At Peterborough the high proportion of wall to window was disguised by the application of close-set vertical fins. Around the same time, standard-sized stores typically alternated brick panels with pale, rendered window bays, as at Congleton, Barry and Stourport-on-Severn, all dating from 1969, and Lichfield in 1970.

Several mammoth stores opened in the late 1960s, rivalling those in Blackpool and Birmingham. They included Huddersfield

Fig 7.32
On 12 November 1970,
Store 445 in Wrexham,
just inside the Welsh border,
moved to a new-build store.
The row of close-spaced,
part-blind, elongated
window openings without
frames – an approach
adopted widely by
Woolworth's in the late
1960s – evoked earlier
American Woolworth stores
such as Houston (1949).
While the old Wrexham
store had offered 7,600 sq ft
of sales space, the new store
had 39,700 sq ft.
[FWW01/01/0445/002]

(1967; 40,615 sq ft), Harlow (1967; 40,000 sq ft, Figs 7.33 and 7.34), Norwich (1968; 42,670 sq ft), Wolverhampton (1968; 70,456 sq ft), Croydon (1969; 42,700 sq ft), Aylesbury (1969; 69,000 sq ft) and Ipswich (1969; 56,844 sq ft). To put this in a wider context, the largest Woolworth store in the world opened in Boston, Massachusetts, in 1970 with sales floors of 133,410 sq ft and 1,000 car parking spaces.[23] By now Woolworth's had introduced a classification system based on sales turnover rather than size, the best – such as Wrexham – being designated 'Super A Class'. This lasted until 1977, when the categories changed to classes 1 to 14, relating to the amount of display space in lineal feet.

The store on The Broadwalk in the new town of Harlow occupied a large box of a building that had been planned by the Development Authority as a department store; Woolworth's took on the shell, and transformed the interior with its now-familiar blue-and-white look and laminated finishes (see Figs 7.33 and 7.34). Harlow was a seedbed for new ideas.[24] Instead of strip lighting, for example, the store had square illuminated ceiling panels, and although the 'diamond W' featured prominently on the façade, the walls of the sales floors were adorned with a new symbol, a stylised coronet in the form of a 'W', with pearls balanced atop the spikes. There was a carpeted soft goods section, a clothing department with mantle rails, a Hat Bar, a Music Shop that sold instruments as well as records, a Camera Shop, a Bath Shop and Baby Care. Most influential of all was the 132-seat restaurant on the

lower ground floor. This was luxurious when contrasted with the hard-edged Guildford-type cafés of old. Laid with a dark green carpet, it had green upholstered seating with, in the middle, round tables surrounded by chairs for family groups. This was probably the first of Woolworth's 'Harvest House' restaurants, fitted by Curtis, which endured into the early 1980s. That in Harlow was enlivened by a valance, set over the self-service bar and decorated with horses. The Harvest House in Liverpool, in 1968, was adorned with glass-fibre murals on 'Warerite' laminate, depicting harvesting scenes.[25] That in Aylesbury, in 1969, was the first licensed restaurant in the business: its 'corn stook' motif was meant to signify the agricultural importance of the town.

Wolverhampton was a collaboration between Woolworth's architect, W A Draysey, and the architects responsible for the city's Mander Centre. It trumped Harlow: with 1¼ miles of counters, this was the largest Woolworth's store in Britain. New departments here included a Wig Bar, a wallpaper department, an office equipment section, a complete demonstration kitchen, bikes and go-karts, and a Dr Scholl's Foot Health Bar.[26] The restaurant was twice the size of Harlow's. Woolworth's was now selling anything and everything. Croydon – which expanded into the Whitgift Centre in 1971 with the slogan 'It's well worth shopping at Woolworth' – sold washing machines, refrigerators and freezers, and offered a free delivery service within a 15-mile radius.[27] All of these stores had extensive Food Halls, stocked increasingly

Figs 7.33 and 7.34 Store 990 in Harlow: the innovative fabric department and the Food Hall. [Courtesy of woolworths museum.co.uk, © 3D and 6D Pictures Ltd]

169

with chilled and frozen, as well as fresh and canned, foods.

The spiky coronet that appeared at Harlow (*see* Fig 7.33) can be seen in photographs of several stores around 1968. It may have been a short-lived experiment, for in Woolworth's Diamond Jubilee year, 1969, it was dropped in favour of a different 'corporate symbol' which wholly superseded the old 'diamond W'. This looping 'W' was a reworking of the 1959 basket logo, and was often referred to as the Winfield logo. It was produced by the Graphic Design and Packaging Department of Woolworth's, probably by the senior designer B Fox.[28] In the early 1970s it began to appear on company documentation, on the exterior of stores and on own-label packaging.

The advent of Woolco

Out-of-town hypermarkets and malls were multiplying throughout North America by the early 1960s. They pandered to customers with private cars who wanted to shop in bulk, perhaps just once a week, ideally paying with a credit card and storing foodstuffs in a fridge or freezer to prolong their life. American Woolworth invested heavily in this phenomenon, setting up its first out-of-town Woolco store in Columbus, Ohio, in 1962, rivalling S S Kresge's K Mart stores. The Woolco chain expanded rapidly throughout North America, with 67 stores by 1967 and 300 by the mid-1970s. As Woolco grew, Woolworth executives began to neglect their established

Fig 7.35
Boys playing outside
Woolco, Thornaby (Store
2002), on 19 August 1968.
One boy points out the
tyre bay.
[JLP01/08/079168]

downtown variety stores, firmly believing that the growth demanded by their shareholders would be delivered, in future, by the out-of-town hypermarkets.

British shoppers had become familiar with town-centre shopping precincts and malls by the mid-1960s, but they were still not fully prepared for the arrival of out-of-town shopping. Although 40 per cent of households now owned a car, the very idea of shopping outside urban centres was alien. Even grocery shopping was still a purely urban activity. Buying food in bulk was impractical for most people: just 47 per cent of households had a fridge, and as late as 1973 only 6 per cent owned a freezer.

American Woolworth nevertheless pressed its British subsidiary to steal a march on its rivals by spearheading out-of-town shopping. Consequently, in 1966 the decision was taken to establish a Woolco 'check-out department store' chain in Britain. There was reason to question the wisdom of this step. Recent experiments in off-centre shopping, though they were not numerous, had mixed results. An American company named GEM had set up out-of-town 'supercentres' near Nottingham and Leeds in 1964, and Asda (Associated Dairies) had opened a superstore near Wakefield in 1965.[29] GEM struggled for a couple of years, battling both planning restrictions and the 'innate conservative outlook' of English shoppers and traders, before giving up and selling its supercentres to Asda.[30]

It was evident that while some car-borne British shoppers were prepared to undertake their weekly food shopping at a superstore like Asda, they still preferred to buy non-food items on the high street. Nevertheless, Richard Evans, the newly appointed General Manager of the Woolco Division, made several trips to America to study the Woolco stores there.[31] Before long Woolworth's was building its first 'Woolco Department Store' at Oadby, near Leicester. Essentially a large single-storey shed, with a flat roof and ribbed steel cladding, this utterly functional building was designed by S Penn-Smith, Son & Partners, under the auspices of Woolworth's construction superintendent, L V Fox.[32] As far as the choice of site was concerned, accessibility by road – in this case the A6 and M1 – was critical. Oadby had a potentially large customer catchment area, regarded as a 15-mile radius encompassing much of the east Midlands, and the surrounding car park was laid out optimistically with 800 spaces. Due to lack of space, this was arranged on two tiers connected by a ramp.

With the opening of the Oadby Woolco on 10 October 1967, Woolworth's initiated a new numerical store sequence: this became Store 2001. Customers parked their cars and entered the industrial-looking building through a brightly lit portal, positioned beneath six red squares spelling out the name 'WOOLCO'. At the time, 'Woolco' meant little to British shoppers. For decades this had been the brand name for products – mainly haberdashery – in America, but not in Britain.[33] To add interest, Woolco's long windowless façade was punctuated by bold panels of abstract, geometric design. The interior comprised a vast air-conditioned and artificially lit sales area of 64,000 sq ft. The centre, comprising 55 per cent of the space, was taken up by a gargantuan self-service version of a Woolworth's store selling a wide range of products, including food, furniture, clothing and white goods. Customers used wheeled trolleys (rather than the wire baskets they had become accustomed to in urban supermarkets), and could avail themselves of a Woolco credit card. There was a Red Grill restaurant and, around the edges of the 'mass display central checkout unit', concessions such as a butcher's shop and a Dixons outlet. In addition, there was a tyre bay.

Woolworth's high street rivals did not rush to move away from the high street. Marks & Spencer's, Boots, C&A and others took a cautious stance, watching with interest as Woolworth's and the large supermarket chains – Asda, Tesco, Carrefour and eventually Sainsbury's – persevered with the construction of ever-larger units through the late 1960s and early-to-mid-1970s. In 1967, Woolworth's executives hoped to open another 20 Woolco outlets, but progress was slow. Just two opened in 1968, occupying large units in pioneering off-centre shopping centres. Store 2002 at Thornaby-on-Tees (Figs 7.35–7.38) had a sales area of 68,000 sq ft and was served by 900 parking spaces. This development was initiated by the Thornaby-on-Tees Corporation, and the unit was designed by Elder, Lester & Partners for Woolworth's.[34] Store 2003 occupied a unit in The Hampshire Centre (otherwise known as Castlepoint, Fig 7.39), Bournemouth, a shopping centre designed by Lionel E Gregory of Poole for the developer Second Covent Garden Properties Ltd. An

innovation here in 1969 was a 'super money box', or cash dispenser, which allowed National Westminster Bank customers to withdraw £10; this may have been the first such service in a retail store. In the late 1960s plans for further Woolco stores came unstuck as applications were turned down by local authorities: West Riding, for example, rejected plans for a Woolco at Swallownest, Sheffield, in 1969. As a result, Woolworth's was sometimes lumbered with land which it had purchased and could not, subsequently, develop.

Fig 7.36 (top)
Woolco, Thornaby, 19 August 1968: mannequins in the clothing department. [JLP01/08/079174]

Fig 7.37 (above)
Woolco, Thornaby, 19 August 1968: the Red Grill, which featured in all Woolco stores. [JLP01/08/079184]

Fig 7.38
Woolco, Thornaby, 19
August 1968: checkouts.
[JLP01/08/079183]

Fig 7.39
The opening of Woolco
at Bournemouth (Store
2003) in 1968.
[FWW01/01/0054/003]

The sleeping giant of the high street, 1970–1982

Reversing fortunes

Woolworth's profits grew year on year after the war, until 1966, when they entered a downward trajectory. Executives faced increasing dissatisfaction from shareholders, and from their American masters, who maintained a keen interest in their subsidiary's performance. Meanwhile, British shoppers still cherished the high street red-fronts. In 1970 these numbered 1,131, employed around 90,000 people, and remained, by most standards, extremely profitable.

Saturation point, however, had been reached. Not only did new openings grind to a halt, but management began to weed out under-performing stores – four had already closed in 1969 – while continuing to modernise the remainder.[1] In the quest for long-term growth, the board increasingly pinned its hopes on spin-off formats such as Woolco, and on the expanding overseas operation. Additional stores opened in the West Indies, and in Nicosia, Cyprus (built 1973–8),[2] but ambitions to open in Western Europe were thwarted. New ventures required heavy investment. Large loans were taken out, but a ready source of capital lay to hand in the hundreds of freehold and leasehold stores owned by the company. The inherent value of the high street chain was, ultimately, to prove its downfall.

Ernest Lionel Gorst ('Bill') Medcalf (Chairman, 1969–73) believed in the potential of Woolco, planning a further 18 outlets, while declaring that 200 of the high street stores were 'old fashioned'.[3] A study initiated in 1970 identified towns in which Woolworth's had two stores, such as Southampton (Stores 24 and 128), Croydon (Stores 12 and 234) and Stevenage (Stores 747 and 1008), where they could consolidate in the best location. In addition, unprofitable branches were targeted for closure. Around 57 stores had closed by the end of 1972.[4] While most of these were in suburbs, they included some long-established city-centre stores, notably Union Street in Glasgow, Deansgate in Manchester and King's Road in London. Seeking alternative ways of raising capital from Woolworth's rich property portfolio, Medcalf began to discuss sale-and-leaseback arrangements with property companies, and decided to create rentable office space over some stores, starting with a pilot development at High Wycombe. The redevelopment potential of several extremely valuable London sites was explored: the store on Cheapside was sold to make way for an office block, but no buyer was found immediately for the large branches on Kensington High Street and Oxford Street (near Oxford Circus; Store 161).[5] A few years later, in October 1977, Woolworth's announced that the store at the east end of Oxford Street (Store 463) had been acquired by developers for conversion to the Oxford Walk shopping centre.[6]

Meanwhile, the character of the high street stores was in the throes of dramatic change. The imminent arrival of decimalisation accelerated the implementation of self-service. 'Cash and wrap' – with sales girls presiding over large sales desks, as in Marks & Spencer's stores, rather than seated at individual checkouts by the exit, in supermarket fashion – was tried out in 100 food departments in 1970 before being introduced to 777 stores (rather than the 560 originally envisaged) by the end of 1971 (Figs 8.1–8.3).[7] The smallest stores had a simpler self-service system, with three or four checkout points close to the exit. The so-called 'crash conversion programme' was piloted in 1970 at Pinner in north-west London, which closed for just four days for transformation to self-service: 54 stores had been converted in this manner by August 1971.[8] Crash conversion involved compromises and economies,

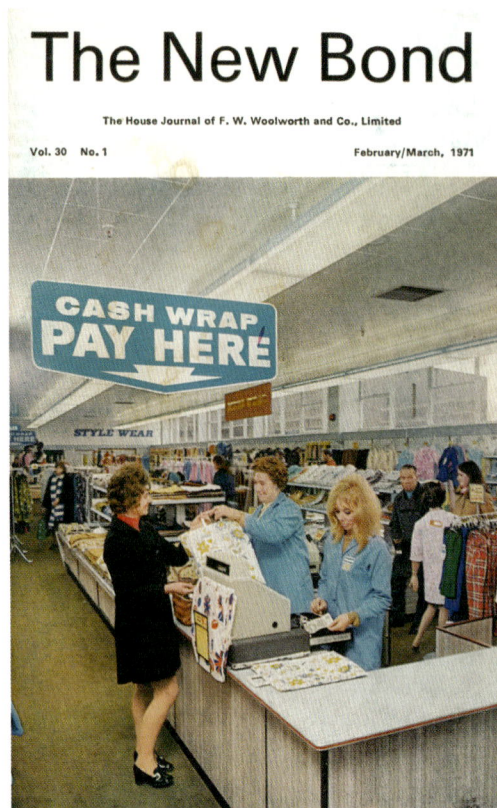

The New Bond

The House Journal of F. W. Woolworth and Co., Limited

Vol. 30   No. 1   February/March, 1971

Fig 8.1
A 'cash and wrap' counter at Store 107, Basingstoke, illustrated on the cover of The New Bond, **30,** *1, February/March 1971. This branch had relocated on 23 October 1970 from its old premises at Nos 5–7 London Street to Nos 1–13 Chiswick House in the town's new shopping precinct.*
[Author's collection]

recycling old fittings alongside the introduction of modern shelving supplied by Chromesh Ltd.

The main driver for change was the need to replace every till in the chain. Woolworth's was the country's largest user of cash registers and had thus been compelled to formulate plans for Britain's conversion to decimal currency several years ahead of the event.[9] The process of equipping stores with dual-currency cash registers began in 1968 and was completed in phases leading up to conversion in 1971. The expense of over £1 million was borne entirely by the company, since no government compensation was forthcoming. In parallel with this, however, some saving was made through the adoption of self-service. Not only did the number of tills fall, but the headcount dropped from 90,000 to approximately 70,000 by 1975, and to just 52,000 (or 37,000 full-time equivalents) by 1982. In a publicity stunt that signalled the enormity of the impact of decimalisation on Woolworth's, Lord Fiske, Chairman of the Decimal Currency Board, chose to go 'decimal shopping' at the Strand branch on the morning of the switchover, on 15 February 1971 (Fig 8.4).[10]

Fig 8.2
Customers wait to enter the new-look Store 405 in Andover, in 1972. The sign hanging outside informs them: 'New! Shopping made easy with cash-wrap service'.
[FWW01/01/0405/001]

Fig 8.3
A bright red 'cash and wrap'
desk in Store 59, Belfast,
September 1978.
[JLP01/10/05738]

Conversion to self-service triggered nostalgia for Woolworth's old interiors. When the Museum of London was being planned in 1971, just as Woolworth's was transforming its stores, the Assistant Keeper Colin Sorensen acquired a mahogany counter, shelving, floorboards and other items dating from 1937–8, from the North Cheam and Whetstone branches.[11] He explained: 'I wanted a tiny slice of the original Woolworth's to be shown, to illustrate what the stores were like. So much is lost or destroyed with today's rapid changes and advanced technology, that people tend to forget or don't know what went before.'[12] Sorensen issued a call to Woolworth's staff for donations of pre-war merchandise,[13] and a fully stocked counter

Fig 8.4
Lord Fiske 'decimal shopping'
(for Imperial Leather soap)
at Woolworth's Store 188,
the Strand, London, on
15 February 1971. All items
were dual-priced in both
old and new money between
August 1970 and August
1971.[a]
[George S Hales/Getty
Images]

Fig 8.5
In 1971 the Museum of London acquired fixtures and fittings from Woolworth's, to recreate an old-style store in miniature. The wooden counter dated from c 1936 and was of standard type: 8ft long and 3ft 6ins deep, stained mahogany red, with decorative scroll brackets and an understock cupboard to the rear. Glass and wood counter dividers and price signs were also acquired, as well as gas ceiling lamps, lampshades advertising 'roasted nuts', and scoops and balance scales for weighing loose confectionery.
[© Museum of London]

formed a permanent display when the museum opened on the Barbican Estate in December 1976 (Fig 8.5). By then, every Woolworth's store in the country had been converted to self-service: the last being Stone, Staffordshire, in 1975.[14] As Sorensen clearly realised, the extreme makeover undergone in the course of conversion to self-service stripped the quintessential character from Woolworth's premises; the atmosphere was lost, along with the familiar soapy smell and the bustling conviviality of the counters, qualities which could not be recaptured in any museum display, no matter how authentic.

Stephen J Owen, who took over as Chairman in 1973, had to contend with particularly harsh trading conditions. Woolworth's faced intense competition from supermarkets like Tesco and Asda and, like all retailers, had to deal with rampant inflation, the introduction of VAT and the three-day week, brought in to conserve energy during the miners' strike of 1974. Overheads such as wages were higher than ever before. At the same time, Woolworth's advertising budget expanded, although commercials featuring particular products were 50 per cent funded by manufacturers or suppliers. From 1975 until 1977, adverts used the memorable slogan 'the Wonder of Woolworth'. But despite the best efforts of the PR agents, Allen Brady & Marsh, Woolworth's

performance remained lacklustre, especially compared with the remarkable progress of its former arch-rival, Marks & Spencer's, which had been warmly embraced by the expanding middle class.

The range of goods on sale had become all-encompassing since the abandonment of fixed prices, but now began to contract. Medcalf eliminated goods with low profit margins, such as cut-price cigarettes, handkerchiefs and cheap jewellery. By the mid-1970s the main lines were clothing, household textiles, gardening, audio and records/cassettes, furniture, leisure/DIY (Fig 8.6) and fresh food.[15] It had been a decade since the Windsor experiment (*see* p 154), but now purpose-built garden centres were established next to several stores (*see* Fig 4.14). Woolworth's was still the country's leading retailer in fields such as music and confectionery. Haberdashery was a particular strength: the largest stores sold fabric from rolls, and from 1971 the company published a popular knitting and crocheting magazine. New items that appeared on shelves in the course of the decade included electronic calculators and portable televisions.

Food, despite its slender margins and limited shelf life, had become vitally important to Woolworth's since the war. This came under severe threat in June 1977, when Tesco, at that time a chain of 730 supermarkets, launched a drastic price-cutting war following its abandonment of Green Shield trading stamps. Unable to compete, Woolworth's chose to refocus on items with a higher profit margin. Toiletries were also affected by supermarket price-cutting, but cheap cosmetics such as Evette remained popular.

By the mid-1970s, full-time sales assistants earned around £27.50 a week, or £29 in city centre stores. The gender profile of Woolworth's employees was still polarised, with only five female store managers in 1974. But in October 1975 Woolworth's appointed its first ever female director, Pat Downs, the Personnel Director.[16] Several female buyers were also recruited in the 1970s.

Woolworth's up-to-date distribution network was sorely tested on 6 May 1971, when fire broke out in the Castleton warehouse, prompting a frantic dash to save the records

and IT equipment (see Fig 7.8), and causing millions of pounds of damage.[17] Shortly before this calamity, the company had commissioned a second distribution centre of 430,000 sq ft on the Dorcan Industrial Estate, Swindon, to service 650 stores south of Birmingham. This opened in July 1972, and the Castleton facility, rebuilt to a design by the Lyons Group, reopened in 1974.[18] Whereas Castleton – which handled stock for the north of England, Scotland, Ireland and the Isle of Man – had originally made use of the railway system, from 1974 both centres relied on road haulage. Stock was distributed by a fleet of lorries operated by National Carriers Ltd, with trailers painted in Woolworth's bright red livery. Following a report from consultants PW International, who mapped Woolworth's 300 suppliers, four transhipment centres opened in June 1978: at Radlett (Herts), Patchway (Bristol), Warrington

Fig 8.6
Houseproud, Beaconsfield (Store 972), opened on 26 October 1973. Woolworth's had developed a strong reputation for DIY products and trialled this specialist format in 1973. The yellow corrugated plastic fascia was set with white letters and the Winfield logo. No further branches appear to have opened.
[FWW01/01/0972/001]

another major new initiative was introduced in response to the establishment of Argos, originally conceived as Green Shield Stamps catalogue shops. Woolworth's began to plan a chain called 'Shoppers World', based on the 'Woolco Catalogue Stores' operating in Canada. While Argos was based largely in the south, Shoppers World deliberately concentrated on the Midlands and the North.[20] The first opened in the Merrion Centre in Leeds, in September 1974, and was given the store number 4001. Lettering on shopfronts was lower case and italicised, preceded by a large scrolled 'S', but this was superseded by new blocky lettering in 1979. In the first year, 14 Shoppers World outlets were converted from existing Woolworth's stores. Eventually there were 28 free-standing Shoppers World stores, plus 17 in Woolworth's stores (Figs 8.7 and 8.8), all served by a distribution warehouse at Heywood, Lancashire. Another spin-off formula followed the purchase, by American Woolworth in 1975, of Footlocker. In the late 1970s and early 1980s four experimental Footlocker shoe shops, with the sequence 3001 onwards, opened in shopping centres in Tamworth, Birmingham, Chester and Wolverhampton.

Nine Woolco stores had opened by 1975, and two more were in the pipeline. The process of opening these hypermarkets had been painfully slow and laborious due to difficulties in obtaining planning permission from local

Fig 8.7
Store 968 opened in a parade designed by T P Bennett & Son at Nos 138–142 Queensway, Paddington, London, in 1957.[b] This stood opposite Whiteley's department store. Part of the store was converted into a Shoppers World, Store 4030, around 1979, with shopfitting carried out by Curtis. [FWW01/01/0968/001]

(Cheshire) and Cumbernauld (Scotland). Each had a conveyor system enabling goods, now carrying new-fangled bar codes, to be moved in and out quickly rather than warehoused for long periods.

The opening of the Swindon warehouse was followed, in September 1972, by the launch of 'Woolworth by Post'. Though catalogues were not produced, newspaper advertisements listed goods that could be ordered from Swindon.[19] This was discontinued a year later, when

Fig 8.8
The interior of Shoppers World, Queensway. This included displays of goods, catalogue stands, a counter for payment and collection, and a vast stockroom. [FWW01/01/0968/002]

authorities who, quite rightly, foresaw the devastating effect that such developments would have on their high streets.[21] Thus most Woolcos opened in new, expanded or overspill towns, such as Killingworth to the north of Newcastle (1970), Middleton to the north-east of Manchester (1971), Hatfield in Hertfordshire (1972) and Washington near Sunderland (1973). The last of the Woolco outlets, and one of the most successful, opened in June 1976 at Newtownards in Northern Ireland, nine miles from Belfast. Designated Store 2014, this was an experimental Woolco Hypermarket. Built at a cost of £1.25 million as an anchor tenant in the Ards Shopping Centre, it featured 24 checkouts, 900 trolleys, unusually high gondolas, wide aisles and even, in an arrangement with Esso, a petrol filling station with the Woolco fascia edging the canopy. This Woolco Hypermarket remained very profitable, right up to the sale of the chain in 1986,[22] quite a turnaround for Ireland which, at the height of the Troubles in the early 1970s, had struggled to contribute to company profits.[23] By December 1977, however, there were signs that Woolworth's managers had lost faith in Woolco. It was announced that the Greater Lancastrian Co-operative Society would take over two Woolco sites: one at Kirkby on Merseyside, which closed in January 1978; the other a site with planning permission in Blackpool.[24] An experimental 'Savermarket' opened at Kings Heath, Birmingham (in the former Store 554) in March 1978: half was devoted to food, the remainder to a combination of Woolco and Shoppers World. Plans were laid for a Woolco at Tallaght, Dublin, in 1980, but no further outlets ever opened.[25]

Facing adversity

At the beginning of the 1970s, Woolworth's operated 41 Irish stores: 23 in the south and 18 in the north. In circumstances reminiscent of the early 1920s, the Troubles caused great disruption, with staff ever alert for incendiary devices. Barbara Walsh, the historian of Irish Woolworth's, has recounted the appalling statistic that 'No Woolworth store in Ulster escaped an attack at one time or another'.[26] Woolworth's Construction Department was kept busy, refurbishing or rebuilding damaged stores. The Bangor store, for instance, had to be completely rebuilt after a device exploded on

the sales floor on 30 March 1974; fortunately a warning was given and the store had been evacuated. The flagship Belfast store (*see* Figs 3.49 and 4.20) was badly damaged by fire when devices exploded in April 1974 and January 1976. On 3 May 1976 a 200lb car bomb in the garrison town of Lisburn (*see* Fig 8.21) wrecked Woolworth's. Although compensation was available for such events, some sites, such as Omagh and Belfast North Street, were simply abandoned. Tipperary closed for different reasons in 1977: the façade had been undermined by recent shopfitting and would cost too much to repair.[27] The premises soon reopened under the name Wellworths, much to the annoyance of the Moore brothers, whose stores traded under the same name. Having assumed the name of a retailer that had, itself, imitated Woolworth's branding, Tipperary's Wellworths thrived in the hands of Woolworth's former manager and sales staff.

The single most traumatic experience for Woolworth's in the post-war period happened not in Ireland, but in Manchester, where a serious fire caused 10 deaths on Tuesday 8 May 1979 (Fig 8.9). Store 4 (*see* Fig 3.26) had been modernised in 1967–70 and was reopened, like so many others, by one of Woolworth's favourite celebrities, the 'Opportunity Knocks' TV host Hughie Green. It had four vast sales floors connected by escalators, and included a 208-seat Harvest House restaurant on the second floor, with prints of old Manchester adorning the walls. Astonishingly, it had no smoke

Fig 8.9
A devastating fire claimed 10 lives at Store 4, Manchester, in May 1979. This shows the damaged building in the aftermath, on 15 August 1979 (compare Fig 3.26). Other Woolworth's stores affected by fire included Colchester and Faversham in 1973, both possible victims of arson attacks,[c] North Finchley in 1977 and Worcester in 1979. [JLP01/10/06600]

detectors or sprinkler system. When fire broke out in the furniture department next to the restaurant (compare with Fig 8.10), staff did not immediately raise the alarm and it was left to passers-by to phone the fire brigade. Those trapped were rescued with difficulty through the barred windows of the second-floor offices and from the roof. Most of the victims were

found just outside the restaurant at the head of a staircase, where they had been blinded and overwhelmed by dense toxic fumes from polyurethane foam sofas.[28] Woolworth's reputation suffered a terrible setback.

The Manchester fire, which led to new regulations regarding furnishings, did not deter Woolworth's from selling furniture. Plans for a 'furniture centre' had already been drawn up by Doug Hardy, and the first in a new chain of furniture superstores, 'Furnishing World' (Fig 8.11), opened in Southampton as Store 2101 in June 1980. Nine more openings were planned in 1980–1, but in the event only five opened.[29] These beige, brown and red sheds were located on a single level close to car parks. The company also began to plan stand-alone DIY and garden centres. Designs were prepared for 'DIY World' (Fig 8.12), including a detailed scheme for Forstal Road, Aylesham, and the first was set to open in Hull in summer 1980.[30] Ideally, these would stand next to Furnishing World, with 25,000 sq ft allocated to DIY and 10,000 sq ft to gardening, in addition to a petrol filling station, car parking, a play area and a restaurant. However, everything changed just weeks later, when Woolworth's bought a ready-made DIY chain from B&Q (see p 186).

Fig 8.11 (right)
The livery of Woolworth's
new spin-off chain,
Furnishing World, which
was launched in 1980. The
fifth and last branch, Store
2105, opened in December
1982 in Gillingham,
next to B&Q and MFI.
[FWW01/02/2104/001]

Fig 8.12
George Reid's 1976 design
for 'DIY World' – a standard
retail warehouse of portal-
frame construction with a
corrugated asbestos roof –
a highly developed concept
that was scuppered by the
purchase of B&Q in 1980.
[FWW01/02/9999/001]

Store buildings in the 1970s

The 1970s was a time of transition in British retailing. Shops were just beginning to shift away from urban centres into edge-of-town malls, such as Weston Favell in Northamptonshire and Brent Cross in north London. Additionally, off-centre supermarkets became increasingly common as people adopted the habit of driving to the shops and buying foodstuffs in bulk. Urban shopping centres continued to be erected on a large scale, notable examples being Eldon Square in Newcastle, the Arndale Centre in Manchester and the sleek modernist mall in the new town of Milton Keynes. By and large, however, faith in modernism was crumbling and a new traditionalism took hold. By the middle of the decade, new commercial buildings often assumed a rather brooding character, dominated by dark red or brown brickwork, smoky tinted windows and pitched (though often fake) roofs. Arches and other Classical elements crept back, somewhat apologetically, into architectural designs (Fig 8.13). Alongside this, however, an industrial warehouse aesthetic prevailed, usually involving the cheapest permissible forms of construction and cladding, and sometimes exposing structural elements externally in a nod to the emergent high-tech style.

Doug Hardy remained Woolworth's architect throughout the 1970s, with George Reid as his deputy.[31] In the course of the decade, this team worked on a mere handful of new branches: Kingswinford, Dudley (1970), Chelmsley Wood, Birmingham (1971), Swanley (1971), Linwood (1971) and Belle Vale, Liverpool (1973). They installed Store 1139, the last new opening of the decade, in Milton Keynes Shopping Centre in 1979. In addition, they oversaw the extension and relocation of many older branches (Figs 8.14 and 8.15), usually into covered shopping centres, as at Luton, Basingstoke, Exeter and Derby, and they rebuilt several after fires. But, by and large, the department's workload must have significantly reduced once the modernisation programme associated with the self-service rollout (see pp 173–4) was complete.

New standard-sized stores usually had undemanding vertical-pane frontages, typically alternating panels of brickwork with rendered 'Sandtex' panels containing aluminium-frame windows (see Fig 9.22). The façades of larger stores, such as Hanley and Barnsley (Fig 8.16), often adopted similar vertical panes, but deployed a wider variety of materials, colours and textures. Some abandoned windows altogether (Figs 8.17–8.19). At a practical level, windowless fronts were ideal for Woolworth's

Fig 8.13
Store 317 in Wellingborough had a typical vertical-panel front, but with the addition of miniscule arches at the top: a tentative postmodern touch. Note the new-style fascia and logo, the recessed 'arcade' shopfront and the 'Hartlepool' doors. This photograph probably dates from around 1977. [FWW01/01/0317/002]

Fig 8.14
The Chippenham store, Store 493, opened after rebuilding in 1975. For its predecessor, see Fig 4.78. The architectural press considered that this bland building restored the 'geometric integrity' of the street, but noted disparagingly, 'It could be anywhere.'[d] The reopening here was attended by Anne Aston of TV's The Golden Shot. This photograph was taken during the last few weeks of trading in 2008. [DP025261]

Fig 8.15
Store 473 moved to Nos 44–48 High Street, Maldon, Essex, in 1971. The unusual design – with a bronze shopfront, slate mansard roof and mahogany window frames – was supposedly produced 'to comply with planning requirements of a Conservation Area'.[e] Posters advertised its opening on 12 August by Miss England. At this time, Woolworth's was a joint sponsor of the Miss England, Miss Scotland and Miss Wales beauty contests. Other sponsorship deals involved rally cars, the Great Britain II (an entrant in the Transatlantic Tall Ships Race of 1976) and the European Community Youth Orchestra. [FWW01/01/0473/001 Keith Yuill Photographic]

181

Fig 8.16
Store 360 in Barnsley was enlarged and rebuilt in 1971–3, occupying most of a triangular site. The Queen Street elevation, shown here, had fibreglass cladding panels set on a black brick background. The elevation to Eldon Street was more conventional.
[FWW01/01/0360/002]

Fig 8.17
Store 322 relocated to a new shopping centre in Hartlepool on 26 February 1970. The shell of the building was erected by Costain's and adapted by Woolworth's.ʃ Its blind elevation was relieved solely by a gigantic 'W', prefiguring the 'Big W' format of 1999 (see Fig 9.19). The doors were a new type, with a red 'W' symbol on the horizontal push bar, henceforth known as 'Hartlepool doors'.
[FWW01/01/0322/001]

Fig 8.18
Store 138 in Gillingham opened on 25 November 1971. The industrial-style façade – flanked by much older and more traditional buildings on the High Street – was of 'vulcaplast reinforced plastic panels' set with yellow illuminated letters, 2ft high. Stores such as this – as ever, constructed with Truscon floors and steelwork by Banister Walton – represent the nadir of Woolworth's high street building programme. Note the new logo, stuck onto the glass of the doors. [FWW01/01/0138/001]

Fig 8.19
Store 70 in Walthamstow, north London, opened on 15 June 1972. The frontage was clad in light and dark grey striped aluminium panels set with individual box letters. In retrospect, it is obvious that such designs were more suited to industrial parks than urban shopping streets. The windows display an intriguing mixture of popular art, plastic buckets and musical instruments. [FWW01/01/0070/001]

favoured arrangement of first-floor stockrooms, which did not require much natural light. Around 1970, many air-conditioned stores with blind elevations were built on shopping streets, not just by Woolworth's, but by other large chains, such as Littlewood's, C&A and BHS. Emulating out-of-town American stores of the 1950s, these buildings had a disastrous impact on the character of many provincial high streets, leaving a problematic legacy for future generations.

Shopfronts continued to evolve (Fig 8.20). Around 1970 Woolworth's began to clad pilasters and external structural piers in white oblong tiles supplied by Langley's and laid in soldier stack bond. Such tiling was common on retail developments through the late 1960s and early 1970s, most famously on the façade of Manchester's Arndale Centre, once described as 'the longest lavatory wall in Europe'.[32] Fascias were normally of mosaic tiles, Stelvetite (plastic-coated steel, usually white) or fibreglass. Towards the end of 1971, the oversized red or yellow Egyptian-style lettering that had been favoured since 1965 was abandoned, and new italicised sans serif letters – either white on a bright red ground, or vice versa – were substituted. This was

accompanied by the looping 'W', usually known as the Winfield logo, which had first appeared on packaging and company documentation in 1969. Replacing the 'diamond W', it adorned fascias, projecting signs and, by 1973, the push plates of a new design of stainless steel doors, referred to as 'Hartlepool doors' (see Fig 8.17). It was not represented in the tiles of lobby floors, which were now plain. The new red-and-white look was not imposed on the entire portfolio, just on new and remodelled stores, and so many outlets continued to display older forms of lettering, sometimes with the obsolete 'diamond W', for years to come. The new look changed little before the mid-1980s, but from around 1976 fascias were made of reinforced plastic sheeting called Duraform (Fig 8.21). By 1982, over 120 Woolworth's stores had been fitted with Duraform fascias in 'Woolworth Red' with a matt finish.[33] Among them was the hugely extended branch in the new St David's Centre, Cardiff (1979–82).

Woolworth's sales areas had been brought up to date, as described above (see pp 173–4), in the late 1960s and early 1970s. As the decade progressed, Woolworth's catering operation also changed dramatically (Fig 8.22). The introduction of ready-prepared food meant

Fig 8.20
A new-look Woolworth's shopfront being fitted at Store 535, Dovercourt, Harwich, in the 1970s. This store, with its unusual channelled rustication, was built in 1934 and extended in 1937 by the local contractor Percy H Hawkins. [FWW01/01/0535/001]

Fig 8.21
Store 343 in Bow Street, Lisburn, Northern Ireland – which had been rebuilt on an enlarged footprint in 1966 but was badly damaged by a bomb in 1976 – repaired and fitted out with one of Woolworth's new Duraform fascias in 1977.
[FWW01/01/0343/001]

Fig 8.22
This cafeteria opened in Store 29, Derby, when it relocated to the Eagle Centre (now Westfield Derby) in 1975. With their carpets and plush leatherette seats, Woolworth's restaurants had become more comfortable and welcoming (compare Fig 7.30). The warm orange-brown colour scheme and boldly patterned walls were typical of the mid-1970s, and the air of intimacy was enhanced by the lighting: individual lamps hanging over the tables and spotlights set into the suspended ceiling. Most of Woolworth's cafés and takeaway units were fitted by Curtis of Leeds.
[FWW01/01/0029/003]

185

that vast, labour-intensive kitchens were no longer required. By 1977, out of 47 restaurants, just 5 retained their own bakery. The old tea bars vanished, though a 'Diamond Bar' installed in Jersey in 1966 remained a talking point into the 1980s. By and large, the tea bars were replaced by takeaway units, such as 'Kwik Snax', which opened in Kingston upon Thames after refurbishment in 1972. By 1977 there were 120 similar takeaways.[34] One of the last Harvest House restaurants opened in Leamington in 1980. In the early 1980s they seem to have been superseded by restaurants named 'Maxi', for example in Reading and Wolverhampton, but these were short-lived.

The B&Q venture

Geoffrey Rodgers, who succeeded Stephen Owen as Chairman of Woolworth's in November 1979, was keen to build up a DIY division. Previously, Woolworth's had diversified by starting up new businesses, such as Woolco and Shoppers World. Rodgers fully intended to develop a new chain of DIY stores (*see* p 180), but an approach from B&Q changed his mind. Founded as Block & Quayle in Southampton in 1969, B&Q had built up a chain of 33 stores, which was purchased by Woolworth's in August 1980 for £16.7 million.[35] The acquisition of a mature business was a new departure for the company. American Woolworth, on the other hand, had experience in this area, having acquired the shoe manufacturer and retailer G R Kinney in 1963, the menswear chain Richman Brothers in 1969 and Footlocker in 1975. Yet another

purchase made by British Woolworth's in November 1980 was Dodge City, a chain of 32 DIY stores in the north-east and Wales. Costing £20.1 million, these were added to the B&Q chain.

The hugely expensive purchases of B&Q and Dodge City were funded by the sale of six large Woolworth's stores, including Princes Street, Edinburgh (for £11.5 million), Cornmarket, Oxford (for £11 million) and High Street, Bromley (for £4.5 million).[36] By April 1982, 23 additional stores – including the flagship superstores in Blackpool, Dublin, Manchester, Nottingham, Leeds, London and Liverpool – were up for sale with a combined price tag of £90 million.[37] Rodgers explained: 'All the stores are profitable … But they are not providing a satisfactory return on investment and we can use the funds more effectively elsewhere.'[38] In addition, the Kensington Regional Office closed and the rolling refurbishment programme for high street stores was curtailed. If there was any doubt that B&Q was the top priority, that was answered by the watering down of lucrative DIY lines in the 960 high street stores, opening up the market for B&Q. Some effort to revitalise high street sales was made with 'Crackdown', a year-long price-cutting campaign starting in February 1981, but this had little effect. In May 1982 two American executives were despatched to London to join the British board. Ostensibly this was to help the company resolve its problems – one of the Americans, John Sullivan, was cast in the role of chairman designate. But it soon became apparent that these men had a hidden agenda. Within months, the American parent had sold its offspring.

9

After the divorce, 1982–2009

America sells up

In the centenary year of Woolworth, 1979, the Canadian Brascan Corporation launched a £550 million takeover bid for the company. Although this proved unsuccessful, it highlighted the vulnerability of Woolworth. The American parent still owned 52.7 per cent of British Woolworth's, but was deeply in debt. Crucially, loans taken out to fund expansion after the Second World War were due for repayment.[1]

A solution was found in October 1982, when the company's full shareholding in British Woolworth's was sold to Paternoster Stores plc, a consortium of around 30 City institutions, masterminded by the merchant bank Charterhouse Japhet (address: Paternoster Square, London). Costing £310 million – although the value of Woolworth's store property alone was around £500 million – this was one of the biggest retail takeovers to date in Britain, and one of the first management buy-ins.[2] The board of directors was replaced and John Beckett stepped in as Chairman. Formerly of British Sugar, Beckett, like most of his colleagues, had limited retail experience.[3]

One of Beckett's first acts was to restructure, creating eight small regional offices accommodated over stores or at the Executive Office. The four regional Construction Departments were merged into a single Architects' Department, based in London under the Company Architect, George Reid (Fig 9.1), who had taken over from Doug Hardy in 1980. Inevitably, this entailed many redundancies, mainly affecting construction staff in Liverpool and Birmingham. Before long the new department was split to create a separate Planning and Fixtures Department, headed by newly recruited ('non-Woolworth's') employees.[4]

Fig 9.1
George Reid had been Doug Hardy's deputy for many years, before taking over as Woolworth's Chief Architect from 1980 until around 1988, a period when few new stores were built. This photograph dates from 1979.
[Author's collection]

Disposing of its British subsidiary was not enough to save American Woolworth in the long term, though it struggled on for a further 17 years. Shortly after the British sale, the loss-making US Woolco division closed, but Canadian Woolco kept going until 1994, when the stores were sold to Wal-Mart. After 1982, Woolworth concentrated on its speciality shops, especially its shoe shops. The variety stores shrank in number and lost money. Briefly, in 1996, a modern F W Woolworth & Co format was tested in three stores.[5] It was even suggested that Woolworth might revert to the old counter layout, with vintage decor, to appeal to customers' nostalgia.[6] But this came to nothing. The closure of the last remaining 400 or so red fronts, primarily in Woolworth's original heartland of New York City, was announced in July 1997. A year later, the F W Woolworth Corporation was reinvented as the Venator Group (later Foot Locker) and the Woolworth Building in New York was sold for $137.5 million.[7] At that time Woolworth's was still a ubiquitous presence on British shopping streets.

Property disposal

Woolworth's was Britain's fifth top retailer when it was cut adrift by its American parent in 1982, but its 955 or so stores had fared poorly in recent years. Pre-tax profits had tumbled from £46.5 million in 1978 to £22.1 million in 1981 and £6.1 million in 1982.[8] Paternoster, swiftly renamed Woolworth Holdings plc, declared that it would take seven years to turn business around. It had assumed control in the midst of Geoffrey Rodgers' ambitious sale-and-closure programme. Of 26 stores put on the market in March 1982, five had been sold by November, and negotiations were under way regarding the superstores in Guildford, Liverpool, Manchester, Blackpool and Watford.[9]

Property disposal was a recurring theme over the next few years. Although Woolworth Holdings announced that it would put Rodgers' programme on hold for a year while it undertook a review, no fewer than 17 stores were sold in the course of 1983. The highest profile casualty was the flagship store in Liverpool, Store 1, which closed on 4 June 1983. Meanwhile, the property portfolio was transferred to a new division called Woolworth Properties, which began to charge F W Woolworth's a full market rent. Woolworth Properties was staffed by Woolworth's former Real Estate Department. An independent assessment in 1983 revalued Woolworth's portfolio at £578.4 million.[10] Subsequently, the annual rent bill increased from £33.3 million in 1984 to £48.5 million in 1985. This put a colossal strain on Woolworth's, as stores which failed to deliver stringent – some might argue, more realistic – trading targets were picked off. These included some of the largest city-centre stores, the very properties that would fetch the highest prices on the open market. Woolworth's had effectively become a property bank on which its owners could draw to fund the expansion of B&Q and other ventures.

By March 1984 the chain had shrunk to 930, while B&Q had grown to 115.[11] In May 1984, a further 34 stores were sold for around £70 million. Gerald Ronson's Heron Corporation bought 32 of these sites, including the Nottingham, Leicester, Cardiff and Guildford stores, for just £50 million.[12] The Middlesbrough store and Store 161 in Oxford Street were also sold. Immediately, another six stores were put on the market, including Harlow and Wigan. Ironically, a short-lived concession called 'The Property Shop' was established in a number of Woolworth's stores, starting with Northfield, Birmingham, in May 1984, at a time when the property value of the chain was itself being plundered.[13] This went into liquidation in winter 1985.

The millions raised from property sales enabled Woolworth Holdings to buy the electrical retailer Comet for £177 million in May 1984. Before long, an experimental version of Comet called 'Electronic World' had opened within nine Woolworth's stores, including Aylesbury, Coventry and High Wycombe.[14] This was the first serious attempt to develop synergy between the different brands owned by Woolworth Holdings, but it was short-lived, having being abandoned by 1987.

In spring 1986 it was announced that a further 23 stores would close.[15] This time the majority were in what the firm deemed 'declining suburbs', often areas entered by Woolworth's in the 1950s. Two, however, were on main thoroughfares in central London, on Holborn and the Strand, which saw little weekend trade. Condemned stores outside London included Manchester (Piccadilly), Birmingham (Bull Ring), Swansea, Sheffield, Cheltenham and Letchworth. Most of these closed on the same day: 28 June 1986. By December 1986, just 811 Woolworth's stores were trading in Great Britain.

Meanwhile, Woolworth Holdings reviewed Woolworth's sub-chains: Shoppers World, Furnishing World and Woolco. At the time of the takeover, yet another new format was being developed by the former Woolworth's management, led by the non-executive director David Quayle. Quayle, the man who put the 'Q' in B&Q, had been given a consultancy contract to develop fresh ideas for Woolworth's large city-centre stores. In a pilot exercise costing £1 million, Quayle revamped the Woolworth's store in Broadmead, Bristol, under the name '21st Century Shopping', which was proclaimed on a silver and black fascia.[16] This sold half of Woolworth's normal lines of merchandise. It had carpeted departments, an American-style cafeteria called 'Rendezvous 21' and a food court with concessions, something which was still novel in the UK. The *Woolworth News* explained: 'Think of an Italian piazza and you will have the look and "Mediterranean feel", as Mr Quayle likes to put it.'[17] The timing of this experiment, launched in October 1982, was spectacularly unfortunate: it was quietly abandoned in 1983 and Quayle left the company.

Also in 1983 the 45 Shoppers World outlets, including 28 in free-standing shops, closed. By this time the Shoppers World chain, which had lasted 10 years, employed 500 people, about half of them part-time.[18] The outlets had been losing roughly £1 million a year on a turnover of £25 million. Many Shoppers World stores were sold to Argos, while others reverted to the Woolworth's format. Furnishing World held out for another two years. Eventually, in 1985, satellite Furnishing World units opened within existing Woolco and Woolworth's outlets as a prelude to transferring its free-standing stores, rather predictably, to B&Q.[19] Woolco itself was sold off in 1986 (see p 197).

Though it was not immediately publicised, Woolworth Holdings decided to withdraw completely from the Republic of Ireland. Nineteen properties were sold for an estimated £9 million, beginning with £4.75 million for the store on Grafton Street in Dublin.[20] In July 1984, shocked Irish managers were presented with a fait accompli: of the 18 remaining stores, 12 had been sold to House & Land Ltd, 5 to Primark (which traded in the Republic of Ireland as Penney's) and 1 – on Henry Street, Dublin – to the Royal Life Insurance Company. The withdrawal would be completed by 6 October. While the unions engaged in arguments about redundancy pay, the staff organised sit-ins which were reported by a sympathetic press. As a postscript, in 1996 Woolworth's undertook market research to examine the possibility of re-entering the market in the Republic of Ireland, identifying 32 potential store locations, but did not proceed.

By 1990 the foreign stores in Cyprus, Zimbabwe and the West Indies had suffered the same fate as the stores in the Republic of Ireland. In Britain, however, the disposals programme took a new twist in 1987, when Woolworth Properties began to sell stores not as vacant properties, but with Woolworth's as the sitting tenant. Between 400 and 500 stores had been sold on this basis by 2001.[21]

To most observers, it was clear that its owners considered the chief value of Woolworth's to reside in its properties rather than in its established position as a high-street retailer. The disposal programme was, consequently, viewed in some quarters as plain, old-fashioned asset stripping. Just one new branch was added to the chain in the period 1980–5, to offset the rash of disposals. Opening in 1983, this was Store 1140 in the port of Porthmadog, terminus of the Ffestiniog Narrow Gauge Railway and gateway to Snowdonia (Fig 9.2). This was one of the first stores to demonstrate that the Winfield logo had been unceremoniously dropped by Woolworth's new owners.

Fig 9.2
Store 1140 on the High Street of Porthmadog in Wales opened in 1983. It had a pitched slate roof and very dark brickwork. The first-floor window hoods on shaped brackets offered a heavy-handed nod to a neighbouring building, signalling the effort to contextualise the design. The Winfield logo did not feature on the exterior of this building, and appears to have been jettisoned. With the largest store in Porthmadog, Woolworth's expected to reap good profits from the summer tourist trade.
[FWW01/01/1140/001]

'Cornerstone' and 'Operation Facelift'

After taking stock, Woolworth Holdings attempted to reinvigorate Woolworth's, or at least keep it on life-support until stores could be drip-fed onto the market. The 'Cornerstone' corporate strategy was implemented in spring 1984. In stores of under 20,000 sq ft, products were to be brigaded into six categories: DIY, leisure/play, household, general convenience (such as toiletries and stationery), clothing and daily provisions.[22] Planograms were issued to stores, dictating where and when products were to be displayed, leaving local managers with no freedom to improvise.

Hand in hand with Cornerstone, funding was released for 'Operation Facelift'. This was probably developed by consultants rather than George Reid's in-house team.[23] As it transpired, this was little more than an unfocused sequence of experiments, playing with the look and layout of the stores, suggesting that management had no clear idea about the image they wanted to project. At the prototype store in Hounslow, the most striking features were 'the use of geranium red on the walls and fixtures, wider shopping aisles, new wall signage, full lighting, and perimeter cash desks'.[24] The orange signs had distinctive white lettering in a rounded font.

The next experiment, in Halifax, reflected the twee tendency of 1980s shopfitting to hark back to the Victorian era. With its red and gold fascia, wrought-iron entrance portico and arching light fittings, it sought to evoke the idea of a traditional arcade.[25] The refurbishment of Goole after a fire provided an opportunity for further experimentation (Fig 9.3). Here a dark blue slatted fascia was set with white lettering and a gigantic, red, crossed 'W'. Most significantly, this was the first time any store had been identified on its main fascia as 'WOOLWORTHS', with an 'S'. Inside, the 'facelift' was cheaper than at Halifax: there was a similar 'shop within a shop' arrangement, but with diffused fluorescent lights and slatted departmental signage. Subsequent refurbishments, such as Coventry, included 'Quick Snacks', a revamping of the old 'Kwik Snax' takeaway units of the 1970s. By December 1984, 18 stores – including Caerphilly and Orpington – had received a facelift 'to reflect the principles of the commercial strategy', but all were regarded as experimental.[26] This approach continued through 1985, when the facelift was applied to superstores for the first time. Among these were Kingston upon Thames, Swindon and the most profitable store in the company at that time, Aberdeen. Instead of being straight, aisles were now laid out on the 'racetrack' principle, with grey walkways

Fig 9.3
Store 505 in Goole first opened in 1933. It suffered a fire two weeks before Christmas in 1983, and the opportunity was seized to experiment with a new style of shopfront. This 'facelift from the ashes' was unveiled in summer 1984.[a]
[FWW01/01/0505/001]

flanked by high gondolas that maximised floor space.

The new shopfronts of 1984–5, being experimental, were very variable. Most bore a very simple 'WOOLWORTH', in white on a geranium ground. Goole, however, triggered debate about the trading name. A correspondent to *Woolworth News* expressed the view that 'the word "Woolworth" conjures up visions of stores in their pre-war days with a Dickensian appearance'.[27] Bob Willett, in charge of store operations, explained the preference for 'Woolworths': 'We believe that it fits our new customer profile: C1, C2, 25–44 years of age.'[28] Yet another experiment was a V-shaped modular red-framed shopfront at Stockport, designed to funnel shoppers into the store just as deep lobbies flanked by displays of goods had nudged customers into Edwardian shops. Similar shopfronts at Dover and Maidenhead had bright red slatted fascias with 'WOOLWORTHS' in white lettering accompanied by a large gold 'W'. Before long, however, all of these 'Facelift' experiments were superseded.

'Weekend', 'General Store' and 'Operation Focus'

Obviously confused about its image under its new owner, Woolworth's looked beyond its own ranks for assistance. Two specialist formulas were devised by Piper Trust, formed by the consultant Crispin Tweddell, formerly joint managing director of Fitch & Co, one of Britain's leading retail design consultancies. Launched in September 1985, these were 'Woolworths Weekend' and 'Woolworths General Store',[29] comparison and convenience formats respectively. Weekend was suited to stores of 10,000 to 20,000 sq ft, while General Stores were under 10,000 sq ft. New uniforms accompanied the introduction of these concepts: red striped blouses for Weekend and blue for General Stores.

The first Woolworths Weekend opened on 12 September 1985 in Hitchin (Fig 9.4). The 16,000 sq ft store was divided into eight areas, colour-coded in pastel shades, and had circular 'cash and wrap' points. A mid-blue 'Weekend' banner ran beneath the 'Woolworths' fascia, and there was a V-shaped lobby, as at Stockport. Significantly, the doors and window frames were coloured peppermint blue. Hitchin was followed by St Albans and Preston on 3 October and Yeovil (with a Tea Bar restaurant), Uxbridge and Walton-on-Thames on 10 October. After a lull, the 'Weekend' suffix was dropped, for example at Spurriergate, York, which reopened on 16 May 1986 with a modern version of the 'diamond W' adorning the fascia.

The General Stores were smaller and had a more traditional look (Fig 9.5). The words 'General Store' were suspended beneath the main fascia, with gold lettering on a red

Fig 9.4
Woolworths Weekend opened in Hitchin, Store 452, in September 1985: the outline of the old lettering can still be seen above the entrance (see Fig 7.25). After Woolworth's regional structure changed in 1987, this branch housed the new Thames Valley Regional Office.
[AL2407/011/02]

Fig 9.5
Woolworth's General Store in the market town of St Neots. The original single-storey Store 645 was rebuilt in 1970 with unusual panels under the windows, described as 'Mink Stone'. This branch was converted to the 'General Store' format around 1986.
[AL2407/023/01]

Fig 9.5
Woolworth's General Store in the market town of St Neots. The original single-storey Store 645 was rebuilt in 1970 with unusual panels under the windows, described as 'Mink Stone'. This branch was converted to the 'General Store' format around 1986.
[AL2407/023/01]

ground. Among the first to open in 1985 were Dunstable (26 September), Egham (17 October), Faversham (17 October) and Leigh (24 October). Remarkably, other initiatives were going on in the chain at exactly the same time. A revamped store in Reading opened in September 1985 as 'The Woolworth Mall'. This must have been regarded as a failure, since a second Woolworth Mall, planned for Croydon, was abandoned.[30]

Meanwhile, in January 1985, Fitch & Co had been commissioned to create a new retail strategy for the chain.[31] The image they devised in the course of 1985 was unveiled in 1986 as 'Operation Focus', largely presented to the world as a timely response to an aggressive takeover bid by Dixons (*see* p 197). Focus was described as an attempt at 'giving the chain the specialist appeal that customers want', with merchandise marshalled into six areas.[32] This differed more radically from the established Woolworth's range than Cornerstone. Food, adult clothing and electrical goods were eliminated, leaving the following: children's toys and clothing ('kids'); gifts and sweets; entertainment; home and garden; kitchens; and cosmetics and fashion accessories ('looks'). Instead of carrying 50,000 lines, stores would stock 20,000; instead of dealing with 8,000 suppliers, Woolworth's would work with just 1,000. Stock was to be more tightly controlled.

To illustrate the problem, it was reported that Woolworth's held a 20-year supply of lime green zips.[33] By 1987, however, it transpired that Focus had been rather too narrow, and lines of merchandise began to expand once again.

Piper's best ideas for the Weekend stores, notably the peppermint blue colour scheme, were rationalised to create a stable visual identity for Operation Focus. This was pioneered at the Edgware Road store in London in June 1986, then rolled out across the chain. A budget of £43 million was assigned for the purpose, allowing 140 stores to receive a Focus makeover by September 1986.[34] As this speed implies, old shopfronts were rarely replaced wholesale, and many older doors – the stainless steel 'Gibbons' doors of the 1950s and 1960s – remained in place. For brand new shopfronts, the design evolved from the Hitchin experiment, having aluminium surrounds, powder-coated in peppermint blue, with push-plates discreetly adorned by the revived red 'diamond W', but without the V-shaped lobbies (Fig 9.6). Fascias were sprayed with buff-coloured 'Wallglaze', set with acrylic red-faced, gold-edged 'WOOLWORTHS' lettering, and sometimes given blue edging. After a period of uncertainty, the trading name had changed officially in March 1986. The company explained, 'We dropped the cumbersome "F. W. Woolworth" as

a signal that changes in the stores were fundamental.'[35] In fact, the 'F. W.' had been dropped around 1967, making 'WOOLWORTH' the trading name, but the old company hadn't replaced all its existing signage.

The peppermint blue and red colour scheme extended to store interiors, to cash desks and wire baskets (Figs 9.7 and 9.8). Highly polished pine-effect flooring replaced the hard, chequered terrazzo of the 1950s and 1960s. Distinctive free-standing gondolas with tiered shelving were piled with colourful pic 'n' mix sweets (Fig 9.9). New 'First Choice' tea bars were introduced, later superseded by 'The Café' (Fig 9.10). Writing on the eve of the transformation of her own branch in Bury St Edmunds, local resident Jacinth Whittaker commented on the Focus revamp:

Fig 9.9
Pic 'n' mix in Store 1139, Milton Keynes, after refurbishment under Operation Focus, photographed on 20 September 1988. The entertainment section is to the rear, and stationery to the right. This store had first opened in Milton Keynes Shopping Centre on 9 August 1979. [JLP01/10/33763]

My local store is to close for a few weeks while the alterations are carried out. The food is going because, although it sells well, it doesn't make enough profit for the floor space … I am sure there will be many of us who will mourn the passing of the Woolworth we knew and loved.[36]

The implementation of Focus had far-reaching repercussions. Shorn of their adult clothing and food departments, many superstores were far too big: the maximum size now required was 25,000 sq ft, but some provided up to 75,000 sq ft. Consequently, stores like Rotherham were cut down, and the surplus accommodation rented to other retailers. By May 1986 schemes of this nature were in the pipeline for Coventry (where JJB Sports opened a store in the basement), Norwich, Dorchester, Uxbridge, Birmingham and Paignton.[37] Around 70 stores, for example Burton-on-Trent, handed surplus space over to Superdrug after Woolworth Holdings acquired that chain in 1987 (see p 197).[38]

One observer in The Times suggested, 'In the longer term it is hard to see the Woolworth focus strategy as being more than a propagator for seedling free-standing specialist chains.'[39] By the start of 1987 Woolworth's was planning just such a 'limited story' chain, concentrating on children. It was still a market leader, but Toys R Us, with its huge, colourful edge-of-town superstores, was making significant inroads. Furthermore, Mothercare had recently been rejuvenated and Boots had announced the launch of a chain called 'Children's World'. Woolworth's retort was 'Kidstore', a formula devised in the Ealing store, which was taken into central control for the purpose of the exercise. This opened in spring 1987 (Fig 9.11), followed by a second branch in Lewisham (Fig 9.12): both were regarded as trials. Although few Kidstores opened, Woolworth's cemented its strength in this field of retailing by acquiring exclusive rights to the Ladybird brand name, which it bought outright 14 years later, in 2000. It also purchased Chad Valley, the toymaker, in

Fig 9.10
In the early 1990s a new
generation of restaurants
was introduced. Simply
called 'The Café', as shown
here at the Milton Keynes
store around 1993, they
had a peppermint blue and
natural wood colour scheme,
in keeping with the Focus
aesthetic. There were 55
of these cafés by 1998.
[FWW01/01/1139/002]

1988. It was rumoured in 1987 that Woolworth's might take over Mothercare as part of a joint bid with the Burton Group for Terence Conran's Storehouse, but this never materialised.

In tandem with revamping existing stores, from the late 1980s Woolworth Holdings began to open new branches. Plans were unveiled in January 1986 for up to 30 new (smaller, more compact) stores in city centres from which the firm had withdrawn.[40] Subsequently, units were leased either in malls (such as the Arndale Centre, Manchester, 1988; St John's Centre, Liverpool, 1990; Bon Accord Centre, Aberdeen, 1990) or in old high street buildings, such as a former Burton's store in Norwich (1990, see Fig 9.6). Others opened in the vast mega-malls that were being erected on brownfield sites outside many of Britain's biggest cities as a result of the Thatcher government's encouragement of out-of-town development, for example in the MetroCentre at Gateshead (c 1986), Merryhill at Dudley (1989), Meadowhall at Sheffield (1990) and Lakeside at Thurrock (1990, Fig 9.13). Unlike the first Woolworth's stores to open in shopping centres in the 1960s, these were not anchor stores, and they failed to thrive. By this time Reid had retired and the small architects' team (just two 'technicians' under Peter Dunn) was transferred to the Planning and Fixture Department.[41]

Other new stores opened as a repercussion of development projects undertaken by Chartwell Land, as Woolworth Properties had been renamed in 1988. More than just a change of name, this involved a change of role: Chartwell's objective was 'unlocking development potential and releasing cash for investment elsewhere in the Group (particularly in the growth of B&Q)'.[42] Until now, other developers had milked the value of former Woolworth's stores, which they had bought

Fig 9.11
The Kidstore format for
children aged up to 13 years
was developed in Store 1149
in Ealing. It opened in
March 1987 and lasted
until 1992.
[FWW01/01/1149/002]

Fig 9.12
The interior of the second prototype Kidstore, Store 1150 in the Riverside Centre, Lewisham, photographed on 29 July 1987.
[JLP01/10/28120]

Fig 9.13
The short-lived Store 1167, at Lakeside, Thurrock, opened in 1990 and relocated in 1993.
[FWW01/01/1167/001]

relatively cheaply. Now, around 60 store sites with potential for redevelopment, by and for the company, were identified. In autumn 1987, Chartwell began to work with the developer Rosehaugh/Sheerwater to maximise the potential of five of these stores, beginning with a scheme in Southampton. One of the biggest of Chartwell's schemes was in Lincoln, where the development of the Waterside Centre – opened in 1991 by Princess Diana – spread beyond the footprint of the old store, onto adjoining land.

Mulcahy and the Dixons bid

John Beckett retired in March 1986, announcing that the Woolworth's chain was at last making reasonable, if not stellar, profits: £17 million (with 850 stores), compared with £32 million (with 176 stores) at B&Q.[43] Sir Kenneth Durham of Unilever was appointed the new Chairman of Woolworth Holdings, while Geoff Mulcahy became Chief Executive. Mulcahy was a key figure. He had been Beckett's colleague at British Sugar. He moved with him to Woolworth Holdings in 1982, and was appointed Managing Director of the F W Woolworth's subsidiary in August 1984, masterminding Operation Focus. On his promotion, he was replaced by a woman, Mair Barnes, previously from House of Fraser, as the head of the Woolworth's operation.

Shortly after his retirement, Beckett was blamed for starting a rumour that the electrical retailer Dixons Group (Dixons having bought Currys in 1984) was about to launch a takeover bid for Woolworth Holdings. Subsequent rumours suggested that another company, Dee Holdings (the owner of Gateway and Carrefour supermarkets) might also make a bid. Woolworth's shares rose dramatically, from 545p to 638p. Dee Holdings soon showed that their interests lay elsewhere, but in April 1986 Dixons – which had operated photographic concessions in several branches of Woolworth's in the 1960s – fulfilled expectations by launching an aggressive £1.8 billion bid, prompting Woolworth's shares to soar to the new high of 920p.

As Mulcahy engaged in a vicious public spat with Stanley Kalms, the Chairman of Dixons, Operation Focus was proffered in Woolworth's defence. One of Dixons' main criticisms of the existing Woolworth's management team was their disposal of prime high street sites to retail rivals. Woolworth Holdings, proud of its own out-of-town B&Q and Comet chains, retaliated by criticising Dixons' failure to relocate from town centres. Dixons eventually unveiled its future plan for Woolworth's as 'Operation Ramrod', predictably renamed 'Operation Ramshackle' by Woolworth's. Ramrod envisaged a reduction in the number of Woolworth's stores from 811 to 650. The equivalent of 2 million sq ft of Woolworth's trading area would be handed over to the Dixons and Currys chains. Moreover, in remaining Woolworth's stores the average retail space would fall from 8,900 sq ft to 7,500 sq ft. High-priced goods would be placed to the fore, with sweets to the rear: a complete reversal of the traditional Woolworth's arrangement.

Ironically, it was while debating the pros and cons of out-of-town retailing with Dixons that Woolworth's announced the sale of the Woolco chain to the Dee Corporation for £26 million.[44] Woolco had not expanded since the 1970s; it comprised 12 stores and employed 3,000 people. It was unfortunate that Woolco, which had struggled against restrictive planning in the 1960s and 1970s, folded just as the government was displaying a more laissez faire attitude that made hypermarkets of this type viable propositions for the first time.

The excitement generated by Dixons' predatory bid lasted from March until July 1986, when Woolworth's finally batted away the threat and the share price resumed its normal pattern. This epic takeover battle had cost both companies millions, but did much to enhance the profile of Geoff Mulcahy.

As Chief Executive, Mulcahy oversaw a number of acquisitions in the late 1980s, starting with Record Merchandisers in December 1986. This distribution firm had been founded in 1966 by EMI Records, and Woolworth's had become a major customer. It was renamed Entertainment UK (usually known as EUK) in 1988, leading to the creation of new music departments in stores to compete with other high street music chains such as Virgin, HMV and Our Price. Additional acquisitions in March 1987 were Charlie Brown Autocentres, with 42 outlets in northern England bought for £19 million,[45] and Superdrug, a national chemist's chain with 297 outlets bought for £257 million. Superdrug subsequently expanded, in many cases by carving out space within existing Woolworth's stores. In February 1988 it was announced that at least 10 per cent of Woolworth's selling space would be handed over to other group outlets.[46] Maximising the redevelopment potential of Woolworth's allowed Mulcahy to buy 94 Ultimate electrical shops to add to the Comet portfolio, and 110 Tip Top chemist's shops and 490 Share Drug outlets to augment Superdrug.

The 'Kingfisher' years, 1989–2000

The 'Kingfisher' name and logo, devised by the design consultancy Wolff Olins at a cost just short of £1 million, was launched by Mulcahy in February 1989. This supposedly marked the end of the turnaround phase of the business's progress, but it also signalled a shift away from the centrality of Woolworth's to the company. The Kingfisher name officially replaced 'Woolworth Holdings' on 17 March 1989. Woolworth's was just one of many retail chains under the vast Kingfisher umbrella, but it still accounted for 43 per cent of group sales and 33 per cent of its profits.[47] New acquisitions under Kingfisher included Laskys (1989), Medicare (1989), Unipart (1993), MVC (Music and Video Club, 1993) and several Continental businesses, notably Darty (1993). A bid to add Dixons to the group in 1989/90 was blocked by the Monopolies and Mergers Commission. Mulcahy continued at the helm, either in the role of Chief Executive or (from 1990 until 1995) Chairman.

Several specialised Woolworth's formats were devised in 1989. New 'Music & Video' stores opened (Figs 9.14 and 9.15). These occupied smaller units than standard Woolworth's stores, but inside they had the same polished pine floors, suspended ceilings set with flush square lights, and peppermint blue fixtures and signage: the Focus look that had been introduced in 1985–6. In mall settings, 'Music & Video' was added to fascias, beneath 'WOOLWORTHS', in blue neon tubing. The same approach was used for 'Sweets and Cards' and 'Kids at Woolworths', both in the Barbirolli Mall in Manchester's Arndale Centre. Most of these specialised shops had closed by 1994.

Optimism that Woolworth's, now with around 750 stores, had turned a corner lasted through the recession of the early 1990s: 'Charles Darwin would be surprised at how successfully the dinosaur of the high street has been transformed' commented *The Times* in March 1991, when annual profits of £63 million were announced.[48] In that year the Hounslow branch was extended and refitted as the store of the future, with touch-screen ordering kiosks.[49] A new-style café – The Café – was launched (*see* Fig 9.10). New stores continued to open in towns that Woolworth's had vacated a decade earlier: the company actively sought outlets, publishing its property 'shopping list' in a brochure entitled 'Woolworths Tomorrow's Retailer'.[50] Ideally, it looked for ground-floor sales areas of between 8,000 sq ft (for example, Winchester and Harlow) and 14,000 sq ft (for example, Glasgow and Edinburgh). New high street stores in Blackpool (Fig 9.16) and Sutton (both 1994) occupied purpose-built anchor units in large Chartwell developments, built in dark red brick and conceived in a chunky postmodern idiom current at the time. They were not, however, designed by the company architects.

By the mid-1990s, things did not look quite so rosy. In a management shakeup, Mair Barnes was replaced as Managing Director by Jonathan Weeks, followed in 1995 by Roger Jones. Jones, a rare and much-respected survivor from the pre-Paternoster days, brought in a new strategy to rejuvenate the brand. He classified Woolworth's stores as 'city' (116 stores), 'heartland' (226 stores) or 'local' (437 stores), each having a different range of goods and

Fig 9.14

Music & Video, Merryhill Shopping Centre, Dudley (Store 1153). The shopfitting for this format, as usual, was by Curtis. When Music & Video was wound up in 1994, Kingfisher concentrated on its sub-chain, MVC (Music and Video Club), which had 36 branches by 1996. MVC was sold in 2004, and went into administration a short time later. [FWW01/01/1153/001]

Fig 9.15

Browsing inside the Music & Video store in Woolwich (Store 1156) around 1990. Woolworth's stopped selling vinyl LPs in 1993, and singles in 1994, concentrating thereafter on CDs and cassette tapes. The store shown here closed on 5 June 1993. [FWW01/01/1156/001]

a distinctive store layout.[51] The prototype city store opened in Regent Street, Swindon, in 1995, followed by Doncaster and Luton, and included new departments such as a 'Kitchenshop'. Ideas for the heartland stores were trialled in the small market towns of Boston, Grantham and Huntingdon. These introduced dry cleaning, pet care, video rental and newspapers. In Chippenham, an old 1970s garden centre was brought back into use, and Congleton was given an experimental in-store post office. It was the 'local' stores, however, that were the most profitable: by 1999, around 300 stores in small towns and suburbs had been converted to this concept, reopening with vast bunches of balloons to create a celebratory feel. 'Local' stores had their own distinctive fascias (Fig 9.17 and see Fig 9.22). The peppermint blue 'Focus' colour scheme was dropped and vertical red and white signage with sideways 'WOOLWORTHS' lettering was widely adopted. In the 'city' stores these signs flanked entrances in the manner of goalposts.

By 1998, when it was announced that the company intended to open 50 new high street branches of between 15,000 and 20,000 sq ft,

there seems to have been an element of uncertainty or ambivalence whether Woolworth's should concentrate on town centres or move into retail parks. Most of the new openings were 'Local' branches, in town centres such as Letchworth. But the store in Monks Cross Retail Park, York, which opened in autumn 1998, was hailed by the concept planning manager as 'truly a blueprint for the future of Woolworths' (Fig 9.18).[52] Around the same time, Woolworths Direct was set up, allowing customers to place telephone orders for goods seen in catalogues or on TV.

Big W marked a confident return to hypermarket retailing (Fig 9.19). The concept, hailed as a copycat Wal-Mart, was launched in June 1999 at Kinnaird on the outskirts of Edinburgh, where a redundant B&Q store was converted to the new format.[53] The idea was to collect all Kingfisher brands – Woolworth's, Comet, Superdrug and B&Q – in one large outlet, typically over 80,000 sq ft. In addition, Big W had a garden centre, sold clothes from Peacock (in a 10,000 sq ft corner kitted out in Peacock's high-street style), and had a Burger King restaurant, but the fact that it did not sell

Fig 9.16
Bank Hey Street, Blackpool, Store 1191, opened on 2 September 1994 on a site previously occupied by Lewis's store, on the north side of the Tower. Woolworth's was the anchor tenant in this new development by Chartwell Land and enjoyed a favourable rent until demerger in 2001: the store was sold and Woolworth's, the sitting tenant, was burdened with a higher rent and a 30-year lease.[b] Historically, there were three other Woolworth's stores in Blackpool: Store 66 to the south of the Tower; Store 309 which opened in 1928 in Bond Street; and Store 851 (later 2016) which opened in 1954 in Talbot Road. [AL2408/002/01]

Fig 9.18
Store 1204 opened in a
retail park called Monks
Cross, on the periphery
of York, in 1998.
[FWW01/01/1204/001]

food excited much comment: 'I don't see why everyone is so fascinated about it,' said Mulcahy. 'There are many retailers around the world who manage to compete very effectively without selling any food.'[54] In reality, Mulcahy hoped that a merger with Asda would plug this gap. Plans were laid to open ten Big Ws by the end of 2000, with ambitions for 70 or 80 by the end of 2003. The stores had a distinctive orange, white and blue livery, and the logo included a lower-case 'big' followed by a white 'W' in a blue circle. From available evidence, it appears that Big W made a steady profit. But with corporate change (see below) it did not fit the profile of the organisation and was abandoned. It has been suggested that the borrowing of the

name Big W from Australia was poetic justice, since the Australian company had copied Woolworth's name in the first place, back in the 1920s.[55]

'General Stores' had been developed before, in 1985. Resurrected in 2000, 'Woolworths General Stores' was a chain of convenience stores, loosely modelled on American drugstores, open from 7am to 11pm (see Fig 4.23). This marked a brief return to retailing food (initially supplied by the cash and carry business Booker), which had been abandoned in 1985. In partnership with Superdrug, the stores had in-store pharmacies, as well as health and beauty lines, and facilities for photo processing, faxing and photocopying. The pilot store, Palmers Green in north London (February 2000), was followed by Muswell Hill and Balham, all conversions of existing Woolworth's outlets which were, confusingly, renumbered using the old Woolco sequence.[56] Later examples included New Malden and Chiswick. The first outside London, and one of just two to occupy a new unit, opened in Southgate Retail Park, Derby, in 2001. As many as 400 General Stores were envisaged, but only 22 ever existed. In March 2002, Spar was awarded the contract to supply food, alcohol and tobacco lines to the General Stores and four 'Locals', but in July Woolworth's called the trial off, declaring, 'At the end of the day customers do not want to buy food from Woolworths.'[57]

In spring 1999 a planned merger of Kingfisher with Asda was announced: this would have created the tenth-largest retail group in the world, run by Mulcahy, and might have seen Asda's 'George' clothing range sold in Woolworth's and food in Big W.[58] This ambitious plan fell through following intervention by Wal-Mart, which swooped in to take over Asda. This was a heavy blow for Mulcahy, and Kingfisher's shares fell dramatically. Had the

merger with Asda gone through, the future of Woolworth's might have been very different.

Woolworths group plc, 2000–2008

Before Kingfisher's promising new retail formats could become established, the structure of the company changed. In autumn 2000 Kingfisher planned to float the entire business, but in March 2001 the former Railtrack Chief Executive Gerald Corbett was head-hunted to oversee a demerger of the lucrative DIY/electricals arm (including B&Q and Comet) from the general merchandise arm. Corbett embarked on a series of meetings with venture capitalists. As a result, Superdrug was sold and Woolworth's was floated on the stock market – on 28 August 2001, at 25p a share – as an independent company. In addition to Woolworth's and Big W, this included MVC's 88 shops, the wholesaler Entertainment UK and music publisher Video Collection International (VCI). Corbett remained as Chairman of Woolworths Group after demerger until he was replaced by Richard North in 2007.

Woolworths Group inherited an overdraft of £200 million and a lot of expensive leases. Disastrously, Kingfisher had retained Chartwell Land, which held the remaining Woolworth's store freeholds. In August 2001 it was announced that the remaining portfolio of around 182 sites, worth £614 million, would be sold. These included Woolworth's Belfast flagship (see Fig 4.20), sold to Dunnes for £17.3 million in April 2003. Even Woolworth's Marylebone Road headquarters (see Fig 6.45) was sold. The new owners of these properties were guaranteed leases of 30 or more years, at market-based rentals, by Chartwell Land. As Nigel Stretch, of Woolworth's Estate Department, observed: 'Woolworths had no control over the buildings that they had

Fig 9.19
Big W, Newport, Wales (Store 1251). This hypermarket format was launched by Kingfisher in 1999, combining Woolworth's with Comet and B&Q, but not – unlike the previous Woolco chain – including food. It had a restaurant called Big Café. The stores were costly to set up and each employed around 200 people. They used the main store numbering sequence. [Courtesy of woolworths museum.co.uk, © 3D and 6D Pictures Ltd]

originally designed and built other than a responsibility as tenant. Sad times!'[59] A small team within the Property Services Department now looked after these stores.

Conceptually, General Stores and Big W had depended on collaboration with other Kingfisher chains, and after the demerger they were much less viable. General Stores was the first casualty. Without in-house expertise to run the pharmacies, from July 2002 the General Stores were converted back into standard Woolworth's outlets. It took longer to deal with Big W: seven were sold to Tesco or Asda in 2005, but those which did not attract a buyer were converted into Woolworth's stores, albeit in larger-than-usual premises at off-centre locations. The format was referred to as 20/20,[60] after the agency that produced it, and both mirrored and magnified developments within the high-street chain.

New Chief Executive Trevor Bish-Jones – who had worked with Corbett in the past, at Dixons – decided that the high street chain of 808 stores should develop a tight focus on 'kids and celebrations', appealing primarily to young families with a reasonable household income. A new store design called 10/10 was developed to suit this more specialised format, and managers were determined to test this as fully as possible before rolling it out across the chain. In October 2002 the first pilot store, in Hemel Hempstead, Hertfordshire, was unveiled: the opening seems to have been planned for the 10th of October, hence the name of the format.[61] The fascia displayed 'Woolworths' in red neon lower-case letters (this had always been upper case in the past) and a projecting sign introduced a new corporate logo, a red 'W' under a curling banner referred to as the 'swoosh'. The number of doorways was reduced to maximise internal space. The main pathway running through the store was floored in red, while the remainder was tiled in beige. Counters were arranged at an angle to the gangway, and included specialised display fittings, lit by spotlights. This proved successful, and so further trials were held at medium-sized Kettering and smaller Market Harborough, clarifying that the format worked best in stores of over 12,000 sq ft. It was tweaked yet again at three stores in outer London in the course of 2003: at Redhill, Uxbridge and Kingston upon Thames. Ultimately the fascia lettering reverted to upper case and the 'swoosh' was reconfigured in white on a red ground. This was rolled out to 200 stores, sometimes with a new-look red and yellow café, evidently designed to appeal to children (Fig 9.20). As many as 150 stores were earmarked for relocation, to suit the 10/10 format better. As Bish-Jones explained:

> What we are starting to do is tidy up the estate, because there are stores where we are clearly under-spaced ... For example, at King's Lynn (Norfolk) we are trading out of 1,000 sq ft (95 sq m) but there's a shopping centre opening and we're taking a 14,000 sq ft (1,300 sq m) store there.[62]

This referred to the new Vancouver Centre, where Store 1262 opened in 2006. Many small branches, however, were untouched and beginning to look grubby. Paradoxically, these neglected stores were often the ones that generated the greatest profits.

A new concept was eventually developed for smaller stores, called 5/5 and piloted at Kingswood, outside Bristol. Essentially, a mass of rather expensive purple signage explained that Woolworth's entire range of 300,000 products could be ordered in store, using touchscreens or laminated catalogues. In-store ordering systems had recently been tried out elsewhere, notably at Mold and Heswall, with good results. Woolworth's historian Paul Seaton has referred to this retail approach as the 'elastic walls concept'.[63] The launch of Kingswood in November 2005 was attended by Wooly the sheep and Worth the sheepdog, mascots which featured in Woolworth's promotions from 2003 until 2008, and fronted the introduction of the 'Worthit!' basic range in 2007 – a year in which the chain converted a loss of £12 million, for 2006, into a profit of £3.4 million: a short-lived turnaround.

The in-store catalogue trials of 2005 led, a year later, to the introduction of Woolworth's Big Red Book. In a serious attempt to compete with Argos, order and collection points were set up in every store, but without the expensive refit seen at Kingswood. The system did not work well: not only were many catalogue items unavailable, but catalogue prices were not maintained in stores, to the annoyance of customers.

Woolworth's was now in dire straits. Overtures from Apax (in 2005), Baugur (in 2006) and Malcolm Walker of the frozen food company Iceland (in 2008) had been fended off, but the future of Woolworth's was

Fig 9.20
A new style of Woolworth's café, designed to appeal to kids, in Big W, Byker, Newcastle (Store 1256). [Ken Trimmer]

constantly questioned by business analysts. The company had been worth £350 million when it demerged from Kingfisher, but by summer 2008 its value was just £110 million. After the fleeting recovery of 2007, a loss of £20 million was predicted for 2008. The Group's reserves had been depleted by the purchase of Total Home Entertainment Ltd (in 2006) and Bertram Books (in 2007), to boost the Entertainment UK division. In January 2008 Woolworth's refinanced, with over £350 million loans based on its assets: this was, at the time, the largest asset-based loan made in Europe.[64] Paul Seaton has observed that this arrangement 'went from being the talk-of-the-town as an incredibly clever Board strategy to outright disaster in just six months'.[65] Assets included just two freehold properties – the stores in Guernsey and Jersey, which had not been transferred to Woolworth Properties in 1982.[66] In addition to its debts, the company had a pension fund deficit estimated at £100 million. Hopes for a turnaround were slim. The trading environment was increasingly difficult: just about everything sold by Woolworth's

could be picked up on a family's weekly supermarket shopping trip. Moreover, changes in merchandising policy had allowed rivals like Wilkinsons to encroach onto traditional Woolworth's territory. A consultant observed in The Times:

> In the last five years, the likes of Poundland, Home Bargains and 99p Stores have been growing at around 15 per cent a year. They're doing exactly what Woolworths used to do. It's things, for example, like having a value hardware range. It doesn't sound very exciting, but things like fixtures, fittings, paint, door handles.[67]

Last-minute efforts were made to revive Woolworth's. Trevor Bish-Jones announced that 10 per cent of the stores were too large.[68] Shortly before being ousted as chief executive in favour of Steve Johnson, formerly of Focus DIY, he tried to entice other retailers to 'buddy up', or share space in Woolworth's stores. As a result, in April 2008 a deal was struck with Somerfield whereby Woolworth's would open 3,000 sq ft concessions in 11 Somerfield stores, starting in Cheadle, while Somerfield would operate food concessions in three city-centre Woolworth's stores. In tandem with this, a programme called 'Simplification' introduced drastic price cutting: children's jeans for £2, for example. Four leasehold stores in London were sold to Waitrose for £25.5 million, bringing the chain down to 817.[69] Evidence of corner-cutting was increasingly obvious to staff behind the scenes. Duncan Stephen, a sales assistant in the Glenrothes branch, never received his uniform and reported that stock levels were low, broken air conditioning was not fixed, and they frequently ran out of basic supplies such as carrier bags or guns to price stock.[70] The final new Woolworth's store, Store 1275, opened at Bitterne on 30 October 2008, and was to have a fleeting existence.

Finale, 2008–2009

On 19 November 2008 a deal was announced whereby the restructuring specialist Hilco would buy the retail arm of the Woolworths Group for the nominal sum of £1. Possibly, by this act, managers hoped to save its other businesses, including Entertainment UK. The market value of Woolworth's fell to £18 million, and its debts were estimated at £385 million.[71] One of the largest single debts was £106 million

owed to Entertainment UK for stock supplied to Zavvi (previously Virgin Megastores). This happened against the background of the 'credit crunch', when the world's banks appeared to be on the brink of collapse and had to be recapitalised by governments, plunging many countries into recession. The Woolworths Group's banks rejected the Hilco solution and recalled their loans, forcing the retail arm of the company and Entertainment UK – and also Zavvi – into administration. On 26 November trading in the shares was suspended, and it became evident that 30,000 jobs were at risk at the stores, the four distribution centres and at Entertainment UK. Although Deloitte, the administrators, and Hilco, as their agent, actively began to wind down the business, staff and public alike assumed that someone would intervene at the eleventh hour to rescue Woolworth's. The alternative was unthinkable.

In early December 2008, with many suppliers refusing to deliver to Woolworth's stores, Deloitte reported interest in parts of the business from 10 or so potential bidders, some of whom expressed an intent to keep the brand on the high street despite the impending recession. Among them, reportedly, were Theo Paphitis (of the Rymans and La Senza chains), Ardeshir Naghshineh (an Iranian property developer who, with a 10.2 per cent stake

Fig 9.21

Deloitte, the administrator, appointed Hilco to oversee and maximise stock disposal in the last weeks of trading. A former Woolworth's employee claimed Hilco 'brought with them a range of tacky, luminous posters, loudly advertising "Woolworths biggest ever sale" … I am quite sure that most of the various posters and signs that were supplied to us were generic and designed for use in any store.'[c] A selection can be seen here at Store 150, Kilburn, north London, in the throes of the closing sale on 17 December 2008. According to Hilco, 'The largest retail inventory liquidation ever carried out within Europe was executed and completed within six weeks, recovering some £280 million of cash, after all operating expenses.'[d] [DP077954]

in Woolworths Group plc, was the largest shareholder), Sir Richard Branson and Sir Geoff Mulcahy. Simultaneously, executives inside Woolworth's, notably Tony Page,[72] began to hatch plans to resurrect the chain after closure. Woolworth's stores continued trading through the busy Christmas period (Figs 9.21–9.23), with 20 per cent off marked prices from mid-November, and a closing-down sale from 11 December. With takings of £27 million, 5 December 2008 was reportedly the best trading day in Woolworth's history. As well as selling stock, the increasingly bare stores began to dispose of fixtures and fittings (Fig 9.24). One company insider observed that this was the ultimate blow, claiming that the cost of refitting out the stores would have been 'beyond the reach of just about any private investor, particularly at the height of the credit crunch'.[73]

Deloitte (with Hilco) closed the remaining 807 stores between 27 December 2008 and 6 January 2009, with 27,000 job losses. Some 207 stores closed on 27 December; 37 on 29 December; 164 on 30 December; 200 on 3 January, and the rest – approximately 200 branches – on 6 January. The following day, 7 January 2009, dawned with no Woolworth's store trading in the British Isles, for the first time in over 99 years. On 27 Jan 2009 Woolworths Group plc, unable to pay its debts, went into administration.

Fig 9.22
Store 393, Faversham: store closing, 30 December 2008.
[DP069295]

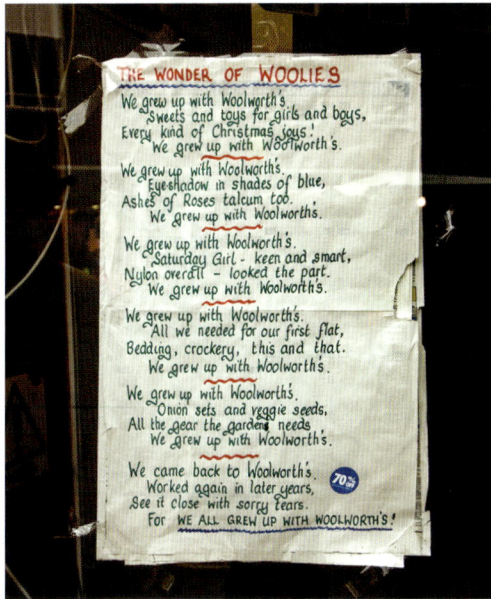

Fig 9.23
'The Wonder of Woolies': a poem, complete with 70 per cent off sticker, posted by staff in the window of Store 109 in Canterbury, photographed on 31 December 2008.
[DP069304]

Fig 9.24
The Faversham store: fixtures for sale on 30 December 2008.
[DP069296]

10

Aftermath, 2009–2014

Taking Woolworth's place

Following Woolworth's demise the leases on its prime stores were quickly taken up by other retailers. By the end of 2009 many had been transformed into branches of Poundland (Fig 10.1), Poundstretcher (Fig 10.2), Iceland (Fig 10.3), Wilkinsons, QD Stores, B&M Bargains, 99p Stores and other 'value' or 'discount' chains. Some, such as Driffield, were replaced by new buildings. Others, including Ilkeston and Margate, remained empty for several years, with increasingly faded and lopsided 'WOOLWORTHS' lettering over the doors.

Unfortunately, the 'Woolworths' name was not sold to Tony Page or any of the other companies or individuals who had expressed an interest in keeping it alive on the high street. On 2 February 2009 it was announced that the Shop Direct Group, owned by David and Frederick Barclay, the proprietors of the *Daily Telegraph*, had purchased the Woolworths and Ladybird brands, which would survive within an internet-based shopping company. The Chad Valley brand was bought by the Home Retail Group, the owner of Argos.

From January 2009 a number of ersatz Woolies rose phoenix-like from the ashes, opened by former Woolworth's staff, often in former Woolworth's premises. The most publicised venture was that undertaken by the Dorchester store manager, Claire Robertson, who recruited Radio 2 DJ Chris Evans to reopen her store, 'Wellworths', on 11 March 2009. This was staffed with ex-Woolworth's employees. Robertson's endeavour drew widespread admiration and was the subject of a BBC1 documentary. Following pressure from Shop Direct, however, the store was renamed Wellchester.[1] After trading for three years, it closed and became a branch of Poundland.

A more ambitious spin-off was Alworths, which opened in the old Woolworth's premises in Didcot on 5 November 2009, exactly 100 years to the day after F W Woolworth & Co Ltd had first opened on Church Street in Liverpool. Alworths, with its purple and blue fascias, was set up as a chain by Andy Latham, who had worked as Woolworth's Head of Store Concessions and Development. It sold toys, confectionery and household goods. Branches opened in Amersham, Evesham, Hertford and elsewhere, but Alworths didn't meet with success. It faced legal action from the Barclay brothers for trading off the goodwill of the Woolworth's business.[2] Alworths went into administration in 2011, and 15 of its 18 stores were bought by Poundstretcher. Another failure was 'Wee W' in Stornoway, set up by former

Fig 10.1 (right)
Store 233, Nos 13–15
High Street, Inverness,
was rebuilt in 1964. It is
now one of two Poundland
shops in the town centre.
[Ron Baxter]

Fig 10.2 (far right)
Store 1066 in Lochee,
a suburb of Dundee, is now
occupied by Poundstretcher.
The store sits in the shadow
of what was once the
world's largest jute mill. The
artificial stone-slab front,
the glass mosaic infill panels
and much of the shopfront
have survived from 1962,
when this branch –
photographed in April 2014
– first opened.
[Ron Baxter]

Woolworth's staff. But some legacy stores have endured until the time of writing. Thus the Ledbury branch still houses a store with a brash red fascia, named 'Wellworth It!' (Fig 10.4).

Ironically, it was a version of the original Woolworth's retail model that proved most resilient on Britain's recession-hit high streets in the period 2009–14. Pavements were lined by multiple stores with a 'pile it high, sell it cheap' ethos – Wilkinsons, Home Bargains, Poundland, Poundworld, Poundstretcher, 99p Stores – many with a fixed-price policy, not a million miles removed from the business plan hatched by Frank W Woolworth in 1879. This is an old style of variety retailing that died out around the time of the Second World War, but made a strong comeback once out-of-town shopping had, predictably, devastated town centres in the 1990s. Recently, it has thrived cheek by jowl with charity shops, pawnbrokers (or 'cash for gold' shops) and cafés: a combination that characterises many modern high streets.

Fig 10.3
Store 503 in The Brittox, Devizes, was one of 51 Woolworth's stores bought by Iceland in January 2009. Woolworth's had opened in this unusual building in 1933. It was photographed in March 2014.
[DP161372]

Fig 10.4
Wellworth It! in Woolworth's old Store 696 in Ledbury retains the 1930s shopfront.
[Ron Baxter]

Looking at Poundland and its ilk, successfully ensconced in former Woolworth's stores, one cannot help but wonder what might have happened if Woolworth's had stood its ground, unchanged, awaiting the return of the particular genre of variety retailing that had always been its strongest suit.

What if?

What if Woolworth's had not confused and alienated its customers by chopping and changing its merchandise? What if the parent company had not diversified into a series of expensive retail formats in a quest for higher returns? What if profits had continued to be channelled back into the high street stores and investors had been content with a slower rate of growth? What if the properties had not been sold off, and the stores had not been lumbered with high rentals? A glance at Marks & Spencer's, which has had its ups and downs but still stands proud on British high streets, suggests that such questions might not be quite as naïve as they appear at first sight. But bearing in mind the pressures to which Woolworth's management was subjected – the insistent demands of their American masters, of their shareholders, and of the vultures that circled the company's assets, not to mention competition from price-cutting rivals such as Tesco – maintaining the status quo through the decades was never going to be an option. Nevertheless, the relatively simple task of keeping the high street stores in good order, with a stock of attractive merchandise that met customers' expectations, should not have proved such a challenge.

In hindsight, it is clear that Woolworth's took a great many wrong turns. One of the most regrettable developments regarding the stores was the conversion to self-service. This could not have been avoided, yet it annihilated the special character and atmosphere of the stores. The experience of shopping and working at Woolworth's became more mundane, since there is scant opportunity for chit-chat at a checkout desk. Worst of all, little effort was expended on the self-service rollout. Fitted out in cheap laminates, with hard terrazzo floors and harsh fluorescent strip lighting, the stores were undifferentiated from other modern high street shops. Not enough was done to recreate the welcoming shopping environment that Woolworth's offered in days gone by, or to

invoke the glamour of the company's American roots, something which had been achieved to perfection in the 1930s.

The high value of the stores – built in prime locations over the years, to designs by North & Robin, Priddle, Donaldson, Winbourne, Hardy and others – also played a crucial part in the company's downfall. Their worth surpassed that of the retail operation, and during the shopping revolution of the late 20th century it was inevitable that this would be exploited, one way or another. As it turned out, the buildings were sold off in batches to fund new, often mistimed and short-lived, commercial ventures. These absorbed the attention of executive management, which increasingly neglected the Woolworth's operation. Consequently, Woolworth's became moribund long before the 'credit crunch' and the dark days of winter 2008–9.

The departure of Woolworth's left many provincial town centres adrift, without their commercial anchor. Following Woolworth's collapse, the very concept of the high-street shopping centre seems under threat as never before.

Former employee and company historian Paul Seaton has suggested one way in which Woolworth's could, conceivably, make a return to British shopping streets in the future:

> F W Woolworth GMBH of Germany went into administration in spring 2009. Under German law that business was allowed to restructure and today is one of that country's great success stories, profitable and expanding rapidly. It goes to show that the basic Woolworth formula continues to be a winner with European consumers. Maybe one day they will expand overseas to the UK.[3]

Meanwhile, British and Irish high streets retain hundreds of former Woolworth's stores. But how can these buildings continue to be valued and appreciated, now that their red signboards have been dismantled? Architecturally, few are distinguished. By and large they were cast in the mainstream fashions of their day, rather than being in the avant garde. Despite this, they formed part of the backdrop to daily existence for most of the British population, spanning at least four generations. Multiple retailers are often accused of churning out the same shop designs all over the country, but a glance through this book will demonstrate that Woolworth's architectural house style was, at all times, fairly loosely conceived. Nevertheless, with their standardised shopfronts and familiar interiors, as well as their comprehensive geographical spread, the stores embodied collective experience and cultural memory on a national scale, something few buildings can claim. Thus Woolworth's was a unifying influence, offering an experience that could be shared and relished by people from places as far flung as Kirkwall and Penzance.

Many old Woolworth's stores were designed originally to be slick and modern, but over time have acquired a patina of period charm. Even with buddleia sprouting from cracks in their faience fronts, they are regarded with affection by former customers in local communities. But it must be acknowledged that values dependent on sentiment and memory are transient; they will fade with the passage of time. It is only by comprehending the centrality of Woolworth's stores to life in 20th-century Britain and Ireland – their unrivalled status as high-street icons – that future generations who don't have fond recollections of pic 'n' mix, Embassy records or Miners lipstick might be moved to preserve, and even cherish, something of the company's presence in the fabric of our towns and cities, as part of Britain's and Ireland's shopping heritage.

Postscript

Just as this book is going to print, the news has broken that the website www.woolworths. co.uk has been taken down, and customers have been directed to Shop Direct's other online shopping site www.very.co.uk. This has given rise to speculation that the brand name 'Woolworths' might be sold, and possibly applied to a new high street chain. We might not, after all, have reached the end of the story.

APPENDIX 1

Timeline of significant events

1879	Frank W Woolworth opens his first five-cent store in America
May 1909	Woolworth sets sail from America, to open a British subsidiary
Nov 1909	Woolworth's first British store opens on Church Street, Liverpool
1913	Cass Gilbert's Woolworth Building is completed in New York
c 1913	North & Robin begin to design stores for Woolworth's
Aug 1914	At the outbreak of war, Woolworth's operates 34 British and Irish stores
1919	William Priddle takes up the role of Woolworth's Chief Architect
1921	Woolworth's 100th store opens in Mansfield
1923	William L Stephenson takes over as Managing Director
	The new Liverpool superstore opens
1931	Shares in British Woolworth's are floated on the London Stock Exchange
Early 1930s	Woolworth's opens its first self-service cafeterias
1932	Bruce Campbell Donaldson is appointed Woolworth's Chief Architect
1933	Woolworth's 500th store opens in Eltham
1938	The rebuilding of the Blackpool superstore is completed
1939	At the outbreak of war, Woolworth's operates 759 stores
1944	The New Cross store is hit by a V-2, with great loss of life
	Harold Winbourne is appointed Woolworth's Chief Architect
1955	Woolworth's first self-service store opens at Cobham
1958	Store 1000 opens in Portslade
1960	Doug W Hardy is appointed Woolworth's Chief Architect
1961	Woolworth's first garden centre opens in Windsor

1962	The Winfield brand name is introduced
	Woolworth's opens in Birmingham's Bull Ring Centre
1967	The first Woolco opens in Oadby, Leicester
1974	The first Shoppers World catalogue store opens in Leeds
1974 and 1976	The Belfast store is damaged by bombs during the Troubles
1979	A fire in the Manchester superstore causes 10 deaths
1980	Furnishing World opens in Southampton
	DIY World is planned
	Woolworth's buys B&Q
	George Reid is appointed Woolworth's Chief Architect
1982	Paternoster Stores (Woolworth Holdings) buys Woolworth's
1984	The 'Cornerstone Strategy' and 'Operation Facelift' are implemented
	Woolworth's withdraws from the Republic of Ireland
1985	Two new formats – 'Woolworths Weekend' and 'Woolworths General Store' – are introduced
	A new strategy is developed by Fitch (launched in 1986 as 'Operation Focus')
1986	Dixons launches an aggressive bid for Woolworth's
	Woolco is sold
1987	Kidstore is launched
1988	Woolworth Property Ltd is renamed Chartwell Land
1989	The Kingfisher name is adopted
1999	The first Big W opens in Edinburgh
2000	General Stores is reintroduced in Palmers Green
2001	The Woolworths Group demerges from Kingfisher
2007	The Worthit! brand name is introduced
Nov 2008	Woolworth's enters administration
Jan 2009	The last stores close

APPENDIX 2

Woolworth's Store List

Woolworth's stores are listed by their number and name. This is followed – only when required for disambiguation – by additional geographical information. Full addresses have been omitted, since both addresses and locations changed over the years. In the main numerical sequence the year of opening (not building) has been added. This has been included only when supporting evidence has been available. Most missing dates, however, can be determined approximately from the position of stores in the sequence. Note that store numbers were occasionally reallocated to new branches after the original store had closed.

The information here has been gleaned from newspaper reports, company documentation, the store gallery at www.100thbirthday.co.uk and a spreadsheet compiled by Paul Seaton. Occasionally these sources conflict and no doubt some errors have crept in. A few gaps remain, where the identity of stores could not be discovered.

Historical store lists from 1972 and 1995, as well as a complete alphabetical list of stores operating at the end of 2008, can be downloaded from www.woolworthsmuseum.co.uk. Additional lists were supplied to the author by former Woolworth's employees.

1	Liverpool, Church Street, 1909	34	Clapham Junction, London, 1914	68	Watford, 1916
2	Preston, 1910	35	Portsmouth, Commercial Road, 1914	69	Devonport, 1916
3	Liverpool, London Road, 1910	36	Nottingham, 1914	70	Walthamstow, 1916
4	Manchester, Oldham Street, 1910	37	Bradford, 1914	71	Sutton, 1916
5	Leeds, 1910	38	Swindon, 1914	72	Ramsgate, 1916
6	Hull, Whitefriargate, 1910	39	Glasgow, Union Street, 1914	73	Brighton, Western Road, 1916
7	Brixton, 1910	40	Colchester, 1914	74	Ealing, 1916
8	Middlesbrough, 1911	41	Hammersmith, London, 1914	75	Aberdare, 1917
9	Woolwich, 1911	42	Cricklewood, London, 1914	76	Dublin, Henry Street, 1918
10	Bristol, 1911	43	Kingston upon Thames, 1914	77	Manchester, Stretford Road
11	Harlesden, 1912	44	Norwich, Rampant Horse Street, 1914	78	Streatham, London, 1918
12	Croydon, North End, 1912	45	Putney, 1915	79	Aberdeen, St Nicholas Street, 1919
13	Wolverhampton, 1912	46	Walsall, 1915	80	Bromley
14	Swansea, 1912	47	Dover, 1915	81	Weston-super-Mare, 1919
15	Peckham, 1912	48	Stockport, 1915	82	Walworth Road, London, 1919
16	Bolton, 1912	49	Leicester, 1915	83	Cork, 1920
17	Chatham, 1912	50	Southsea, 1915	84	Poole, 1920
18	Grimsby, Freeman Street, 1913	51	Huddersfield, 1915	85	Londonderry, 1920
19	Ilford, 1912	52	Luton, 1915	86	Stratford, London, 1920
20	Lewisham, 1913	53	Northampton, Gold Street, 1915	87	Acton, London, 1920
21	Wimbledon, 1913	54	Bournemouth, 1915	88	Torquay, 1920
22	Warrington, 1913	55	Hanley, 1915	89	Worthing, 1920
23	Richmond, London, 1913	56	Plymouth, 1915	90	Kingstown (Dun Laoghaire), 1920
24	Southampton, East Street, 1913	57	Deptford, 1915	91	Chiswick, 1920
25	Cardiff, 1913	58	Wandsworth, 1915	92	Wakefield, 1920
26	Wood Green, London, 1913	59	Belfast, High Street, 1915	93	Portadown, 1921
27	Newcastle-upon-Tyne, Northumberland Street, 1913	60	Cheltenham, 1915	94	Hackney, 1921
		61	Stoke Newington, 1915	95	Jersey, St Helier, 1921
28	Darlington, 1913	62	Peterborough, 1915	96	Greenock, 1921
29	Derby, 1913	63	Stroud, 1916	97	Limerick, 1921
30	Edgware Road, London, 1914	64	Tooting, 1916	98	Pontypridd, 1921
31	Dublin, Grafton Street, 1914	65	Worcester, 1916	99	Belfast, North Street, 1921
32	Dudley, 1914	66	Blackpool, 1916	100	Mansfield, 1921
33	Southend-on-Sea, 1914	67	Gravesend, 1916	101	Dewsbury, 1921

102	Kingsland High Street, London	166	Stirling, 1924	230	Manchester, Exchange Arcade, 1926
103	Birmingham, Bull Ring, *c* 1923	167	Boston, 1924	231	Rushden, 1926
104	South Shields, 1921	168	Paisley, 1924	232	Berwick-upon-Tweed, 1926
105	Bangor, Gwynedd, 1921	169	Hull, Hessle Road, 1924	233	Inverness, 1926
106	Hounslow, London, 1921	170	Smethwick/Cape Hill, Birmingham	234	Croydon, Church Street
107	Basingstoke, 1921	171	York, 1924	235	Blackburn, 1926
108	Barry Dock, 1921	172	Eastbourne, 1924	236	Green Lanes/Hornsey, London
109	Canterbury, 1922	173	High Holborn, London, 1924	237	Pontefract, 1926
110	Taunton	174	Dundee, 1924	238	Dumfries, 1926
111	Reading, 1922	175	Tottenham Court Road, London	239	West Ealing, London, 1926
112	West Bromwich, 1922	176	Kentish Town Road, London, 1924	240	Holloway Road, London
113	Lowestoft, 1922	177	Maidstone, 1924	241	Folkestone, 1926
114	Leamington, 1922	178	Worksop, 1925	242	Barrow-in-Furness, 1926
115	Bridgwater, 1922	179	Boscombe, 1925	243	Horsham, 1927
116	Bishop Auckland, 1922	180	Leith, Edinburgh, 1925	244	Ryde, 1927
117	Rugby, 1922	181	Oldham, 1925	245	Kidderminster, 1927
118	Glasgow, Argyle Street, 1922	182	Port Talbot/Aberavon, 1925	246	Ilfracombe
119	King's Lynn	183	Shepherd's Bush, 1925	247	Woking, 1927
120	Bridgend, 1922	184	Bedford, 1925	248	Aldershot, 1927
121	Glasgow, Charing Cross	185	Newport, Wales, 1925	249	Ashford, 1927
122	Dumbarton, 1922	186	Wolverhampton, 1925	250	Abergavenny, 1927
123	Coventry, 1922	187	Wigan, 1925	251	Hastings, 1927
124	Dunfermline, 1922	188	Strand, 1925	252	Coatbridge, 1927
125	Gloucester	189	Oxford, 1925	253	Whitehaven, 1927
126	Palmers Green, London, 1922	190	Accrington, 1925	254	Chichester, 1927
127	East Ham, London, 1923	191	Clacton-on-Sea, 1925	255	Southwark Park Road, London, 1927
128	Southampton, Above Bar, 1923	192	Margate, 1925	256	Strood, 1927
129	Leyton, London, 1923	193	Doncaster, 1925	257	Tottenham, London, 1927
130	Pontypool, 1923	194	Cambridge, 1925	258	Longton, 1927
131	Harrogate, 1923	195	Bedminster, 1925	259	Westcliffe-on-Sea
132	Halifax, 1923	196	Upper Norwood, London, 1925	260	Penge, London, 1927
133	Herne Bay, 1923	197	Perth, 1925	261	Tunbridge Wells, 1927
134	Great Yarmouth, 1923	198	Kilmarnock, 1925	262	Deal, 1927
135	Swansea, 1923	199	Crewe, 1925	263	Slough
136	Lancaster	200	Hereford, 1925	264	Ashton-under-Lyne, 1927
137	Birmingham, Aston Road North	201	Sheerness, 1925	265	Macclesfield, 1927
138	Gillingham, 1923	202	Maidenhead, 1925	266	Birmingham, New Street, 1927
139	Weymouth, 1923	203	Harrow Road, London	267	Chester-le-Street, 1927
140	Merthyr Tydfil, 1923	204	Barnstaple, 1925	268	Keighley, 1927
141	Ilkeston, 1923	205	Enfield, London, 1935	269	Llandudno, 1927
142	St Helens, 1923	206	Yeovil, 1925	270	Guernsey, St Peter Port, 1927
143	Sheffield, The Moor, 1923	207	Bath, 1925	271	Kentish Town, London, 1926–7
144	Sunderland, 1923	208	Widnes, 1926	272	Ebbw Vale, 1927
145	Kirkcaldy, 1923	209	Stourbridge, 1926	273	Salisbury, 1927
146	Hamilton, 1923	210	Buxton, 1926	274	Rochdale, 1927
147	Burton on Trent, 1923	211	Ayr, 1926	275	Redcar, 1927
148	Ipswich, 1923	212	Ballymena, 1926	276	Byker
149	Pen-y-Craig	213	Edinburgh, Princes Street, 1926	277	Whitley Bay, 1927
150	Kilburn, London, 1924	214	High Wycombe, 1926	278	Spennymoor, 1927
151	Exeter, 1923	215	Leigh, 1926	279	Hockley, Nottingham
152	Birkenhead, 1923	216	Staines, 1926	280	North Finchley, London, 1927
153	Bargoed, 1923	217	Bury, 1926	281	Scunthorpe, 1927
154	Gateshead, 1923	218	Montrose, 1926	282	Eastleigh, 1927
155	Sutton Coldfield, 1923	219	Northwich, 1926	283	Glasgow, Sauchiehall Street
156	Lincoln, 1923	220	Fulham, London	284	Eccles
157	Grantham, 1924	221	Kettering, 1926	285	Guildford, 1927
158	Douglas, Isle of Man, 1924	222	Enfield Highway, London	286	Wembley, London, 1927
159	Carlisle, 1924	223	Castleford, 1926	287	Llanelli, 1927
160	Burnley, 1924	224	Caerphilly, 1926	288	Brighton, London Road, 1927
161	London, 311 Oxford Street, 1924	225	Redditch, 1926	289	Portsmouth, Fratton, 1927
162	Kensington High Street, London, 1924	226	Loughborough, 1926	290	Congleton, 1927
163	Chester, 1924	227	Nuneaton, 1926	291	St Austell, 1927
164	Redhill, 1924	228	Aberdeen, Union Street, 1926	292	Brighton, St James Street, 1927
165	Scarborough, 1924	229	Ashington, 1926	293	Upton Park, London, 1927

294	Grays, 1927	353	Islington, London, 1929	416	Penrith, 1930
295	Windsor, 1927	354	Lambeth, London	417	Caernarvon, 1930
296	Catford, London	355	Chelmsford, 1929	418	Waterford, 1930
297	Maesteg, 1927	356	Letchworth, 1929	419	Waterloo, Liverpool, 1930
298	Sittingbourne, 1927	357	Newmarket, 1929	420	Evesham, 1930
299	Handsworth, 1928	358	Chesterfield, 1929	421	Penarth, 1930
300	Newcastle-under-Lyme, 1928	359	Winchester, 1929	422	Hendon, London
301	Market Harborough, 1928	360	Barnsley	423	Willesden, London, 1930
302	Poplar, London, 1928	361	Colwyn Bay, 1929	424	Wellington, Shropshire, 1930
303	Newport, Isle of Wight, 1928	362	New Cross, London, 1929	425	Louth, 1930
304	Camborne, 1928	363	Lewes, 1929	426	North Shields, 1930
305	Balham, London	364	Kings Road, Chelsea, London, 1929-30	427	Bromsgrove, 1930
306	Falmouth, 1928	365	Falkirk, 1929	428	Banbury
307	Newbury, 1928	366	Saltcoats, 1929	429	Gainsborough, 1930
308	Rhyl, 1928	367	Upper Edmonton, London	430	West Hendon, London
309	Blackpool, Bond Street, 1928	368	Romford, 1929	431	Abertillery, 1931
310	Camberwell, London, 1928	369	Haverfordwest, 1929	432	Felixstowe, 1931
311	St Albans, 1928	370	Uxbridge, London, 1929	433	Clerkenwell, London
312	Shrewsbury, 1928	371	Burslem, 1929	434	Jarrow, 1931
313	Newington Butts, Elephant & Castle, London, 1928	372	Farnham, 1929	435	Salford, 1931
313	Arnold, 1965	373	Smethwick/Bearwood, Birmingham, 1929	436	Henley-on-Thames, 1931
314	Bow, London, 1928			437	Birmingham, Lozells Road, 1931
315	Manor Park, London	374	Brecon, 1929	438	Kendal, 1931
316	Bishops Stortford, 1928	375	Southall, London, 1929	439	Morpeth, 1931
317	Wellingborough, 1928	376	Lichfield, 1930	440	Cardiff, 1931
318	Spalding, 1928	377	Godalming, 1930	441	Shirley, Southampton, 1931
319	Sheffield, Haymarket	378	Walton-on-Thames, 1930	442	Clapham, London
320	Stafford, 1928	379	Tredegar, 1930	443	Sale
321	Durham, 1928	380	Bangor, Co Down, 1930	444	Beverley, 1931
322	Hartlepool, 1928	381	Wallasey, 1930	445	Wrexham, 1931
323	Bridlington, 1929	382	Workington, 1930	446	Clonmel, 1931
324	Stoke-on-Trent, 1928	383	Nantwich, 1930	447	Saltley, Birmingham
325	Bury St Edmonds, 1928	384	Whitby, 1930	448	Bristol, Gloucester Road, 1931
326	Tonbridge, 1928	385	Rotherham, 1930	449	Cradley Heath, Warley, 1931
327	Wisbech, 1928	386	Bootle, 1930	450	Leek, 1931
328	Barking, 1928	387	Liverpool, Great Homer Street	451	Brentwood, 1931
329	Camden Town, London, 1928	388	Consett, 1930	452	Hitchin, 1931
330	Skegness, 1928	389	Erdington, 1930	453	Dorking, 1931
331	Dundalk, 1928	390	Bexleyheath, London, 1930	454	Newark-on-Trent, 1931
332	Mexborough, 1928	391	Brompton Road, London, 1930	455	Liverpool, Wavertree Road
333	Twickenham, London, 1928	392	Braintree, 1930	456	Neath, 1931
334	Muswell Hill Broadway, London, 1928	393	Faversham, 1930	457	Caterham, 1931
335	Elgin, 1928	394	Cirencester, 1930	458	Moss Side
336	Stockton-on-Tees, 1928	395	Runcorn	459	Golders Green, London, 1932
337	Commercial Road, London, 1928	396	Edgware/Burnt Oak, 1930	460	East Sheen, London, 1932
337	Tipperary, 1954	397	Erith, 1930	461	Liverpool, Walton Vale
338	Coventry Road/Small Heath, Birmingham	398	Nelson, 1930	462	Altrincham, 1932
		399	Radcliffe	463	London, 150–154 Oxford Street, 1932
339	Portobello Road, London, 1928	400	Southport, 1930	464	Monmouth, 1932
340	Newcastle-on-Tyne, Clayton Street, 1928	401	Beckenham	465	Uttoxeter, 1932
		402	Carmarthen, 1930	466	Teignmouth, 1932
341	Dartford, 1928	403	Dorchester, 1930	467	March, 1932
342	Wednesbury, 1928	404	Tiverton, 1930	468	Nottingham, Radford Road, 1932
343	Lisburn, 1928	405	Andover, 1930	469	Coulsdon, 1932
344	Bognor Regis, 1929	406	Harrow, 1929	470	Aylesbury, 1932
345	Retford, 1929	407	Kilkenny, 1930	471	Batley, 1932
346	Whitechapel, London, 1929	408	Morecambe	472	Long Eaton, 1932
347	Littlehampton, 1929	409	Chorley, 1930	473	Maldon, 1932
348	Trowbridge, 1929	410	Darwen	474	Coalville, 1932
349	Bilston, 1929	411	Colne	475	Aberystwyth, 1932
350	Northampton, Abington Street, 1929	412	Motherwell, 1930	476	Cardiff, Albany Road, 1932
351	Wallsend-on-Tyne, 1929	413	Hawick, 1930	477	Paignton, 1932
352	East Grinstead, 1929	414	Sligo, 1930	478	Ulverston, 1932
		415	Coleraine, 1931	479	Liverpool, Walton Road

480	Greenwich, London	544	Blyth, 1934	608	Huntingdon, 1935
481	Longsight, Manchester	545	Horley, 1934	609	Cannock, 1935
482	Bacup	546	Seven Kings	610	Prescot, 1935
483	Tunstall	547	Forest Hill, London, 1934	611	Armagh, 1935
484	Cardiff, Clifton Street, 1932	548	Saffron Walden, 1934	612	Hindley, 1935
485	Glossop, 1932	549	Heanor, 1934	613	Fleetwood, 1935
486	Galashiels, 1932	550	Hornchurch, 1934	614	Stornoway, 1935
487	Oswestry, 1933	551	Christchurch, 1934	615	Surbiton, 1935
488	Houghton-le-Spring, 1933	552	Haywards Heath, 1934	616	Hucknall
489	Whitstable, 1933	553	Hythe, 1934	617	Leven, 1935
490	Melton Mowbray, 1933	554	Kings Heath, Birmingham, 1934	618	Maryport, 1935
491	Leigh-on-Sea, 1933	555	Cromer, 1934	619	Ellesmere Port, 1935
492	Ripon, 1933	556	Norwich, Magdalen Street, 1934	620	Hoylake
493	Chippenham, 1933	557	Frome, 1934	621	Tavistock, 1935
494	Stratford-on-Avon, 1933	558	Pwllheli, 1934	622	Ely, 1935
495	Wick, 1933	559	Peterhead, 1934	623	Liskeard, 1935
496	Wilmslow, 1933	560	Prestatyn, 1934	624	Ashby-de-la-Zouch, 1935
497	Alton, 1933	561	West Wickham, 1934	625	Bexhill-on-Sea, 1935
498	Morden, 1933	562	Petersfield, 1934	626	Clitheroe, 1935
499	Sparkhill, Birmingham	563	Marlow	627	Urmston, 1935
500	Eltham, 1933	564	Cliftonville	628	Winsford
501	Barnet	565	Hoddesdon, 1934	629	Normanton
502	Esher	566	Mitcham	630	Totnes, 1935
503	Devizes, 1933	567	Swadlincote, 1934	631	Cosham, 1935
504	Kenton, Harrow	568	Stone, Staffs, 1934	632	Sevenoaks, 1935
505	Goole, 1933	569	Bodmin, 1934	633	Romsey, 1935
506	Porth, 1933	570	Ross-on-Wye, 1934	634	Cheadle
507	Thornton Heath	571	Dunstable, 1934	635	Sandbach, 1935
508	Tamworth, 1933	572	Old Kent Road, London	636	Chesham
509	Brighouse, 1933	573	Havant	637	Wimborne, 1935
510	Exmouth, 1933	574	Shoreham-by-Sea, 1934	638	Dereham, 1935
511	Canning Town, London, 1933	575	Birmingham, Harborne	639	Hemel Hempstead, 1936
512	Greenford, 1933	576	Ruislip, 1934	640	Sutton-in-Ashfield, 1936
513	Winton, 1933	577	Tewkesbury	641	Richmond, Yorkshire, 1936
514	Ripley	578	Stalybridge	642	Cowdenbeath, 1936
515	Chepstow, 1933	579	Skipton, 1934	643	Waltham Cross, 1936
516	Lower Edmonton, London, 1933	580	Helensburgh, 1934	644	Newtown, Montgomeryshire, 1936
517	Holywell, 1933	581	Withernsea, 1934	645	St Neots, 1936
518	Gorleston-on-Sea, 1933	582	Brierley Hill	646	Tolworth, 1936
519	Arbroath, 1933	583	Feltham, 1934	647	Seaford, 1936
520	Alloa, 1933	584	Gosport, 1934	648	Loughton, 1936
521	New Ferry, Wirral, 1933	585	Leominster, 1934	649	Seaham
522	Newton Abbot, 1933	586	Rugeley, 1934	650	St Andrews, 1936
523	Neasden, London	587	Beeston	651	Penzance, 1936
524	Ludlow, 1933	588	Newport, Shropshire, 1934	652	Malvern, 1936
525	Solihull, 1933	589	South Norwood	653	Stamford, 1936
526	Chingford Mount	590	Hertford, 1934	654	Yiewsley, 1936
527	Blaenau Ffestiniog, 1933	591	Malton, 1934	655	Selly Oak, Birmingham
528	Hyde, 1933	592	Witham, 1934	656	Shanklin, 1936
529	Crook, 1933	593	Acock's Green, Birmingham, 1934	657	Falloden Way, Hampstead Garden Suburb, London, 1935
530	Leytonstone, London, 1934	594	Fraserburgh, 1934		
531	Sidcup, 1934	595	Lurgan, 1934	658	Frinton-on-Sea
532	Orpington, 1934	596	Morley, Leeds	659	Stamford Hill, London, 1935
533	Worcester Park	597	Cowes, 1934	660	Hockley, Lodge Road, Birmingham
534	Barnard Castle, 1934	598	North Harrow	661	Atherstone, 1936.
535	Dovercourt, Harwich, 1934.	599	Chertsey, 1934	662	Whitchurch, 1936
536	Fareham, 1934	600	Wallington, 1934	663	Selby, 1936
537	Rickmansworth	601	Halstead, 1935	664	Denbigh, 1936
538	Kingsbury, London, 1934	602	Norbury, London	665	Glasgow, Kilmarnock Road, 1936
539	Edgware, 1934	603	Kingswood, 1935	666	Welling, 1936
540	Mill Hill Broadway, London, 1934	604	Morriston, Swansea, 1935	667	Addiscombe, 1936
541	Hayes, 1934	605	Wellington, Somerset, 1935	668	Beccles, 1936
542	Hinckley, 1934	606	Southbourne, 1935	669	Minehead, 1936
543	Rutherglen, 1934	607	Rawtenstall, 1935	670	Wokingham, 1936

671	Beacontree	735	Whetstone, London, 1938	798	Debden, 1953
672	New Malden, 1936	736	Petts Wood, 1938	799	Boreham Wood, 1953
673	Camberley, 1936	737	Banstead, 1938	800	Victoria, London, 1953
674	Edinburgh, Lothian Road, 1936	738	Market Drayton, 1939	801	Bray, Co Wicklow, 1953
675	Airdrie, 1936	739	Ilkley, 1938	802	Old Swan/Prescot Road, Liverpool, 1953
676	Conwy, 1936	740	North Watford, 1938		
677	Wells, 1936	741	Pembroke Dock, 1939	803	Barmouth, 1953
678	Witney, 1936	742	Parkstone, 1939	804	North Berwick, 1953
679	Ashbourne	743	Birmingham, Gooch Street	805	Nairn, 1953
680	Hove, 1937	744	Highgate/Junction Road, London, 1939	806	Holyhead, 1953
681	Hampstead, London, 1936			807	Wishaw, 1953
682	Epsom, 1937	745	Greenford	808	Galway, 1953
683	Mold, 1937	746	Dagenham, 1939	809	Mullingar, 1953
684	Alfreton, 1937	747	Stevenage	810	Cleveleys, 1953
685	Bridport, 1937	748	Sidcup, 1939	811	Hunstanton, 1953
686	Knaresborough, 1937	749	Northfield, Birmingham, 1939	812	Launceston
687	North Cheam, 1937	750	The Hyde, Colindale 1939	813	Redruth, 1953
688	Newport Pagnell, 1937	751	Morecambe, 1939	814	Bridgnorth, 1953
689	Rayners Lane, Pinner, 1937	752	New Brighton	815	Oldbury, Warley
690	Brigg	753	Bathgate, 1939	816	Smethwick High Street, Birmingham
691	Brixham, 1937	754	Otley, 1939	817	Pennywell, Sunderland, 1953
692	Eastcote, 1937	755	Rothesay, 1939	818	Bulwell, 1953
693	Whitton, 1937	756	Stoneleigh	819	Shirley, Birmingham, 1953
694	Prestwick, 1937	757	Clifton, 1939	820	Billingham, 1953
695	Leighton Buzzard, 1937	758	Wealdstone, 1940	821	Thurles, 1953
696	Ledbury, 1937	759	Clydebank, 1939	822	Alnwick, 1953
697	South Harrow, 1937	760	Weybridge, 1946	823	Ballina 1953
698	Rye, 1937	761	Romford, 1940	824	Welwyn Garden City, 1953
699	Southgate, London, 1937	762	Diss, 1939	825	Enfield Highway, 1954
700	Cheapside, London	763	Upminster, 1940	826	Hainault/Chigwell, 1954
701	Downham, Bromley, 1937	764	East Molesey, 1947	827	New Addington, 1954
702	Barkingside, 1937	765	Uckfield, 1940	828	South Oxhey, 1954
703	Sutton, 1937	766	Amersham, 1940	829	Brentford, 1954
704	Heywood	767	Porthcawl, 1940	830	Dursley
705	Driffield, 1937	768	Crawley, 1940	831	Tonypandy, 1954
706	Pinner, 1937	769	Newry, 1946	832	St Leonard's-on-Sea
707	West Norwood, 1937	770	Drogheda, 1950	833	Omagh, 1954
708	Bideford, 1937	771	Woolston, 1951	834	Cupar, 1954
709	Belmont, Harrow, 1938	772	Woodbridge, 1951	835	Gorton, Manchester
710	Hull	773	Wexford, 1952	836	Truro, 1954
711	Sleaford, 1937	774	Cleethorpes, 1952	837	Gloucester, 1954
712	Abingdon, 1938	775	Tralee, 1952	838	Exeter
713	Finchley Road, 1938	776	Cardigan, 1952	839	Dublin, Thomas Street, 1954
714	Sherborne, 1938	777	Liverpool, Allerton Road, 1952	840	Sudbury, 1954
715	Tenby, 1938	778	Burnham-on-Sea	841	North Walsham, 1954
716	Gosforth, 1938	779	Haslemere, 1952	842	Haslingden
717	Ringwood, 1938	780	Broadstairs, 1952	843	St Anne's-on-Sea, 1954
718	Harpenden, 1938	781	Farnborough, 1952	844	Belgrave Road, Leicester
719	Fishponds, 1938	782	Atherton, 1951	845	Ilford
720	Hayes, Kent	783	Forfar, 1952	846	Sydenham, London, 1954
721	Elm Park/Hornchurch, 1937	784	Swanage, 1952	847	Northallerton, 1954
722	South Woodford, 1938	785	Lymington, 1952	848	Sheldon, Birmingham, 1954
723	East Acton, London	786	Thorne, 1952	849	Eastbourne
724	Blackheath, Warley, 1938	787	Bletchley	850	Govan
725	Belper, 1938	788	Southmead	851	Blackpool, Talbot Road, 1954
726	Milford Haven, 1938	789	Stowmarket, 1952	852	Killarney, 1954
727	Ballards Lane/Finchley, London	790	Warwick, 1953	853	Glastonbury, 1954
728	Purley, 1938	791	South Clifton, Bristol	854	Epping, 1954
729	Sidmouth, 1938	792	Wymondham, 1953	855	Portobello, Edinburgh
730	Newquay, 1938	793	Ormskirk, 1953	856	Strabane, 1954
731	Ashford, Middlesex, 1939	794	Liverpool, Park Road	857	Bingley
732	Girvan, 1938	795	Totton, Southampton, 1953	858	Corby, 1954
733	Cheetham Hill, Manchester, 1938	796	Newhaven, 1953	859	Potters Bar, 1954
734	Kenton, 1938	797	St Paul's Cray, 1953	860	Johnstone, 1954

861	Blaydon-on-Tyne	924	Aveley, 1956	987	Peterlee, 1957
862	Wickford, 1954	925	Harold Hill, 1956	988	Quinton, Birmingham
863	St Ives, Cornwall, 1954	926	Leatherhead, 1955	989	Crewkerne, 1957
864	Downham Market	927	Tenterden, 1956	990	Harlow
865	Leyland	928	Lancing, 1956	991	Kirkstall Road, Leeds, 1958
866	Egham, 1954	929	Chorlton-cum-Hardy, 1956	992	Clevedon, 1958
867	Oakengates, Telford, 1954	930	Leigh Park, Havant, 1956	993	Bethnal Green Road, London, 1958
868	Sherwood	931	Hexham, 1956	994	Tottenham, West Green Road, 1958
869	St Ives, Cambs, 1955	932	Selsdon, 1956	995	Glasgow, Byres Road, 1958
870	Clay Cross	933	Hadleigh, 1956	996	Flint, 1958
871	Cobham, 1955	934	Didcot, 1956	997	Southall, London
872	Ladypool Road, Birmingham	935	Coventry, Radford, 1956	998	Great Crosby, Liverpool
873	Stanley, 1955	936	Linthorpe Road, Middlesbrough	999	Salisbury, Silver Street, 1958
874	Crowborough, 1955	937	Moreton, Wirral	1000	Portslade, 1958
875	Teddington, 1955	938	Keswick, 1956	1001	South Elmsall
876	Honiton	939	Matlock, 1956	1002	West Hounslow, 1958
877	Berkhamsted	940	Dawlish, 1956	1003	Irvine, 1958
878	Glasgow, Westmuir Street, 1954	941	Pudsey, 1956	1004	Wantage, 1958
879	Port Talbot	942	Garston, Liverpool	1005	Bitterne Road, Southampton, 1958
880	Rayleigh, 1955	943	Glasgow, New City Road	1006	Dunoon, 1958
881	Troon, 1955	944	Glasgow, Dumbarton Road, 1956	1007	Newton Aycliffe, 1958
882	Leicester	945	Birmingham, Stratford Road	1008	Stevenage, 1958
883	Coventry, Walsgrave Road, 1955	946	Lea Village, Birmingham	1009	New Milton, 1958
884	Sheringham, 1955	947	Gerrards Cross	1010	Glasgow, Springburn Road
885	Cavan, 1955	948	Aston High Street, Birmingham	1011	Hillsborough, Sheffield, 1958
886	Oban, 1955	949	Felling, Gateshead, 1956	1012	Halesowen, 1958
887	Tipton	950	West Worthing	1013	Bartley Green, Birmingham
888	Reigate, 1955	951	Addlestone, 1956	1014	New Washington, 1959
889	Wanstead, London, 1955	952	Hailsham, 1956	1015	Bo'ness, 1959
890	Oxted, 1955	953	Earlestown, Newton-le-Willows, 1956	1016	Kirkwall, Orkney, 1959
891	Burgess Hill, 1955	954	Farnworth, 1956	1017	Forest Gate, London, 1959
892	Caledonian Road, London	955	Luton, Dunstable Road	1018	East Kilbride, 1959
893	Broadwater, Worthing, 1955	956	Bloxwich, 1957	1019	Edgeley, Stockport
894	Westbourne	957	Hull, Anlaby Road	1020	Cambuslang, 1959
895	Fleet, 1955	958	Musselburgh, 1957	1021	Hatfield
896	Larne, 1955	959	Hartcliffe Estate, Bristol	1022	Kirby, Liverpool
897	Royston, 1955	960	Kensington, Liverpool	1023	Newtownards, 1959
898	Hook Road, Chessington, 1955	961	Clifton, Nottingham, 1957	1024	Ashby, Scunthorpe, 1959
899	Crayford, 1955	962	Llanrumney, Cardiff	1025	Shaw, 1959
900	East Dulwich	963	Parkgate, Rotherham	1026	Kenton, Newcastle on Tyne
901	Hatch End, Pinner	964	Shipley, 1957	1027	Longbenton
902	Wembley	965	Middleton, Manchester	1028	Birmingham, West Heath
902	Preston Road, Wembley, 1955	966	Sanderstead, 1957	1029	Bellshill, 1960
903	Liverpool, West Derby Road	967	Hayes End, 1957	1030	Melksham, 1960
904	Glasgow, Paisley Road	968	Queensway/Paddington, London, 1957	1031	Twydall Green, Gillingham, 1960
905	Benwell			1032	Canvey Island, 1960
906	Kingstanding, Birmingham, 1955	969	Huyton, Liverpool	1033	Heswall, 1960
907	Seaton, 1955	970	Slough, Farnham Road, 1957	1034	Stretford, Manchester, 1960
908	Yardley, Birmingham, 1955	971	Waterlooville, 1957	1035	Cinderford, 1960
909	Southampton, Portswood Road, 1955	972	Beaconsfield, 1957	1036	Thurso, 1960
910	Dartmouth, 1955	973	Abergele, 1957	1037	Kents Moat Estate, Birmingham
911	Billericay, 1955	974	Cotteridge, Birmingham, 1957	1038	Ammanford, 1960
912	Chadwell Heath, 1955	975	Shotton, 1957	1039	Radlett, 1960
913	Kingsbridge, 1956	976	Biddulph, Stoke-on-Trent, 1957	1040	Bracknell, 1960
914	Holbeach, 1955	977	Dudley Road, Birmingham	1041	Marylebone High Street, London, 1960
915	Horncastle, 1956	978	Biggleswade, 1957		
916	Norris Green, Liverpool	979	Eastwood, Nottingham, 1957	1042	Mastrick, Aberdeen, 1960
917	Northenden, Manchester, 1956	980	Crouch End, London, 1957	1043	Coldthorpe
918	Oldfield Park, Bath, 1956	981	Grimsby, Victoria Street, 1957	1044	Bramhall, 1960
919	Hull, King Edward Street, 1956	982	Shoreditch, 1957	1045	Sandown, Isle of Wight, 1960
920	Helston, 1956	983	Shirehampton, 1957	1046	Basildon, 1961
921	Warminster, 1956	984	West Brompton, London, 1957	1047	Notting Hill Gate, London, 1961
922	Bicester, 1956	985	Ruislip Manor, 1957	1048	Knutsford, 1961
923	Keynsham	986	Cambridge, Fitzroy Street	1049	Bentilee Estate, Stoke-on-Trent, 1961

1050	Kirkintilloch, 1961	1114	Houghton Regis, 1966		Arndale Centre, 1990
1051	Stranraer, 1961	1115	Seacroft Centre, Leeds, 1966	1170	Sheffield, Merryhill Centre, 1990
1052	Thetford, 1961	1116	Huyton, Liverpool, 1966	1171	Lincoln, Waterside Centre, 1991
1053	Lytham St Annes, 1961	1117	Doncaster, Queensgate	1172	Birmingham, The Pallasades, 1991
1054	Birchington	1118	Wylde Green, Sutton Coldfield	1173	Slough, The Observatory, 1991
1055	Brechin, 1961	1119	Yate, 1966	1174	Bristol, Galleries, 1991
1056	Heckmondwike, 1961	1120	Blandford Forum, 1966	1175	Nottingham, Victoria Centre, 1991
1057	Blackwood, 1961	1121	Kenilworth, 1967	1176	Aylesbury, Friars Square, 1992
1058	Plumstead, London, 1961	1122	Wombwell, 1967	1177	Barnstaple, Green Lanes Centre, 1992
1059	Lanark, 1961	1123	Mountain Ash, Glamorgan, 1967	1178	Lancaster, 1994
1060	Haverhill, 1961	1124	Southwick, Brighton, 1967	1179	Woking, Peacock Centre
1061	Headingley, Leeds, 1965	1125	Bedworth, 1967	1180	Reading, 1992
1062	Fort William, 1962	1126	Enniskillen, 1967	1181	Telford, 1992
1063	Dalkeith, 1962	1127	Bourne, 1967	1182	Barnsley, Alhambra Centre, 1992
1064	Fakenham, 1962	1128	Carlow, 1967	1183	Bromley, 1992
1065	Glasgow, Dalmarnock Road	1129	Cross Gates, Leeds, 1968	1184	Dundee, Wellgate Centre, 1993
1066	Lochee, Dundee, 1962	1130	Swinton, Manchester, 1969	1185	Guildford, 1993
1067	Stafford	1131	Stourport-on-Severn, 1969	1186	Hounslow, 1993
1068	Dungannon, 1962	1132	Castle Douglas, 1969	1187	Cheltenham, 1993
1069	Drumchapel, Glasgow, 1962	1133	Mere Green/Four Oaks, 1969	1188	Glasgow, 1994
1070	Cowley, 1962	1134	Kingswinford, 1970	1189	Taunton
1071	Edinburgh, Dalry Road	1135	Chelmsley Wood, Birmingham, 1971	1190	Ashton-under-Lyne, The Arcades, 1994
1072	Largs, 1963	1136	Swanley Centre, 1971	1191	Blackpool, Bank Hey Street, 1994
1073	Netherton, Bootle, 1963	1137	Linwood, 1971	1192	Sutton, 1994
1074	Cwmbran, 1963	1138	Belle Vale, Liverpool, 1973	1193	Chorley, Market Walk
1075	Swindon Park, 1963	1139	Milton Keynes, 1979	1194	Walsall, Town Wharf
1076	Dingwall, 1963	1140	Porthmadog, 1983	1195	Caerphilly, 1996
1077	Maghull, 1963	1141	Leicester, Haymarket Centre, 1986	1196	Motherwell
1078	Plymstock, 1963	1142	Leeds, Merrion Centre, 1987	1197	Leeds
1079	Armley, Leeds, 1963	1143	Shrewsbury, 1988	1198	Harrow, St George's Shopping Centre
1080	Campbeltown, 1963	1144	Gateshead, MetroCentre, 1988	1199	Livingston
1081	Port Glasgow, 1963	1145	Manchester, Barbirolli Mall, Arndale Centre, 1988	1200	Middlesbrough
1082	Lydney, 1963			1201	Kirkcaldy, Mercat Shopping Centre
1083	Wythenshaw	1146	Derby, Eagle Centre, 1988	1202	Colchester, Culver Square, 1999
1084	Glenrothes, 1963	1147	Newport, Wales, Kingsway Centre, 1988	1203	Banbury, Castle Quay
1085	Broughty Ferry, Dundee, 1963			1204	Monks Cross, York, 1998
1086	Marlborough, 1963	1148	Middlesbrough, Hill Street Centre, 1989	1205	Broughton Park
1087	Perry Barr, Birmingham			1206	Dover
1088	Speke	1149	Ealing (Kidstore), 1987	1207	Oldham, 1999
1089	Cheadle	1150	Lewisham (Kidstore), Lewisham Centre, 1987	1208	Edinburgh (Big W), 1999
1090	Merrion Centre, Leeds, 1964			1209	Blackburn, Cobden Court
1091	Buckingham, 1964	1151	Colchester (Kidstore), Culver Centre	1210	Thame
1092	Bell Green, Coventry, 1964	1152	Derby (Kidstore), Eagle Centre	1211	Stornoway
1093	Lyme Regis, 1964	1153	Dudley, Merryhill Centre, 1989	1212	Chesterfield, Vicar Lane, 1999
1094	West Byfleet, 1964	1154	Lincoln, Sincil Street, 1989	1213	Braehead, Braehead Shopping Centre
1095	Firth Park, Sheffield	1155	Manchester, Barbirolli Mall, Arndale Centre, 1989	1214	Swiss Cottage
1096	Edinburgh, Stockbridge, 1964			1215	Kirkintilloch
1097	Wednesfield, 1964	1156	Woolwich (Music & Video), 1990	1216	Clydebank Shopping Centre.
1098	Blairgowrie, 1964	1157	Putney, Putney Exchange, 1990	1217	Coventry (Big W)
1099	Welshpool, 1964	1158	Norwich, St Stephen Street, 1990	1218	Clapham High Street
1100	Corstorphine, 1964	1159	Aberdeen, Bon Accord Centre, 1990	1219	Weymouth
1101	Nuneaton	1160	King's Lynn, Broad Street, 1990	1220	Camberley, Princess Way
1102	Walton-on-the-Naze, 1964	1161	Sheffield, Meadowhall, 1990	1221	East Belfast, Connswater, 1999
1103	Torquay	1162	Liverpool, St John's Centre, 1990	1222	Letchworth
1104	Elephant & Castle, London, 1965	1163	Winchester (Music & Video), 1990	1223	Bristol, Filton (Big W), Abbey Wood Retail Park
1105	South Shields, Prince Edward Road	1164	Cardiff (Music & Video), St David's Centre, 1990		
1106	Chard, 1965			1224	Rotherham (Big W), Poplar Way, Catcliffe
1107	Banbridge, 1965	1165	Eastbourne (Music & Video), Arndale Centre, 1990		
1108	Walkden, 1965			1225	Honiton
1109	Swaffham, 1965	1166	Watford, Harlequin Centre	1226	Bexleyheath
1110	Lee, London, 1965	1167	Thurrock, Lakeside Shopping Centre, 1990	1227	Ballymena
1111	Rustington, 1965			1228	Redruth (Big W)
1112	Castlemilk, Glasgow	1168	Kirkcaldy, 1990	1229	Fleet, Hart Centre
1113	Brownhills, 1966	1169	Manchester, Barbirolli Mall,	1230	Irvine, Rivergate Centre

1231	Glasgow (Big W), The Forge Retail Park
1232	Stockton on Tees (Big W), Portrack Lane
1233	Bradford (Big W), Victoria Shopping Centre
1234	Watford
1235	Northallerton
1236	Bolton (Big W)
1237	Chester, Foregate.
1238	Gateshead MetroCentre, Garden Walk
1239	Tamworth (Big W), Ventura Retail Park.
1240	Wood Green Shopping Centre
1241	Ilford, Balfour Road
1242	Derby, London Road
1243	Slough, Queensmere
1244	Scunthorpe, Parishes Shopping Centre
1245	Newark (Big W), North Gate Retail Park
1246	Cwmbran (Big W), General Rees Square.
1247	Norwich (Big W), Riverside Retail Park.
1248	Belfast (Big W), Yorkgate, 2001
1249	Coatbridge (Big W)
1250	Birmingham (Big W), St Andrews Retail Park, Small Heath
1251	Newport, Wales (Big W), East Retail Park, Maesglas
1252	Beckton (Big W), Beckton Retail Park.
1253	Manchester (Big W), Cheetham Hill
1254	Loughborough (Big W), The Rushes
1255	Hull (Big W)
1256	Newcastle, Byker (Big W), Fossway
1257	Aberdeen (Big W)
1258	Bristol Imperial Park (Big W)
1260	Ely
1261	Didcot
1262	King's Lynn, Vancouver Centre, 2006
1263	Harlow, The Water Gardens
1264	Putney, High Street
1265	Cumbernauld
1266	Ayr, High Street
1267	Shaftesbury
1268	Antrim, Castle Mall, 2008
1269	Nailsea
1270	Worcester
1271	Brierley Hill
1272	Shepton Mallet
1273	Magherafelt, Meadow Lane, 2008
1274	West Belfast, Park Centre, 2008
1275	Bitterne, 2008

Woolworths concessions (all 2008)

1801	Cheadle
1802	Dronfield or Mitcham?
1803	Downham Market
1804	Norwich, Catton
1805	Dronfield or Mitcham?
1806	Chelmsford
1807	South Norwood
1808	Boston
1809	Hinckley
1810	Southwark
1811	Wicklow

Woolco

2001	Oadby
2002	Thornaby
2003	Bournemouth
2004	Killingworth
2005	Middleton
2006	Hatfield
2007	Washington
2008	Cumbernauld
2009	Sheffield
2010	Cwmbran
2011	Kirkby
2012	Wythenshaw
2013	Livingstone
2014	Newtownards
2015	Kings Heath

General stores

2000	Palmers Green (Store 126)
2001	Muswell Hill (Store 334)
2002	Balham (Store 305)
2003	Hackney (Store 94)
2016	Blackpool (Store 851)
2017	Musselburgh (Store 958)
2018	Twickenham (Store 333)
2019	New Maldon (Store 672)
2020	Brixton (Store 7)
2021	Chiswick (Store 91)
2022	Grays (Store 294)
2023	Greenford (Store 512)
2024	Leyton (Store 129)
2025	Streatham (Store 78)
2026	Waterloo, Liverpool (Store 419)
2027	Wembley (Store 286)
2028	Derby (Southgate Retail Park)
2030	Bournemouth
2031	Edgware Road, London (Store 30)
2033	Lothian Road, Edinburgh (Store 674)

Kidstore

2082	Ealing
2083	Lewisham
2087	Colchester
2088	Derby

Furnishing World

2101	Southampton
2102	Rotherham
2103	Eastbourne
2104	Poole
2105	Gillingham

Footlocker

3001	Tamworth
3002	Birmingham
3003	Chester
3004	Wolverhampton

Shoppers World (from store lists dated 1974 and 1979)

4001	Leeds
4002	Newcastle-under-Lyme
4003	Springhill, Birmingham
4004	Nelson
4005	Leigh
4006	Derby
4007	Liverpool
4008	Morley
4009	Heywood
4010	Sparkhill
4011	Sale
4012	Brownhills
4013	Edgeley
4014	Harborne
4015	Knutsford
4016	Moreton
4017	Stourbridge
4018	Accrington
4019	Kensington High Street, London
4022	Kings Heath
4023	Acton
4024	Stroud
4025	Bromsgrove
4026	Coalville
4027	Evesham
4028	Sheffield
4029	Dudley

Shoppers World (from Woolworth's architects' files)

4041	Swindon
4043	Swansea
4044	Colchester
4045	Bedford

Shoppers World (from store list dated 2003)

4001	Leeds
4002	Preston
4004	Manchester
4005	Leeds
4006	Hull
4007	Brixton
4008	Middlesbrough
4009	Woolwich
4010	Bristol
4011	Harlesden
4012	Croydon
4014	Swansea
4015	Peckham
4016	Bolton
4017	Chatham
4018	Grimsby
4019	Ilford
4020	Lewisham

4021	Wimbledon
4022	Warrington
4023	Richmond
4025	Cardiff
4026	Wood Green
4027	Newcastle
4028	Darlington
4029	Derby
4030	Edgware Road, London
4031	Dublin
4032	Dudley
4033	Southend
4034	Clapham Junction
4035	Portsmouth
4036	Nottingham
4037	Bradford
4038	Swindon
4040	Colchester
4041	Hammersmith
4042	Cricklewood
4043	Kingston
4044	Norwich
4045	Putney
4046	Walsall
4047	Dover
4048	Stockport

Overseas Stores

Jamaica

J1 King Street, Kingston
J2 Slipe Road, Cross Roads, Kingston
J3 Montego Bay
J4 The Village Mall
J5 Mandeville
J6 May Pen
J7 Kings Plaza, Constant Springs
J8 Kingston Mall
J99 Newport (warehouse)

Trinidad

T1 Port of Spain
T2 San Fernando
T3 Princes Town
T4 St Augustine
T5 Arima
T6 Gulf City

Barbados

B1 Bridgetown

Southern Rhodesia/ Zimbabwe

R1 Salisbury (Harare)
R2 Bulawayo
R3 Charter Road
R4 Bank Street

Cyprus

C1 Nicosia

A detail of a typical Woolworth's red mosaic fascia from the 1960s, uncovered at Store 356, Letchworth, during renovations in 2014. [Ron Baxter]

NOTES

Conversion table for measurements

Imperial measurements have been used in this book, metric equivalents are given below:

1 inch = 254mm
1 foot = 304.8mm
1 yard = 0.914m
1 mile = 1.6km
1 acre = 0.4 hectares

Abbreviations

HEA   Historic England Archive (formerly National Monuments Record and then the English Heritage Archive)
LMA   London Metropolitan Archives
RIBA   Royal Institute of British Architects
SPAB   Society for the Protection of Ancient Buildings

Notes to Text

Introduction

1   Information from The National Archives.
2   Information from Paul Seaton, 4 Mar 2013.
3   Phillips 2009.

Chapter 1

1   Winkler 1957 rev edn, 23–4. According to company mythology – for example in the *Fortieth Anniversary Souvenir,* 1919, 4 – this innovation was Woolworth's idea.
2   Winkler 1957 rev edn, 52.
3   Ibid, 69.
4   Ibid, 78–9, 85.
5   Ibid, 118, 122, 130, 136.
6   Boyce 2009, 46.
7   *See,* for example, *Fortieth Anniversary Souvenir,* 1919, 4–11.
8   Winkler 1957 rev edn, 130–1.

Chapter 2

1   Winkler 1957 rev edn, 70–1.
2   From a scrapbook created by David J Davis, an American store manager in the early 20th century, http://museum.woolworths.co.uk (accessed 11 Nov 2013).

3   Gareth Shaw, www.oxforddnb.com (accessed 28 Jul 2013).
4   *The Drapers' Record,* 31 Jul 1909, 294; Winkler 1957 rev edn, 144.
5   Winkler 1957 rev edn, 145.
6   Winkler 1957 rev edn, 145.
7   Kirkwood 1960, 17.
8   Sharples 2004, 175.
9   Manchester City Architects Building Bye-law Plan No: 9740, plans submitted Dec 1909.
10   Several photographs of Miles's shop were published in *The Drapers' Record,* 20 Sept 1902, 729–31.
11   *The New Bond,* **18**, 1, Mar 1959, 83.
12   *Woolworth's First 75 Years,* 1954, 16.
13   Plunkett-Powell 1999, 151. Before long, refreshment rooms had opened in numerous American Woolworth stores, serving food on china branded with the firm's name and logo.
14   *The Observer,* 14 Jun 1931, 8.
15   *The New Bond,* **18**, 1, Mar 1959, 83.
16   Typical newspaper headlines when Woolworth landed in England included: 'New American Invader' (*Dundee Courier,* 8 Jun 1909, 8) and 'A Five-cent American Invasion' (*The Luton Times and Advertiser,* 18 Jun 1909, 6).
17   *The Times,* 23 Feb 1909, 4.
18   Morrison 2003, 159–63.
19   For the Selfridge 'Bargain Basement Theory', *see The Times,* 20 Nov 1923, 12.
20   Morrison 2007.
21   *York Herald,* 13 Oct 1888, 6.
22   *Hartlepool Mail,* 11 Apr 1888, 3.
23   Briggs 1984, passim.
24   Morrison 2003, 229; Briggs 1984, 31.
25   Winkler 1957 rev edn, 147
26   *The Drapers' Record,* 14 Aug 1909, 387.
27   Ibid.
28   Snow 1974, 15.
29   Passenger lists, www.ancestry.com (accessed 19 Dec 2013).
30   www.woolworthsmuseum.co.uk (accessed 28 Jul 2013).
31   R J Berridge, quoted in Plunkett-Powell 1999, 113.
32   Briggs 1984, 46.
33   Winkler 1957 rev edn, 148; Pederson J P and Grant T 2007, 467.
34   *Western Daily Press,* 28 Sept 1911, 7.
35   *Nottingham Evening Post,* 16 Jan 1914, 6.

36   Manchester City Architects Building Bye-law Plan No: 11767.
37   A brochure published by Hillier Parker May & Rowden 1981, 63.
38   Kingston upon Thames Museum and Heritage Service KC1/1/449.
39   Ibid KC1/1/451.
40   Bedford Lemere daybook, HEA.
41   Kingston upon Thames Museum and Heritage Service, KC1/1/453.
42   For example, Store 22 in Warrington (plans of 1924, HEA).
43   This identification was made by Paul Seaton: *see* www.woolworthsmusem.co.uk (accessed 1 Mar 2014); email correspondence 4 Mar 2013.
44   *Woolworth's First 75 Years,* 1954, 18.
45   Winkler 1957 rev edn, 142.
46   Winkler 1957 rev edn, 146–8.
47   *The Observer,* 14 Jun 1931, 8.
48   *Derby Daily Telegraph,* 6 Nov 1913, 2.
49   *Hull Daily Mail,* 25 May 1914, 5. Pet departments were maintained in some stores through the years (*see* www.woolworthsmuseum.co.uk/lostdepts). They seem to have lapsed by 1972, when a pet department formed 'an exciting new addition' to the Kingston upon Thames store (*Woolworth News,* Aug 1972, 1).
50   *Hull Daily Mail,* 21 Sept 1914, 3.
51   *Hull Daily Times,* 10 May 1912, 10.
52   *Liverpool Echo,* 4 Mar 1914, 1.
53   *Derby Daily Telegraph,* 4 Feb 1914, 2.
54   *Nottingham Evening Post,* 18 Feb 1914, 7.
55   *Fortieth Anniversary Souvenir,* 1919, 24.
56   Denempont is said to have joined the company in 1910, having worked as a location scout in the US. Evidence for this is absent. The 1911 census includes just one 'Louis Denempont': a 23-year-old 'shop assistant', born in Middlesex and residing in Liverpool. Woolworth's architects seem to have been answerable directly to Denempont through the 1920s and 1930s (information from Paul Seaton, 4 Mar 2013).
57   Abel *c* 1960, 20.
58   Shopfront plans for No 35 Princes Street, Stockport, dated 30 Mar 1915 (HEA).
59   LMA GLC/AR/BR/13/186142, architectural drawing for shop at Nos 45–47 High Street, Putney. In 1925 the store spread into Nos 51–53 High Street,

which were rebuilt in matching style in 1934. The store, which had been damaged during the Second World War, was rebuilt in 1970.

60 Temple (ed) 2008, 366.
61 East Sussex Record Office DB/D/7/6538, 21 Jan 1915.
62 Winkler 1957, rev edn, 159–60.
63 *Daily Mail,* 2 Apr 1924, 9.
64 With regard to the Egyptian style of the mausoleum, it is interesting to note that several Woolworth stores were accommodated on the ground floors of Masonic temples. Woolworth may have been a freemason.
65 *The Times,* 9 Apr 1923, 11.

Chapter 3

1 *Hull Daily Mail,* 20 Oct 1924, 5.
2 *Daily Mail,* 29 Jan 1923, 7.
3 *Aberdeen Journal,* 3 Mar 1919, 3. Plans of the shopfront by John Curtis are dated 27 Mar 1919 (HEA).
4 Census of 1911, www.ancestry.co.uk. It is possible that Priddle had worked with North & Robin.
5 Essex Record Office, D/BC 1/4/12/9155.
6 LMA GLC/AR/DS/06/540.
7 Passenger lists, www.ancestry.co.uk.
8 When the Dundee store was being built, the bricklayers and masons were paid 1s 9d per hour, rather more than normal local rates, causing a fuss; *Dundee Courier,* 17 Sept 1924, 5. Woolworth's undoubtedly encouraged such tactics to ensure speedy construction.
9 LMA GLC/AR/BR/06/053813, drawings dated May 1924. Interestingly, the initial design for the rebuilt Woolwich store, dated 1929, was very similar to that for Tottenham Court Road, *see* LMA GLC/AR/ BR/17/073481. For information on Dollar *see* RIBA Biographical File.
10 LMA GLC/AR/BR/17/037798/01, plans of 1923–5.
11 Sharples 2004, 175.
12 *The Builder,* 19 Jan 1923, 116.
13 *The Architectural Review,* Nov 1935, 193.
14 In a letter to Priddle, dated 25 Sept 1923 (HEA), S Gordon Jeeves suggested alterations to the elevation, writing: 'A building of this magnitude, with such a frontage on to one of the most important streets in London, must of necessity be imposing, and no expense spared in the designing of the Elevation, and if it were not necessary from a constructional point of view to introduce the piers as shown, I think you will agree that both from a Shopman's and Architect's point of view, that these piers would be a necessity.' Unfortunately the drawing attached by Jeeves has not survived.

15 *The Builder,* 21 Jan 1927, 112.
16 West Yorkshire Archive Services, Building Regulation Plan, 3 Apr 1928, No 95; City of Manchester City Architects Building Bye-law Plan No: 18021, 1929.
17 LMA GLC/AR/BR/17/042448.
18 Planning Committee Book, 1919–26, 2 Mar 1925, Cambridge Record Office.
19 Pevsner 1973, 579.
20 Drawings dated 1924 and 1925, HEA.
21 *Daily Mail,* 22 Apr 1920, 5.
22 *The Times,* 22 May 1928, 22.
23 Walsh 2011, 42; *Daily Mail,* 18 Oct 1921, 8.
24 *The Times,* 14 Mar 1921, 9.
25 *The Times,* 13 Dec 1927, 13.
26 *The Times,* 18 Dec 1928, 16.
27 As at the Strand, London, in 1925, LMA GLC/AR/BR/06/032856.
28 Walsh 2011, 40.
29 Ibid, 46–7.
30 *The Times,* 25 Mar 1924, 16.
31 *Dover Express,* 17 Jun 1921, 6.
32 *The Times,* 28 Nov 1928, 13.
33 *The Sunday Times,* 5 Feb 1928, 16.
34 Walsh 2011, 86–7.
35 *Manchester Guardian,* 2 Feb 1928, 13.

Chapter 4

1 As predicted in *The Times,* 10 Jun 1931, 23.
2 Winkler 1957 rev edn, 230.
3 www.woolworthsmuseum.co.uk (accessed 8 Jan 2014).
4 *The Times,* 8 Feb 1932, 4.
5 *The Times,* 31 Oct 1938, 22.
6 Hawkins 2009, 124. The Cuban stores were expropriated after the revolution.
7 *The Observer,* 4 Sept 1927, 8.
8 *The Times,* 15 Aug 1932, 9.
9 *The Times,* 10 Mar 1933, 13; 13 Mar 1933, 14.
10 *The Times,* 22 Jan 1938, 16.
11 *The Times,* 8 May 1933, 22.
12 *The Times,* 25 Jan 1936, 16.
13 *The Times,* 24 Jul 1937, 18; 4 Mar 1938, 16; 22 Apr 1938, 7; 19 Jul 1938, 5.
14 Snow 1974, 21ff.
15 Jeremy 1991, 100.
16 *Woolworth News,* Sept 1986, 4.
17 Barbara Hutton's first husband was the self-styled Prince Alexis Mdivani (divorced 1935). Mdivani was followed by: Count Court von Haugwitz-Hardenberg-Reventlow (divorced 1941); the movie actor Cary Grant (divorced 1945); Prince Igor Troubetzkoy (divorced 1951), Porfirio Rubirosa (divorced 1953); Baron von Cramm (divorced 1959) and Prince Raymond Doan Vinh Na Champacak (divorced 1966).
18 *The Times,* 10 Jun 1936, 13.
19 *The Times,* 28 Jan 1939, 19.
20 *The Sunday Times,* 31 Jan 1932, 2.
21 *The Observer,* 14 Jun 1931, 8.

22 *Twenty-six Years of Progress,* 1934, 10.
23 *The Times,* 2 Feb 1932, 1.
24 Hawkins 2009, 123.
25 Anon 1957, 19. One of Woolworth's earliest documented uses of Truscon floors was in Newcastle in 1930 (Plans, HEA).
26 West Yorkshire Archive Service, Burtons 127.
27 Morrison 2003, 225 and 232.
28 On a completely different scale, one other Woolworth's store that seems to have occupied a Burton's development was the small branch in Nelson, Lancashire, of 1930.
29 Seaton 2009, 71. A list of projects undertaken by Shaws of Darwen in the year 1935–6 includes 10 Odeon cinemas, the majority designed by Harry Weedon, and 23 Woolworth's stores, all designed by the staff architects (collection of Shaws of Darwen).
30 *Woolworth's First 75 Years,* 1954, 29.
31 The Preston store has been attributed to Priddle and dated to 1922 despite its evident art deco style (Stansfield 1986, 54). The same source attributed the surviving stores in Blackpool, Preston, Morecambe, Lancaster and Southport to Priddle, stating that he had 'designed a unified standard elevation with much vertical emphasis and reproduced it in various degrees of decoration' (Stansfield 1986, 93). These buildings – like the introduction of Woolworth's art deco style – post-date Priddle's death, yet several publications have perpetuated the error.
32 www.mitchelllibrary.org (accessed 30 Jan 2014).
33 *Dorset Evening Echo,* 20 Apr 1985, 1.
34 William Leslie Swinnerton, RIBA Biographical File (correspondence).
35 *The Times,* 23 Nov 1925, 24.
36 *The Spectator,* 2 Sept 1937,10.
37 All information in this section from 'Blackpool Store 66', photograph album, 1938 (HEA), unless otherwise stated.
38 *The New Bond,* **4**, 3, Mar 1939, 100–2.
39 *The New Bond,* **3**, 10, Oct 1938, 412–13.
40 *Architectural Design & Construction,* May 1938, 189.
41 SPAB Archive, Godalming file; *The Times,* 6 Nov 1929, 10.
42 SPAB Archive, Hampstead file; *The Times,* 3 Jan 1945, 5; *see* http://collage.cityoflondon.gov.uk for a photograph of the site in 1936 prior to redevelopment.
43 SPAB Archive, Hampstead file.
44 SPAB archive, Chippenham file; *The Times,* 28 Dec 1932, 13.
45 *Country Life,* 22 Mar 1946, 540.
46 *Architectural Review,* **CLVIII**, 945, 274–5.
47 *The New Bond,* **2**, 9, Sept 1937, 302.
48 Information from Paul Seaton, 27 Feb 2013: 'In many of the so-called "secondary locations" Woolworth's architects

developed not just the threepenny and sixpenny store but the whole parade, either retaining the freehold and acting as landlord, or often retaining the freehold of the "Woolies" and paying for it by handing on the adjacent buildings to the original owner of the land.' This analysis is based on the board minute books.

49 Store 406, Plans, HEA.

50 Preston & Hoskins have noted that the address given for Marshall & Tweedy on plans for some of Lotery's parades (specifically that in Whitton) was No 22 Conduit Street (Preston, R and Hoskins, L 2013 'London's Suburban Shopping Parades, 1890–1939'. Unpublished report for English Heritage, 220).

51 'Imported from England', *The Architectural Forum,* Aug 1940, 133–6. Interestingly, the architect Charles Marshall sailed to America with Lotery on 26 Nov 1938 (passenger lists, www.ancestry.com).

52 Preston and Hoskins 2013 'London's Suburban Shopping Parades'.

53 'Imported from England', *The Architectural Forum,* Aug 1940, 135.

54 *The Essex Newsman,* 19 Oct 1935, 1.

55 *See, f*or example, *Yorkshire Evening Post,* 12 Jul 1938, 7, recounting an injury sustained in the Scarborough branch, and *The Cornishman and Cornish Telegraph,* 8 Feb 1934, 7, for an incident at Camborne.

56 Drawing dated 1938, HEA.

57 *The Sunday Times,* 29 Jan 1933, 18.

58 *See* www.woolworthsmuseum.co.uk/1930s.

59 Inglis 2005, 163; Phillips 2009, 147.

60 Curtis 1999, 111.

61 *Architectural Design & Construction,* May 1938, 188.

62 www.colinhiggins.com (accessed 10 May 2014).

63 *Daily Mail,* 13 Apr 1932, 5. For a review of the cafeteria *see Daily Mail,* 28 Apr 1932, 7.

64 Museum of London, Accession No 76.55.

65 *Western Daily Press,* 3 May 1932, 5.

Chapter 5

1 Briggs 1984, 104.

2 *The Times,* 27 Apr 1945, 2.

3 http://museum.woolworths.co.uk (accessed 13 Nov 2013).

Chapter 6

1 Annual Report, *The Times,* 14 Feb 1957, 15; Jeremy 1991, 104–5.

2 *The New Bond,* **16,** 5, Oct 1957, 42.

3 Information from Paul Seaton, 4 Mar 2013.

4 *The Edinburgh Gazette,* 22 Aug 1939, 714.

5 *Dundee Courier,* 21 Oct 1943, 3.

6 Information from Paul Seaton, 4 Mar 2013.

7 Hansard, 18 Jun 1947.

8 Hansard, 21 Oct 1952.

9 Annual Report 1954, *The Times,* 10 Feb 1955, 13.

10 Drawings dated Jan to Jun 1939 and 1952–3, HEA.

11 Walsh 2011, 136.

12 *Forty-two Years of Progress, 1909–1950,* 9.

13 Reprinted in *The New Bond,* **9,** 6, Dec 1950, 7.

14 *The Times,* 8 Feb 1951, 10.

15 Reprinted in *The New Bond,* **8,** 1, Apr 1949, 12.

16 Kirkwood 1960, 17.

17 Plans in the HEA show that this store was originally to have had traditional personal service counters.

18 Plans of Store 891, Burgess Hill, HEA.

19 For a good range of illustrations of early self-service stores, *see* www.woolworthsmuseum.co.uk.

20 *The New Bond,* **15,** 3, Jun 1956, 30.

21 *The New Bond,* **16,** 3, Jun 1957, 29.

22 *Architect & Building News,* 3 Dec 1958, 737; Hawkins 2009, 127; *The New Bond,* **17,** 6, Dec 1958, 36.

23 *The New Bond,* **17,** 4, Aug 1958, 13–16.

24 *The New Bond,* **30,** 5, Dec 1971, 24.

25 *The New Bond,* **17,** 5, Oct 1958, 16–17.

26 Annual Report 1959, *The Times,* 11 Feb 1960, 19.

27 For an archive image of the Clarendon, *see* HEA, BL29551.

28 *The Times,* 11 Dec 1939, 6.

29 *The Times,* 14 Dec 1939, 6.

30 *Building,* Jan 1945, 2.

31 Mervyn Miller, 'William Graham Holford', www.oxforddnb.com (accessed 30 May 2014).

32 E M Jope and W A Pantin 1958 'The Clarendon Hotel Oxford', *Oxoniensia,* **XXIII,** 1–129.

33 Sherwood and Pevsner 1974, 69 and 312. Holford was assisted by Howard Mason and worked alongside Woolworth's architects, Harold Winbourne and H W Schofield.

34 *The New Bond,* **17,** 1, Feb 1958, 51.

35 *The Times,* 30 Apr 1955, 8; 5 May 1955, 3.

36 *The Times,* 3 Jun 1957, 3; *The New Bond,* **18,** 1, Mar 1959, 50.

37 Annual Report 1958, *The Times,* 12 Feb 1959, 15.

38 Asbestolux was the trade name for asbestos insulation board, manufactured since 1950 by the Cape Asbestos Co.

39 Annual Report 1959, *The Times,* 11 Feb 1960, 19.

40 *The Times,* 27 Oct 1964, 7.

41 www.woolworthsmuseum.co.uk (accessed 10 May 2014).

42 Annual Report 1959, *The Times,* 11 Feb 1960, 19.

43 American Woolworth also expanded abroad in the 1950s and 1960s, into Mexico (1956) and later Spain (1965).

44 *The Times,* 10 Feb 1954, 13. *See also The New Bond,* **13,** 6, Dec 1954, 4.

Chapter 7

1 *The Times,* 8 Feb 1962, 20.

2 Hardy's construction managers in the 1960s were: G Gilford (Liverpool; R Chatterton from 1968); W A Draysey (Birmingham; Gordon W Lindon by 1969); W B Brown (Kensington) and W A Spinks (Metropolitan, 1951 to 1970). The department has been described as follows: 'In charge was an Architect who headed Architectural Assistants, Estimators, Fixture Clerks, Accountants, Wages Clerks (for site workers), Maintenance Clerks and General Clerks. Outside staff were called Supervising Foremen (who covered allocated areas within their region and the overseeing of all the building programmes),' (information from Peter Dunn, formerly of the Construction/Architects' Department, Woolworth's, 12 Aug 2014). Including builders, there was a labour force of 600 (information from Pat Sullivan, former Project Manager, Woolworth's, 16 Nov 2000).

3 *See,* for example, remarks by former customer Sylvia Fortnum in Phillips 2009, 136.

4 'Arnold Hagenbach', obituary, *The Times,* 8 Apr 2005, 69.

5 *See* www.soultsretailview.co.uk (accessed 14 Feb 2014).

6 Inglis 2005.

7 *The Times,* 8 Feb 1962, 20; *The Times,* 18 Sept 1962, 16.

8 Kirkwood 1960, 11–12.

9 For an illustration of the Windsor Garden Centre *see The New Bond,* **20,** 3, Aug 1961, 18.

10 *The New Bond,* **26,** 3, Aug 1967, 1–2; **29,** 5, Dec 1970, 69.

11 *The Times,* 3 Sept 1988, 31.

12 *The Observer,* 22 Jan 1967, 7.

13 *The Observer,* 22 Jan 1967, 7.

14 *The Times,* 15 May 1961, 26.

15 *The New Bond,* **21,** 5, Oct 1962, 54–5.

16 Foster 2005, 111.

17 *The Times,* 9 Oct 1962, 5; 11 Feb 1965, 17.

18 *The New Bond,* **23,** 6, Dec 1964, 7–8.

19 *The New Bond,* **24,** 6, Dec 1965, 35–9.

20 Brick-faced neo-Georgian stores of this period included Bury St Edmunds (1964), Wisbech (*c* 1965) and, in a remodelling of the mock-timber store of 1930, Kingston upon Thames (*c* 1965).

21 *The New Bond,* **27,** 6, Dec 1968, 26–7.

22 Phillips 2009, 74. It is not absolutely clear what years Peter Taylor was referring to.

23 *The New Bond,* **29,** 5, Dec 1970, 5.

24 *The New Bond,* **26**, 6, Dec 1967, 2–3.
25 Elevation drawings, HEA. For a Warerite advertisement illustrating Woolworth's Watford store and the Woolco at Middleton, *see Journal of the Royal Institute of British Architects,* May 1973, 267–8 (A49).
26 *The New Bond,* **27**, 4, Aug 1968, 33.
27 Croydon Local Studies Library, Redevelopment Box 2 f570 (711) KED.
28 *The New Bond,* **28**, 5, Oct 1969, 16–17. A new blue-and-white 'W' logo came into use in America in 1979 to celebrate the firm's centenary.
29 Morrison 2003, 278 and 324.
30 *Self-service and Supermarket,* **15**, Dec 1966, 15.
31 *The New Bond,* **26**, 6, Dec 1967, 36. Woolworth's architects held plans of the Woolco store in Aurora, Colorado, probably sent over for guidance or collected by Evans in the course of a fact-finding tour (HEA).
32 Woolworths Collection, HEA.
33 'Woolco' had also been the brand name for gramophone records in Germany.
34 The divisional architect for Woolco was Arthur W Lawson.

Chapter 8

1 Annual Report 1969, *The Times,* 12 Feb 1970, 21.
2 The Cyprus store was sold in 1985 to a local businessman who developed an independent 'Woolworths' chain on the island.
3 *The Times,* 11 Apr 1969, 21. In a break from the past, Medcalf began to recruit directors from outside the company, meaning that sentiment was less likely to affect future decision-making.
4 The Store List of 1972 noted 44 closures. However, the Annual Reports recorded 26 closures in 1970, 8 in 1971 and 23 in 1972: a total of 57 by Dec 1972 (*The Times,* 11 Mar 1971, 21; 24 Feb 1972, 23; 15 Feb 1973, 22).
5 Advertisement for Store 161, *The Times,* 28 Jan 1974, 10.
6 *The Guardian,* 19 Oct 1977, 16.
7 *The Times,* 27 Jan 1971, 18; 11 Mar 1971, 21; 24 Feb 1972, 23.
8 *The New Bond,* **30**, 4, Aug 1971, 30; *The Times,* 11 Mar 1971, 21.
9 *The Times*, 20 Jun 1969, 20.
10 *The Times,* 16 Feb 1971, 1.
11 Museum of London, Accession No 71.68/1–31.
12 *Woolworth News,* Jan 1977, 5.
13 *Woolworth News,* Apr 1975, 2.
14 www.woolworthsmuseum.co.uk (accessed 24 Jan 2014).
15 *The Times,* 26 Feb 1975, 20.

16 *The Guardian,* 18 Oct 1975, 13.
17 *Commercial Motor, 1*2 Jul 1980, www.archive.commercialmotor.com (accessed 12 Jan 2014).
18 *The Times,* 2 Jun 1972, 11.
19 In 1971 Woolworth's began to produce Christmas catalogues, published in *Radio Times.*
20 Walsh 2011, 197.
21 *The Observer,* 3 Oct 1971, 15.
22 Walsh 2011, 199–201.
23 *The Times,* 15 Feb 1973, 22.
24 *The Guardian,* 8 Dec 1977, 16.
25 *The Guardian,* 29 Mar 1978, 14; plans of Tallaght in HEA.
26 Walsh 2011, 187.
27 Walsh 2011, 213–5.
28 *The Times,* 21 May 1980, 3.
29 *The Times,* 17 Jun 1980, 20. Schemes were developed for Furnishing World in Mannington, Swindon and Fareham, but these never opened.
30 *The Times,* 21 Jul 1980, 18; drawing dated 29 Sept 1978 (HEA).
31 The construction superintendents in the regional offices were R Chatterton (Liverpool), Gordon W Lindon (Birmingham), C M Davis (Metropolitan, appointed 1970; replaced by Roy S Power by 1979) and W B Brown (Kensington).
32 Morrison 2003, 266.
33 *Store Planning & Design,* Jul/Aug 1982, 26.
34 *Woolworth News,* Oct 1982, 9.
35 *The Times,* 9 Aug 1980, 15.
36 *The Times,* 23 Sept 1982, 17; 2 Oct 1982, 3; 13 Oct 1981, 21.
37 *The Times,* 7 Apr 1982, 13; *Woolworth News*, Apr 1982, 1.
38 *Woolworth News,* Apr 1982, 1.

Chapter 9

1 Seaton 2009, 111.
2 *The Times,* 2 Oct 1982, 11; 27 Oct 1982, 17.
3 *The Guardian,* 26 Jul 1984, 19.
4 Information from Peter Dunn, formerly of the Construction/Architects' Department, Woolworth's, 12 Aug 2014.
5 *The Times,* 18 Jul 1997, 14.
6 Plunkett-Powell 1999, 11.
7 *The Times,* 7 Sept 1999, 28.
8 *The Times,* 15 Oct 1982, 19.
9 *The Times,* 15 Nov 1982, 21.
10 The properties had last been valued in 1978 at £478 million (*The Guardian,* 11 Apr 1979, 14) and would be revalued again in 1985 at £628 million (*The Times,* 29 Mar 1985, 23).
11 *The Times,* 23 Mar 1984, 23.
12 *The Times,* 3 May 1984, 21; *The Guardian,* 3 May 1984, 18.
13 *The Times,* 13 Nov 1985, 2.
14 *Woolworth News,* Nov 1984, 8.
15 *The Times,* 17 Apr 1986, 3.

16 *The Times,* 26 Oct 1982, 21.
17 *Woolworth News,* Aug 1982, 2.
18 *The Times,* 2 Mar 1983, 17.
19 *Woolworth News,* May 1985, 8; Sept 1985, 4.
20 Walsh 2011, 229; *The Guardian,* 26 Jul 1984, 19.
21 Information from Tim Ayre, former Investment Director, Chartwell Land, 18 Jun 2014.
22 www.woolworthsmuseum.co.uk (accessed 1 Mar 2014).
23 *The Times,* 12 Sept 1985, 12; information from Pat Sullivan, former Project Manager, Woolworth's, 16 Nov 2000.
24 *Woolworth News,* Feb 1984, 1.
25 *Woolworth News,* May 1984, 8.
26 *Woolworth News,* Sept 1984, 4–5.
27 *Woolworth News,* Nov 1984, 2.
28 *Woolworth News,* Nov 1984, 2.
29 *The Times,* 12 Sept 1985, 12.
30 Folder of plans by Anko Store Fixtures for the aborted Woolworth Mall, Croydon, dated Apr 1985 (HEA). The Woolworth Mall was to include Electronic World. The yellow-edged stainless steel lettering for the fascia was 'Letraset Plaza inline'.
31 *The Times,* 26 Jan 1985, 3.
32 *The Guardian,* 27 May 1986, 22; Woolworth Holdings plc, Report and Accounts, 1986/87, 18.
33 *The Times,* 23 Jun 1986, 27.
34 *The Guardian,* 26 Apr 1986, 21; 18 Sept 1986, 24.
35 *The Times,* 3 Sept 1988, 31.
36 *The Times,* 1 Oct 1986, 11.
37 *The Guardian,* 19 May 1986, 23
38 *The Guardian,* 8 Feb 1988, 26.
39 *The Times,* 17 Sept 1987, 26.
40 *The Times,* 28 Jan 1986, 13.
41 According to Peter Dunn, Reid continued to work for Woolworth's as a freelance architectural consultant for a short period. Dunn retired in 1994 and Ken Trimmer subsequently became Development Manager, then Architectural Manager, staying in post until Jan 2009 (information from Ken Trimmer, 10 Jul 2014; from Peter Dunn, 12 Aug 2014).
42 According to Tim Ayre, 23 Jun 2014.
43 *The Times,* 27 Mar 1986, 24; 7 Jun 1986, 21.
44 *The Times,* 15 Apr 1986, 21. The Dee Corporation had recently purchased Wellworths from the Moore brothers.
45 The Charlie Brown Autocentres were sold in 1995.
46 *The Times,* 8 Feb 1988, 21.
47 *The Times,* 23 Feb 1989, 23.
48 *The Times,* 28 Mar 1991, 27.
49 www.woolworthsmuseum.co.uk (accessed 7 Feb 2014).
50 Information from Nigel Stretch, formerly of Woolworth's Estate Department, 12 Jun 2014.

51 www.woolworthsmuseum.co.uk (accessed 7 Feb 2014).
52 *Woolies News,* Autumn 1998, 6.
53 *The Times,* 18 Mar 1999, 31.
54 *The Times,* 15 Sept 1999, 27.
55 http://museum.woolworths.co.uk (accessed 11 Nov 2013).
56 *The Times,* 28 Feb 2000, 22.
57 *The Grocer,* 13 Jul 2002, *see* www.thegrocer.co.uk/companies/after-woolies-spar-looks-again/78452.article.
58 *Evening Standard,* 16 Apr 1999, 1.
59 Information from Nigel Stretch, 12 Jun 2014.
60 www.woolworthsmuseum.co.uk (accessed 28 Feb 2014).
61 www.woolworthsmuseum.co.uk (accessed 27 Feb 2014).
62 *Retail Week,* 30 Apr 2004.
63 www.woolworthsmuseum.co.uk (accessed 2 Jun 2014).
64 Information from Paul Seaton, 8 Jun 2014, and www.gordonbrotherseurope.com (accessed 20 Jun 2014).
65 Information from Paul Seaton, 8 Jun 2014.
66 The law in the Channel Islands prohibits selling on leases outside the islands (information from Ken Trimmer, 12 Jun 2014).
67 *The Times,* 15 Sept 2008, 49.
68 *The Times,* 3 Apr 2008, 47.
69 *The Times,* 19 Jun 2008, 45. The four stores acquired by Waitrose were Edgware Road, Chiswick, Islington and Clapham Junction.
70 www.doctorvee.co.uk (accessed 9 Sept 2009).
71 *The Times,* 25 Nov 2008, 45.
72 *Huddersfield Daily Examiner,* 18 Jun 2009.
73 Observation by a company insider who wishes to remain anonymous, by email to author.

Chapter 10

1 www.soultsretailview/2011 (accessed 12 Jun 2014).
2 www.soultsretailview/2009 (accessed 12 Jun 2014).
3 Information from Paul Seaton, 8 Jun 2014.

Notes to Captions

Chapter 2

a Snow 1974, 19.
b *Cheltenham Chronicle,* 7 Oct 1933, 1; *Gloucestershire Echo,* 3 Feb 1934, 1.

Chapter 3

a *The Builder,* 19 Dec 1924, 992.
b *See* correspondence in *The Spectator,* 21 Mar 1925, 12; 28 Mar 1925, 17.
c *The Times, 1*3 Dec 1938, 4.
d *The Architect & Building News,* 5 Apr 1929, 461.
e *Daily Mail,* 9 Apr 1927, 4.
f *The Times,* 7 May 1938, 9; *The New Bond,* **4**, 7, Jul 1939, 244.
g The built design was quite different from those initially submitted to the LCC by A Barton on 7 Dec 1927 (LMA GLC/AR/BR/22/BA/045756).
h *Daily Mail,* 18 Dec 1928, 8.

Chapter 4

a West Yorkshire Archive Service, Burtons 127.
b The unusual Walsall store is listed in an edition of *Faience by Shaws: Illustrating the Progress of Modern Tiling* (*c* 1935; Darwen, np), where it is attributed to Woolworth's 'staff architect' (collection of Shaws of Darwen).
c *The New Bond,* **3**, 7, Jul 1938, 296.
d *Architectural Design & Construction,* **8**, 5, May 1938, 188.
e Caption in Blackpool photograph album, in HEA.
f *The New Bond,* **1**, 3, Mar 1936, 51.

Chapter 5

a *The Builder,* 7 Nov 1924, 736.
b Phillips 2009, 50.

Chapter 6

a Ibid, 60.
b Dated architects' drawings, HEA.

c *Western Morning News,* 27 Nov 1950, 3.
d *The Builder,* 10 Jan 1958, 65–8. This article included plans and photographs of the building.

Chapter 7

a Phillips 2009, 71.
b Information on back of photograph, HEA.
c *The New Bond,* **23**, 4, Aug 1964, 6.
d *The New Bond,* **20**, 3, Jun 1961, 23.
e *The New Bond,* **20**, 3, Jun 1961, 28–9. The extension replaced (and extended) a small purpose-built Woolworth's of the 1920s.
f *The New Bond,* **24**, 3, Jun 1965, 9.

Chapter 8

a www.woolworthsmuseum.co.uk (accessed 24 Jan 2014).
b *The Times,* 22 Jul 1957, 16.
c *The Times,* 16 Oct 1973, 6.
d *Architectural Review,* **CLVIII**, 945, 274–5.
e *The New Bond,* **30**, 5, Dec 1971, 33.
f *The New Bond,* **29**, 2, Apr/May 1970, 70.

Chapter 9

a *Woolworth News,* Jul 1984, 8.
b Information from Paul Seaton, 8 Jun 2014.
c www.doctorvee.co.uk (accessed 9 Aug 2009).
d www.hilco.com (accessed 8 Feb 2014).

BIBLIOGRAPHY

1 Websites

www.woolworthsmuseum.co.uk (created by Paul Seaton)

www.100thbirthday.co.uk (created by Paul Seaton for Woolworths *c* 2008 to complement the Woolworths Virtual Museum – http://museum.woolworths.co.uk; *see* below)

http://museum.woolworths.co.uk (the Woolworths Virtual Museum; this website is now defunct, but was accessed by the author through http://archive.org/web)

www.colinhiggins.com ('Frank Winfield Woolworth's Weblog': transcription of letters and other documents, 1913–16)

www.doctorvee.co.uk ('(Almost) 100 years of Woolworths', series of blog posts by Duncan Stephen, former employee, 2006–2008)

www.soultsretailview.co.uk (created by Graham Soult)

www.flickr.com/photos/ballysundriven (set of 903 photographs of Woolworth's stores)

2 Woolworth's Publications (in chronological order)

Fortieth Anniversary Souvenir, 1919 (US)

Twenty Years of Progress, Christmas 1928 (GB&I)

Twenty-six Years of Progress, Christmas 1934 (GB&I)

The New Bond, 1935–72 (GB&I)

Thirty Years of Progress, Christmas 1938 (GB&I)

Forty-two Years of Progress, 1909–1950, Christmas 1950 (GB&I)

Woolworth's First 75 Years: The Story of Everybody's Store, New York, 1954 (US)

A Career with Woolworth, nd (*c* 1955) (GB&I)

Fifty Years of Progress, 1909–1959, Christmas 1959 (GB&I)

55 Years of Progress, 1909–1964, Christmas 1964 (GB&I)

A Pictorial Record of Executive and Management Personnel, 1974 (GB&I)

A Pictorial Record of Executive and Management Personnel, 1979 (GB&I)

Woolworth News, 1972–82 (GB&I)

Woolworths News, 1982–6 (GB&I)

Woolies News, 1997–2004 (GB&I)

3 Publications

Abel, D *c* 1960 *The House of Sage: 1860–1960.* London: W P Griffith

Anon 1957 *Truscon: The First Fifty Years.* London: Trussed Concrete Steel Company

Boyce, W 2009 *To Build Strong and Substantial: The Career of Architect C Emlen Urban.* The City of Lancaster, Pennsylvania

Briggs, A 1984 *Marks & Spencer 1884–1984: A Century of History.* London: Octopus Books

Brough, J 1992 *The Woolworths.* New York: McGraw Hill

Curtis, P 1999 *Sunderland: A Century of Shopping. Seaham:* The People's History

Fenske, G 2008 *The Skyscraper and the City: The Woolworth Building and the Making of Modern New York.* Chicago: University of Chicago Press

Foster, A 2005 *Birmingham: Pevsner Architectural Guides.* London: Yale University Press

Hawkins, R A 2009 'The Influence of American Retailing Innovation in Britain: A Case Study of F W Woolworth & Co, 1909–1982' in Hawkins, R A (ed) *Marketing History: Strengthening, Straightening and Extending (Proceedings of the 14th Biennial Conference on Historical Analysis and Research in Marketing [CHARM]).* Leicester: University of Leicester

Inglis, I 2005 'Embassy Records: Covering the Market, Marketing the Cover', *Popular Music and Society* **28**, 2, 163–70

Jeremy, D J 1991 'The hundred largest employers in the United Kingdom, in manufacturing and non-manufacturing industries, in 1907, 1935 and 1955', *Business History* **33**, 1, 93–111

Kirkwood, R J 1960 *The Woolworth Story at Home and Abroad.* New York: Newcomen Society

Lebhar, G M 1959 *Chain Stores in America 1859–1959.* New York: Chain Store Publishing Corporation

McBrier, E M 1941 *The Origin of the 5 and 10 Cent Store.* Privately printed

Morrison, K A 2003 *English Shops and Shopping: An Architectural History.* London: Yale University Press

Morrison, K A 2007 'Bazaars and Bazaar Buildings in Regency and Victorian London', *Georgian Group Journal* **XV**, 281–308

Mulcahy, G 1988 'Woolworth Holdings', *in* Nelson, R and Clutterbuck, D (eds) *Turn-Around: How Twenty Well-Known Companies Came Back from the Brink.* London: Mercury

Pederson, J P and Grant, T 2007 *International Directory of Company Histories,* Vol 83. Chicago: St James's Press

Pevsner, N 1973 3rd edn *London 1: The Buildings of England.* Harmondsworth: Penguin

Phillips, D 2009 *The Wonder of Woolies: Memories from Both Sides of the Counter of Britain's Best-Loved Store.* Gosport: Footplate

Plunkett-Powell, K 1999 *Remembering Woolworth's: A Nostalgic History of the World's Most Famous Five-and-Dime.* New York: St Martin's Griffin

Scott, P 2007 *Triumph of the South: A Regional Economic History of Britain during the Early Twentieth Century.* Aldershot: Ashgate

Seaton, P 2009 *A Sixpenny Romance: Celebrating a Century of Value at Woolworths.* London: 3d and 6d Pictures Ltd

Sharples, J 2004 *Liverpool: Pevsner Architectural Guides.* London: Yale University Press

Sherwood, J and Pevsner, N 1974 *Oxfordshire: Buildings of England.* London: Penguin

Snow, V F 1974 JBS: *The Biography of John Ben Snow.* New York: Syracuse

Stansfield, C 1986 *Beside the Seaside.* London: Thirties Society

Temple, P (ed) 2008 *Survey of London, Vol 47: Northern Clerkenwell and Pentonville.* London: Yale University Press

Walsh, B 2011 *When the Shopping was Good: Woolworths and the Irish Main Street.* Dublin and Portland: Irish Academic Press

Winkler, J K 1957 (rev edn) *Five and Ten: The Fabulous Life of F W Woolworth.* New York: Bantum Books

INDEX